T0401479

Fort Worth Characters 2

Richard Selcer

University of North Texas Press
Denton, Texas

10 9 8 7 6 5 4 3 2 1

Permissions:
University of North Texas Press
1155 Union Circle #311336
Denton, TX 76203-5017

The paper used in this book meets the minimum requirements of the American National Standard for Permanence of Paper for Printed Library Materials, z39.48.1984. Binding materials have been chosen for durability.

Library of Congress Cataloging-in-Publication Data is available from the Library of Congress.

ISBN 978-1-57441-968-9 (cloth)

ISBN 978-1-57441-976-4 (ebook)

Fort Worth Characters 2 is number 10 in the Texas Local Series.

The electronic edition of this book was made possible by the support of the Vick Family Foundation.

Typeset by vPrompt eServices.

*Dedicated to all the people who made me want to
be a historian and teacher:
Dean Cozine, Ron Tyler, Colonel Harold B. Simpson,
Virginia Love, Myron Lowe.
I hope I've done you proud.*

Contents

List of Illustrations

Acknowledgments

This book is indebted to many people, but at the top of that list are Rick Miller, Harry Max Hill, and Deran Wright. Rick is a published author himself in the field of Western outlaw and lawman history. He has a demonstrated talent for research and a big heart when it comes to fielding pesky requests for help. Max is a retired Fort Worth librarian who has a talent for research and a nose for a good story. Someday we'll all read his book on Fort Worth nightclubs.

Deran Wright is an artist of rare talent in multiple mediums. He created the beautiful jacket cover art and provided other artistic and technical help with the illustrations in the manuscript. For the professional artist there is not much money or recognition in such work. His true value is as a good friend.

I have worked with these three before, and they still allow themselves to be recruited for another one of my writing projects. Here's hoping they never learn to say "no"!

Coming close behind the Big Three is Quentin McGown, who, as they say, has forgotten more about Fort Worth history than the rest of us will ever know. Quentin served as a reader on the manuscript, catching both grammatical mistakes and historical faux pas with his eye for detail.

Others that played an important role in bringing this book to reality are UNT Press Director Ron Chrisman and *Star-Telegram* editor Steve Coffman. Several of these stories first saw the light of day in the newspaper under Steve Coffman's hand. Those "Fort Worth History" columns have served as test runs of the topics here. This is my fourth book with UNT Press, who have been kind enough to green-light my quirky projects.

Introduction

In 2009 UNT Press published my book *Fort Worth Characters*, a baker's dozen stories about some colorful, oddball, mostly forgotten people in Fort Worth history. The common denominator was that they all achieved some level of fame in their day and, equally important, that they interested me. As an author I am attracted to oddball and forgotten historical figures, the people who have slipped through the cracks of the historical record. You might say I like taking another look at the overlooked.

Now, fifteen years later we are back with thirty-one more characters from Fort Worth history, organized into twenty-five chapters. The criteria for inclusion are the same as before. To be considered a "Fort Worth character" does not mean they were born or died here or even lived most of their lives here. It is only necessary that they have some notable connection to our city that made them newsworthy at some point. Finally, they had to be *interesting* in and of themselves, not because they were part of some great movement or event. That is, after all, the very definition of a "character."

I stumbled across most of the subjects in this book while researching something or someone else. I started a file and eventually decided I wanted to share my findings with others. Some of these people first appeared in one of the columns I have been writing for the *Fort Worth Star-Telegram* since 2019. Limitations on space in those columns limit the stories but do not apply to the chapters in this book, so you may find some familiar characters in much greater detail here—and with source citations, which are unheard of in a newspaper column.

Anybody who has lived in Fort Worth for any length of time has heard the names of our great historical figures like Ripley Arnold, Amon Carter, and "Gooseneck Bill" McDonald. These people interest me less than the figures in the shadows of history, the ones who don't have buildings and streets named after them. Or statues. (One curious thing about those statues: Most of the people who have statues in Fort Worth were not born here and never lived here. See Will Rogers, Quanah Parker, and Bill Pickett.)

There is no particular rhyme or reason to my choices here. Purely by coincidence, it turns out these thirty-one people are fairly representative of our community in terms of race and gender. Counting the headliners only, there are twenty-five men and six women, a mixture of Blacks, whites, and Chinese—with no intention of achieving racial or gender balance. Six of the headliners are African Americans. Tracing their stories in Fort Worth history is a particular challenge because virtually all the historical sources were written by white people about white people. Minorities were "the others." There are one married couple, a father-daughter pair, and a whole football team serving as the Greek chorus to a couple of notables. There are nine entertainers, three songwriters, one martyred hero, and, oddly for a list of Cowtown characters, only one genuine cowboy. There are criminals and law-abiding citizens and some, as the old song says, "we ain't too sure about." (*Paint Your Wagon*, 1969 movie). In short, this is a collection of scalawags, scoundrels, and scamps who may or may not have gotten their requisite fifteen minutes of fame. I want to give them a few (more) minutes of fame.

The chapters are not all the same length. William S. Pendleton, for instance, is seventeen pages long; Townes Van Zandt is just six pages long. This is not a reflection on their relative importance. Some characters made waves; others made just a little ripple. Not everyone lived as large or as long as some others. In general, less documentation exists for those who lived in the nineteenth century. Record keeping got a lot better in the twentieth century. Also, the more famous—or infamous—a person was, the more there was written about them. People of color tended to slip through the cracks in the historical record, unnoticed by census takers, public officials, and newspaper editors. But whether they loom large or small in history, every character in this book has a Fort Worth connection. Maybe they were not born here; maybe they did not die here. But they called Fort Worth home long enough for us to claim them as an adopted son (or daughter).

Unfortunately, photos do not exist for many of the people in this book, or if they do they are in the hands of descendants who have not made them public. They may also be a victim of circumstances. No one bothered to take their picture because they were not deemed newsworthy. Perhaps this book will bring some family photos to light.

All the characters here, be they newsworthy or footnotes in history, have something to say to us today about race and gender, contemporary social norms, and public memory. Bringing their stories to light now gives us a second chance to learn from their experiences.

If this book is the reader's introduction to the Fort Worth story, I hope it encourages you to dig deeper into the history of our wonderful community. You will find lots of colorful characters who made us what we are today, not all of them on the "good" side of the ledger.

Chapter 1

Black Lives Do Matter
The Remarkable Pratts

There are few African Americans in Fort Worth history that we know anything about, and even fewer that we can hold up as role models. For most Fort Worthers, the short list begins and ends with William "Gooseneck Bill" McDonald, who came to Fort Worth years after the first freedmen began creating a community of their own here on the Trinity.

Fort Worth's early Black community is largely unknown because they were barely noticed in the public record. When they do show up in the white press, it is as criminals or for doing something white readers considered laughable. Following a family like the Pratts through public records is made more difficult because ex-slaves typically adopted the surname of their former masters, which surname may have been used by more than one family with no blood connection.

John Pratt was the first African American in Fort Worth to stand out in the Reconstruction era (1865–1876). He was born into slavery in Tennessee about 1841, served with US Colored Troops during the Civil War, then came west afterward. When he arrived in Fort Worth, it was still a frontier village and hardly welcoming to freedmen. In 1870 he was single and living in a boarding house with eight other people, one of whom was Nat Fisher, a freedman from Arkansas. The head of the household was Richard H. "Dick" King, a blacksmith. Pratt apprenticed under King before setting up his own black-smith shop on the public square (corner of Rusk and Weatherford). It was also during these years that Pratt met and married Elletta "Nettie" Fisher (b. 1851), probably the daughter of fellow boarding-house resident Nat Fisher. They started a family that eventually included Mahalia (a.k.a. Mildred), George, Caladonia, James, and Lizzie, all born between 1867 and 1875.[1]

Pratt's high-quality work and exemplary character attracted the attention of prominent white Fort Worthers, specifically former Confederate Major Khleber Van Zandt. Van Zandt and others patronized Pratt's blacksmith shop by choice, not because there was no one else. Their patronage brought him steady business and protected him from the Klan. This success is why he went into the history books as "Fort Worth's first Negro businessman." Where Van Zandt led, others followed, and the friendly feelings were mutual. According to the recollections of an unnamed speaker at a meeting of the Fort Worth Sons of Confederate Veterans (SCV) many years later, Pratt used some of his money to pay for the "college education" of his old master's son, which raises questions about why a free Black man would take such a personal interest in his former master. The SCV speaker went so far as to "pay tribute" to John Pratt, a Black man okay with this white audience.[2]

Pratt was part of the generation of what old-timer Howard W. Peak, Fort Worth's self-appointed historian, called "some mighty faithful negroes," speaking of the war and postwar years. Peak called men like Pratt and Old Dan Hall "reliable in every particular" because they served their "betters," accepting their place in white society without complaint. That was a common attitude among whites who considered themselves respectable and would never have stooped to associating with the Klan.[3]

Not every freedman was so accepting or law-abiding. Whites called Sol Bragg a "bad n— —" because of his long criminal history even before he was convicted of killing a white man. For that the good citizens of Fort Worth hanged him in 1874. Those same people considered Pratt a "good negro" who furnished the iron shackles that Bragg wore on his last walk to the gallows. Those shackles, "heavy enough to hold a herd of elephants," were still on display in the Trinity Saloon twenty years later—a reminder perhaps to other Blacks what would happen to them if they took to crime.[4]

Khleber Miller Van Zandt, ex-Confederate, Fort Worth business leader, and patron of John Pratt's blacksmith shop. Author's collection.

Though it is doubtful that John Pratt could read and write, he saw to it that his second son, James Wellington Pratt (b. 1875), got a good education. The elder Pratt must have picked up a little book-learning because the boy's middle name, Wellington, was so unusual as to be virtually unique in the Black community. It was from British history, made famous by the Duke of Wellington, the man who defeated Napoleon, and hardly an honored figure in the Black community. Getting any kind of education was a challenge for Blacks in those years. Even learning the three Rs was daunting because Fort Worth did not have a public school for Blacks until years later. Pratt Sr. would have had to engage a private tutor.

John Pratt died before his son reached manhood, sometime after 1880. There is no record of his death—no surprise because many Blacks in the nineteenth century died without being noticed by the public record keepers. Nettie and son James continued to reside in Fort Worth. She worked as a nurse for a Black doctor while the son was still living with his mother nearly twenty years later. In the meantime, Nettie remarried, to a man named Payne.[5]

The small Fort Worth Black community was close-knit. Nettie and her children lived next door to Henry Harrison Butler on the block "between Eleventh and Twelfth Streets." He was a pioneer Black educator who opened Fort Worth's first school for Black children in 1873 in the Allen Chapel church building. The city posthumously honored him many years later by naming a public housing project for him. In 1880 38-year-old Butler married 14-year-old Mahalia Pratt. He was a widower whose first wife had passed away two years before. As an educated man and schoolteacher, his only negative was the age difference. He was old enough to be her father. Still, the union of Henry and Mahalia (a.k.a. Mehaly; a.k.a. Mildred) was successful. They had a daughter, Caladonia, born in 1881, and she remained married to him until her death in January 1939. He died six months later, and both were buried in the Old Trinity section of Oakwood Cemetery.[6]

James Pratt was the golden child of the family. From his subsequent career as a teacher, it can be presumed he went to college, attending one of the four historically Black colleges and universities (HBCUs) in Texas in the nineteenth century. In 1894 he took the "[Tarrant] county teachers' examination" in Fort Worth. He was the only Black candidate tested by the county board of examiners. He passed, which should have entitled him to be appointed to a teaching position in the "colored school." But there was a small problem: a vocal group of Black citizens for some reason did not want him placed in their school. Before the 1895 school year began, they petitioned the council not to appoint him. The *Fort Worth Gazette*, which usually did not cover the Black community, was intrigued enough to predict "sensational developments" to follow.[7]

Apparently, James Pratt was not persona non grata in the Black community at large, because he was reported to be a leader in the community years later. He was musically talented and a gifted public speaker, as well as smart. In the 1895 memorial service honoring the passing of African American icon Frederick Douglass, he was a keynote speaker, "arousing the enthusiasm of the audience to a high pitch." He also possessed a fine baritone voice. He was

Henry Harrison Butler, cropped from photo of I. M. Terrell school faculty. Not just a fellow member of Fort Worth's Black community but also a neighbor who became the son-in-law of John Pratt by marrying daughter Mahalia. Billy W. Sills Center for Archives, Fort Worth Independent School District, Fort Worth, TX.

a member of the Negro Harmony Club, entertaining Black and white audiences alike. And he was a member in good standing of the Colored Odd Fellows lodge of Fort Worth. James was carrying on the tradition of his father as a leader in Fort Worth's Black community.[8]

In 1900 James Pratt was 25 and single. His occupation was "schoolteacher," though he had been unemployed for the previous six months before the census taker came around. Ever since the outspoken group in his community had opposed his appointment in 1894, he had found it difficult to find a position. There was no way he would be allowed to teach in a white school. He may have found employment in a Black private school, perhaps Allen Chapel, where his brother-in-law Henry Harrison Butler had started.[9]

James seems to have given up on teaching because he eventually took a job as a mail carrier. Federal employment was one of the very few middle-class jobs open to African Americans at the time. Years later when he was too old and infirm to lug around a mail bag, he got on as a Pullman porter, possibly the most respected employment, outside of the professions, that a Black man could get in the Jim Crow era.

Sometime before 1907 (the records are unclear) James married Lena Johnson. Like John Pratt, Lena's father had been an early entrepreneur in the local Black community, only instead of running a blacksmith shop, he was a barber. James would have been about 30 and Lena about 26 when they tied the knot. There is some suggestion this was his second marriage. Besides their love they also shared their singing talent. She was a soprano who taught music in the Black schools and performed publicly. They also performed together for audiences of Blacks and whites both. Their marriage lasted until death parted them. His jobs as a Pullman porter and a teacher allowed them to buy a house on E. Rosedale, valued at eight hundred dollars in 1930. By that date Lena had moved on to switchboard operator, perhaps at the Jim Hotel. They had one child we know about, James Jr., born in 1908.[10]

In their later years, James and Lena achieved a level of financial security that would have made John Pratt proud. Even as he was still working as a Pullman porter, they owned and operated a restaurant and grocery store on New York Ave. They moved to 1000 E. Verbena. He retired from being a Pullman porter in 1945 or '46 but did not take to his rocking chair. Instead, he started a real estate business. James Pratt was truly a chip off the old block.[11]

James Pratt died on February 3, 1948, of pancreatic cancer. He was 63 years old, though census records over the decades had listed his birth date variously as 1878 and 1884. County physician William M. Crawford made out the death certificate, writing that he had attended the deceased from August 1947 until his death. That latter is unusual since Crawford was white and had no shortage of patients. There is no indication that James was a charity case. Lena provided the information for the death certificate, but her

Left: James and Lena Pratt's grave in the Old Trinity section of Oakwood Cemetery, ca. 1959. Author's collection.

Right: Entry to Old Trinity Cemetery (looking east toward "Gooseneck Bill" McDonald's overpowering marker). Author's collection.

knowledge of her husband's background was shaky. For instance, she gave his mother's maiden name as "Nettie," which is how she had always known her, not as "Elletta." Baker Funeral Home made the funeral arrangements, and James was buried in Old Trinity section of Oakwood Cemetery.

Lena Pratt died in 1959. She had lived alone in their house on E. Verbena since James's death, working as a housekeeper and describing herself as the "widow of J. W. Pratt." As with James, whoever made out her death certificate was a little shaky on the details, giving her age as 68 and her birth date as 1891. They also described her as a simple housewife, which ignored her professional accomplishments as a singer and teacher. She was interred beside James in the Old Trinity. Someone (a family member?) placed a single, upright granite headstone over their graves, almost hidden beneath the overhanging branches of a big oak tree on the east side of the cemetery. Two other family members, Betty and Clifford Steward, are buried in the same plot.[12]

John Pratt as seen in artist Paula Blincoe Collins's historic mural celebrating seventy-five years of African-American history in Fort Worth (panel A). The mural is tucked away in the rear of the Trinity Metro Center. Author's collection.

The Pratt family drops off the radar after James and Lena. This is particularly sad because of what father and son had accomplished in an era of strict racial segregation. They never ran a bank like Bill McDonald, but he had nothing on them when it came to drive and ambition, and, yes, career success.

Of the two, only John's legacy lives on in Fort Worth memory, and that is thanks largely to public art. He is represented in Paula Blincoe Collins's 2002 relief sculpture, "The Historic Wall," on a wall at Fort Worth's Central Station, celebrating seventy-five years of Fort Worth's black history (1865– 1940). Pratt is there as "Fort Worth's first African American businessman," an indistinct figure on the first panel. He is nothing more than an Everyman among all the other African Americans portrayed in the mural.

Curiously, John Pratt does not appear at all on a 2023 public artwork honoring "Black business and entrepreneurial leaders who contributed to the economic development of Tarrant County." Artist Armando Castelan painted the mural on an outdoor wall at 2800 Yeager, the heart of the historic Black neighborhood that was the Near Southside, intending it as "a place for young and old to come and contemplate the history of black businesses in the city." The mural recognizes nearly two dozen Black civic leaders and businesspeople but not John Pratt. The only possible reason for omitting him would be the same reason he appears as only an indistinct figure in Paula Blincoe Collins's mural: there are no known pictures of him—or James Pratt either. It is part of the larger tragedy of Black history that few visual images of historic figures have come down to us. John Pratt is just a name and hand-me-down story in Fort Worth history, which is still more than can be said for James Pratt.[13]

The usual account of the Civil Rights Movement focuses on very public leaders like Rosa Parks and Fort Worth's Opal Lee. But people like the Pratts changed white perceptions in quiet ways by running a successful business and teaching school, ways that do not make headlines.[14]

Chapter 2

Frank James Slept Here. No, Really!

S ome owners of homes on the east coast used to claim that George Washington slept there, whether he did or not, because it gave them bragging rights that none of their neighbors had. Frank James, brother of Jesse James, really did sleep here in Fort Worth, and on more than one occasion. That claim might be suspect were there not so much evidence to back it up. That is because the West from the late nineteenth century was full of imposters claiming to be legendary outlaws, long after the real outlaws were dead and buried. More than one ersatz Billy the Kid scored free food and drink and celebrity treatment in those years, including most notably the man known as Ollie Roberts (nicknamed "Brushy Bill") who asserted his claim to New Mexico Governor Thomas J. Mabry in 1950. Fort Worth had its own copycat "Billy" who blew into town in 1890 and made the rounds of the bars until he was arrested for illegally carrying a pistol. He bonded out and disappeared. As for ersatz Jesse James, at least twenty-six men claiming to be the real Jesse made the celebrity rounds. The most brazen of them was finally exposed by Jesse's daughter-in-law in 1932.[1]

Our Frank James was the real McCoy. The older sibling of the two James brothers by three years, he was born in 1843 in Kearney, Missouri.

The James brothers, Frank (*left*) and Jesse (*right*) as outlaws in Illinois in 1872. Author's collection.

Their parents were a Baptist minister and his wife. Their father died in 1851, and their mother had remarried twice before Frank turned 13. The two boys grew up without a strong parental hand. Though Frank did not have much formal education, he was a bright child who loved to read and reportedly wanted to become a teacher when he grew up.[2]

Those plans were sidelined when the Civil War came along. He was 18 years old and part of a pro-Southern community in politically divided Missouri. Frank enlisted and fought with a guerilla band dubbed "bushwhackers" by their enemies, taking part in the raid on Lawrence, Kansas, in 1863 that killed two hundred. At the end of the war he was paroled, but Frank and brother Jesse continued to wage their personal war against authority in general and the federal government in particular.

Between 1868 and 1876 he rode the outlaw trail robbing banks and trains across several states. In 1876 he was part of the James-Younger gang that was "shot to pieces" trying to rob the banks in Northfield, Minnesota. Frank and Jesse went into hiding and by most accounts retired from their outlaw ways. One source, however, has Frank as the mastermind behind the 1878 robbery of the Union Pacific No. 3 train at Cabon, Wyoming Territory. Reportedly, Frank was going by the name McKinney at the time and did not take part in the robbery itself. Frank certainly had the smarts to plan a heist; whether he and Jesse had actually split up is another matter. This is another part of the endless lore surrounding the James brothers.[3]

Jesse left the outlaw life in 1881 and changed his name to Thomas Howard. Frank also went straight but kept his name. On April 3, 1882, Jesse was shot in the back of the head by Bob Ford for the reward offered by Missouri Governor Thomas Crittenden. Hoping to escape the same fate, Frank turned himself in to the governor, asking for nothing but a fair trial. He got that, first in Missouri, where he was charged with murder and armed robbery, then in Alabama, where he was charged with robbery. He only went to trial in Alabama, but it took two years for his legal troubles to play out, during which time he sat in jail. An Alabama jury acquitted him of all charges. Fort Worth was as fascinated with the story of the James brothers as the rest of the country. The *Fort Worth Gazette* followed Frank's story closely, and the city's newspapers would continue to follow it for the rest of his life.[4]

After making his peace with the law, Frank returned to the family farm near Kearney, where a wife and young child were waiting for him. In June 1874, while still on the run from the law, he had eloped with pretty Annie Ralston of Jackson County, Missouri. Without telling her father, she slipped off to Kansas City to meet him. They were married and hit the road together. They remained happily married for the next forty-one years and had one son, Robert Franklin James.[5]

Though Frank James was done with the outlaw life and lived another thirty years, he could never escape his famous past. All the evidence says that the reformed Frank James never resumed the criminal ways of his youth. Those who knew him characterized him as intelligent, articulate, and well-mannered. However, to the public he was always one-half of the most famous outlaw brothers in history, a celebrity. Reformed outlaws were popular with a public raised on dime novels and Wild West shows. Restless by nature and determined to put his past behind him, he left the family farm, dragging his family from town to town: Nevada, Missouri, then St. Joseph and St. Louis, Missouri, then New Orleans, Louisiana. Eventually they wound up in North Texas, first in Sherman, then in Dallas. He took a shining to Dallas, telling a New Orleans reporter in 1893, "Since my [1882] surrender I have been living in Dallas a good deal." And with Fort Worth only thirty miles away and a direct rail connection, he became a frequent visitor to Cowtown.[6]

As a respectable citizen with above-average intelligence, Frank made enough money to support his family and indulge a fondness for horse racing. His name made him newsworthy wherever he went. He was reported at race-tracks in St. Louis and Chicago, placing modest bets of five and ten dollars on the ponies. According to the same source, he bet "a great deal of money" at some unspecified point in the past. If persistently unlucky, that would explain why he switched to penny ante bets. He was well-known enough around St. Louis to be the subject of an 1898 dime novel, *Frank James in St. Louis*. His fondness for the ponies may have led him to cross paths with another Fort Worth member of the sporting fraternity, Luke Short, who frequented the same racetracks. Frank must not have been a chronic loser, because he was able to purchase a string of horses, elevating his status to "turfman" in the vernacular of the day.[7]

Exactly why Frank James settled in Dallas when he did is unexplained. At the time he had no family in Dallas. Other members of the family, includ-ing his widowed mother, remained in Missouri. In the "George Washington slept here" vein, an Oak Cliff resident, W. W. Bowen, claimed many years later that Jesse James had lived in Dallas in 1868. According to Bowen, he hid the wanted outlaw on his farm "on the McKinney Road." The story is not supported by the known facts of Jesse's life, but it suggests an early connection between the James brothers and the area. In the end, Dallas (and Fort Worth) may have attracted him because in the 1880s both towns were on the rise, and they were congenial to a retired outlaw. Jim Courtright, Doc Holliday, and other hard cases also called one or both cities home at different times.[8]

Dallas and Fort Worth both offered opportunities for someone with an entrepreneurial spirit, and it did not hurt to have been on the right side (as Southerners saw it) of the "Late Unpleasantness." Frank had fought in the Civil War on the Confederate side and afterward joined the United Confederate Veterans (UCV), where he held the title of colonel, unrelated to his actual military rank in the war but a sign of his active role in the organization. His fellow ex-Confederates respectfully referred to him as Colonel James, a nice promotion for the former bushwhacker who had not fought in the regular army.[9]

It was about 1886 that James first turned up in Fort Worth. Historically, we know the James boys had strong connections to Missouri, Minnesota, and Iowa (where they pulled bank robberies), and Tennessee (where Jesse lived for a time), but any connection to North Texas does not show up in the historical record. Perhaps he came here looking for a fresh start, trying to escape his outlaw past. What brought him back to Fort Worth repeatedly was his friendship with former Marshal Timothy "Longhair Jim" Courtright. How they met is yet another mystery, but it could not have been as comrades in the Civil War because they fought on opposite sides. But both men had ridden the outlaw trail, so their paths may have crossed while Courtright was on the run from New Mexico authorities between October 1884 and January 1886.[10]

James came to town to visit Courtright at least twice in the summer of 1886. His presence produced "quite an excitement" in the little town. The *Fort Worth Gazette* reminded readers the old outlaw was someone "you have all read about," adding that he "is here for his health." Whatever the health benefits of Cowtown, James spent his time strolling the streets with his pal, enjoying the attention of the men who wanted to shake his hand. Courtright was likewise a favorite of the locals, so the pair were a kind of Western royalty, part of the wild 'n' woolly West that was passing from the scene. The further removed it got, the more people mythologized it, and though he had been a law-abiding citizen for years, he was still referred to in the newspapers as "the outlaw Frank James." The *Dallas Morning News* was even more impressed than the *Fort Worth Gazette*, doing a headline story about his visit.[11]

One Fort Worther thought of a way to cash in on the two headline-making celebrities. Charles Benton, manager of the Fort Worth Opera House, wanted to pair them up in a Wild West show and take it on tour. He commissioned a script and drew up contracts. Courtright was reportedly "pleased" with the prospect, but James was less than enthusiastic. Reliving his outlaw days was not something he wanted to do. Benton's contracts included stipulations insisted on by each man. Any tour they were on would not play New Mexico, where Courtright was still wanted for murder, or Minnesota, where James was still wanted for the Northfield raid. In the end none of it mattered because the show never came together. In the years to come, James would have reason to reconsider his reluctance to go on the stage.[12]

James was a regular sight around Fort Worth for nearly two years (1886–87), and Longhair Jim was not his only friend. Another was George B. Holland, a "captain" in the local UCV chapter. Captain Holland and Colonel James could reminisce about the war. Holland had been a Fort Worth resident since the end of the war and was the first editor of the *Fort Worth Democrat*. But it was as a theater empresario and racehorse owner that he made his mark. His first theater was the Centennial, opened in 1876, then in 1881 he opened My Theater. His places were among the hottest nightspots in town, and James may have been one of his customers. Holland accumulated plenty of stories about his exploits over the years. When Jim Courtright came back to Fort Worth in 1886 to surrender after being on the lam for a year, it was Holland who escorted him to town. One story related in Holland's 1921 obituary had him arresting Jesse James at some point. That never happened, although it was certainly true that he was a personal friend of Frank James. Besides the ex-Confederate connection, the two men shared a love of good horseflesh and occasionally went to St. Louis together "for the races." Though he was friends with the likes of George Holland and Luke Short, James was no "sport" in the sense of being a gentleman gambler.[13]

James stayed in touch with other old Confederate pals for many years. He was counted among William Clarke Quantrill's bushwhackers that terrorized Unionists in Missouri during the war. Quantrill's veterans held reunions after the war, and James attended them faithfully. In March 1887 he attended one such reunion in the Panhandle, and he was present at their last meeting in Clarendon, Texas, in 1914, one of only thirty-five old-timers still able to travel.[14]

In late winter or early spring of 1887, Frank and Annie settled in Dallas, but Fort Worth still considered him an adopted son. Folks were concerned by a report in August that Annie had come down with dengue fever. The same outbreak also laid Frank low, and his Fort Worth friends feared the worst until October. It was then that the *Fort Worth Gazette* debunked the dire reports that Frank James was "dying," stating with authority, "By those who know [him], he is said to be in good health and at work in Dallas."[15]

As a family man, James was especially proud of his son, who was the kind of boy the father might have been under different circumstances. Young James was described as "bright and intelligent" and an excellent student. In 1891 he won a scholarship to Marmaduke Military Academy at Sweet Springs, Missouri, sponsored by the *Dallas Times-Herald.* Fort Worth was as proud of the boy as Dallas was. The town considered Frank an adopted son.[16]

James was back in Fort Worth in 1892 and back in the news, albeit for a different reason. He brought his family along to visit his "many friends and acquaintances," but, of course, it was Frank that everyone wanted to see. He made the usual rounds of the hotels and saloons, where men lined up to shake his hand and buy him a drink or three. He had been in town a couple of days when a story began circulating that "the notorious Bob Ford" was also in town. This was the man who had assassinated Jesse James, and folks were saying if the two men crossed paths, "one or the other must die." James dismissed the rumor, saying Ford didn't have the "moral courage" to come looking for him, and even if he did, he had five friends in town to Ford's one.

Of course, the rumor proved false. He was right to put no stock in the rumor. Ford, who had made a living doing live reenactments of the murder of Jesse, was living in Creede, Colorado, at the time. One has the sneaking suspicion Fort Worthers would have welcomed a shootout on the city's streets between two such famous Western characters.[17]

The work available for a retired outlaw getting up in years was not the most remunerative. He never had any desire to put on a badge, and teaching tied a man down too much. He drifted between a series of jobs that had no future. At various times he was a shoe salesman, a ticket taker in a burlesque theater, a telegraph operator, and the "betting commissioner" for the New Orleans fairgrounds. In Dallas he sold shoes for the Sanger brothers, who had operated a profitable dry goods store since 1872. He also ran a general store for a time but had to give it up "on account of my health." One person who saw him at work marveled at how the women "flock around him to buy dry goods."[18]

Sometime in the 1890s Frank and family relocated to St. Louis, Missouri. There he took a job variously described as usher/doorman/security guard at the Standard Theater, a vaudeville establishment at Seventh and Walnut Streets. The place was owned by Edward "Boss" Butler, who also ran the St. Louis Democratic party. While here James crossed paths with famous American author-journalist Theodore Dreiser, who called the Standard "a vulgar burlesque theater" patronized by the lowest elements. Frank's duties included "ticket taker." "As dramatic critic of the *Globe-Democrat* . . . I often saw him," recalled Dreiser years later. Though ticket-taker was the humblest of jobs, the former outlaw was not a name or face easily forgotten.[19]

Frank's principal job the last thirty-three years of his life was being a celebrity. His recollections were a rich source of information on outlaw life, offering an insider's take on "long riders" and those who chased them. If you want to understand an outlaw, ask another outlaw. In November 1888, on a visit to Fort Worth, the subject of Eugene Bunch (a.k.a. "Captain Dick Bunch") came up. As the so-called Lone Highwayman, Bunch was even then robbing trains in the area and had been seen in Hell's Half-Acre. Since Bunch had been a Confederate brother-in-arms to the James boys, who had also taken to the outlaw trail after the war, Frank felt free to offer his opinions on Bunch. Years later he also shared his opinions of Bat Masterson and Pat Garrett with a St. Louis reporter.[20]

Promoters were constantly after him to go on the stage, where he would regale audiences with stories of sensational robberies and blazing gun battles. For years he refused to take them up on their offers. He complained to a friend in 1895, "Why is it that everyone looks upon me as a devil past all redemption? God knows I have suffered enough for all I have done. My family has surely suffered enough. Tell the people that Frank James is not a wild man. Tell them that he has feelings, and that in view of his life for the past twelve years, some little consideration is due him."[21]

None of that meant that he was above parlaying his fame into money when the opportunity presented itself. For years he made the rounds of county fairs, starting the horse races even when he didn't have an entry in the race. One Fort Worth acquaintance who saw him at the fair in Burlingame, Kansas, in 1899 told friends back home that he was "the greatest attraction that could possibly be secured" for such events. He added that James easily outdrew the fair's celebrity starter the year before, perennial presidential candidate and "silver-tongued orator" William Jennings Bryan. After starting the race, James hung around to regale the adoring crowd with tales of his past.[22]

Other opportunities demanded more commitment either in terms of time or financial investment. In 1893 he was approached by William Dalton, the law-abiding brother of the famous outlaw Daltons of Oklahoma, about going partners in a "large" Chicago saloon. It is impossible to know how serious the offer was or how interested James was, but the *Fort Worth Gazette* reported the offer as fact. The Wild West show also had some appeal to him, but as an investor, not a performer. Late in life he was reportedly part of a group that purchased Buckskin Bill's Wild West Show, third in size after Buffalo Bill's and Pawnee Bill's shows. The problem with the story is where the cash-strapped James would have gotten the money. Like so many similarly reported episodes, it was the power of his name that got him attached to those ventures.[23]

The middle-aged Frank James was of "slender build," presenting a "gentlemanly" appearance. He had unruly, thinning hair, a "grayish" mustache, and a face tanned and weathered by years out of doors. He was

A middle-aged Frank James in 1898 (*left*) and 1905 (*right*), still an object of curiosity years after going straight and settling in Dallas–Fort Worth. Author's collection.

"a little above" medium height, "slightly stooped in the shoulders," with "as little the look of the bold frontiersman as one could well imagine." On the contrary, he was often described as "gentle and mild-mannered" by reporters who interviewed him. He was a fastidious dresser who favored suits over Western wear, pleasant to one and all, and never prone to braggadocio. There is no record that he ever wore a gun again after giving up the outlaw life. His favorite things were "a good story, a good newspaper, and a good horse." He remained "spry" even into his fifties.[24]

Ultimately, Frank James overcame his reluctance to cash in on his outlaw past. He himself summed it up in 1901 when he said, "I am getting old, and if I am to lay by anything to provide for my old age it must be by this means—the only one which offers itself to me." He sold a saddle that he said he had used in his "bandit days" to a "relic hunter" for $86, a princely sum in those days.[25]

But selling off his relics was a finite source of income. After his saddle and guns and a few more items, he had no more collectibles. He was left with going on the stage after holding out for so many years. He agreed to make his stage debut in a loosely autobiographical melodrama titled, "Across the Desert." The show opened in the fall of 1901 way "out of town" in Zanesville, Ohio, where hopefully audiences wouldn't be too critical of his amateur talents. He insisted on two stipulations in his contract: one, that there was to be no blood and thunder, no outlawry in it anywhere; and two, that he was to have final say on how it was advertised. The producers agreed, and Frank James made his stage debut, apologizing ahead of time: "I don't expect to become an actor in the true meaning of the word, nor do I believe that my manager has any delusions as to my histrionic abilities. My appearance on the stage will therefore be more of a personal exhibit than a dramatic performance."[26]

The show proved to be a hit. Audiences were enthusiastic and "courteous" everywhere it played. The *Fort Worth Record and Register* dutifully reported Frank James's latest endeavor, and it is likely the locals hoped it would come to town. Meanwhile, the *El Paso Times* carried an interview with him where he offered further explanation for why he was taking to the stage at this point in his life: "I can do now, without offense to public sentiment, what I could not have done years ago before I had given indisputable proof by my conduct that the apprehensions of those who had no faith in me were groundless."[27]

In other words, Frank James was truly a reformed man. He was also a man who had come to love the stage lights. The allure of an adoring audience and a paycheck was too much to resist. In 1903 he was one-half of the Great Cole Younger and Frank James Historical Wild West Show with another reformed outlaw who had once ridden with Frank and Jesse as a member of the James-Younger gang. The "Historical" part was very important to James. They spent five months on the road with the show. It came to Fort Worth in October, with general admission tickets priced at twenty-five cents, half of what Buffalo Bill's Wild West Show charged when it came through town a year earlier.[28]

James may have sold out in some eyes, but he was not willing to give up all control over what we would now call his name, image, and likeness. In 1902 a Kansas City theatrical company opened a fanciful drama called

"The James Boys in Missouri." The show's producers did not bother to get James's permission, and their melodrama bore little relation to the facts. When James heard about it, he sought an injunction as the first step to shutting it down, not just because it slandered the reputation he had worked so hard to rebuild but also because it was "harmful to the youth of the country in that it glorified outlawry and made heroes out of outlaws." The injunction would stop the theater from putting on the show while the case worked its way through the courts. James's lawsuit addressed an important legal question that would be fought out in the courts for years to come: Can a private citizen be portrayed on the stage without his consent, whether to his discredit or not?[29]

The reformed Frank James granted an interview to a Kansas City newspaper to explain why he was so opposed to the production. The man who once rode with a murderous gang of outlaws was now concerned for the tender sensibilities of American youth and so polite he could not even bring himself to swear. Said he, "The dad-binged play glorifies these outlaws and makes heroes of them! That's the main thing I object to."[30]

The judge in the case agreed to grant the injunction if the plaintiff (James) put up a bond of $4,000 to "indemnify" the theater owner for lost revenue should James lose in court. In the end, the play went on because James could not pay the $4,000 bond required by the court. "I am a poor man," he said. "I have but a thousand dollars, the fruits of many years of hard work." Friends and supporters offered to pay the rest, but he refused because if he lost the case they would forfeit their bond money.[31]

In 1906 a 65-year-old James moved his family from St. Louis to Fletcher, Oklahoma, in the Big Pasture part of the territory. He announced his intention to "grow up" with the new country. Though Fletcher was home for the next five years, he felt drawn back to the old family homestead in Missouri.[32]

It is no surprise that he chose to return to his roots toward the end of his life. He had grown up on a farm, and in between odd jobs and stage appearances, he became a gentleman farmer. For a time he had a place in McKinney (a suburb of Dallas) where he raised "jacks" (donkeys), proudly showing them at county fairs, perhaps the same fairs where he was the starter at horse races. In 1938 C. J. E. Keller of Fort Worth, in an interview for the

Federal Writers' Project, remembered Frank showing his animals in town. The Fort Worth Stockyards did a booming business not just in cattle.[33]

Neither McKinney, Texas, nor Fletcher, Oklahoma, nor even St. Louis, Missouri, were ever really home to Frank James. He was back home again on the old family farm near Kearney, Missouri (now part of metropolitan Kansas City), where he had spent the first eighteen years of his life. His unmarried niece, Mary (Jesse's daughter), came to live with him and Annie after her mother died. His stage career was over, and he could no longer travel for paid appearances at county fairs. He earned a little money by conducting tours of the "famous James farm" for fifty cents a head, no pictures allowed. Part of the tour was his insistence that he was "innocent of all the charges of outlawry placed against him." He cited his acquittals in Missouri and Alabama as evidence, conveniently forgetting that he had never been tried for the Northfield, Minnesota, raid in 1876 that left five dead.[34]

Even as a septuagenarian, Frank James was still good copy. In 1914 during the United States' trouble with Mexico, a reporter attending one of his Confederate reunions asked him how he would handle things if he were president. Never shy about giving his opinion, he said he would give Mexican dictator Victoriano Huerta twenty-four hours to abdicate, then if he didn't, he would order in the army to "smother the country and annex it to the United States." It is doubtful his advice was relayed to Woodrow Wilson.[35]

Frank James died after a lingering illness at Excelsior Springs, Missouri, on February 18, 1915. The immediate cause was given as either apoplexy (a stroke) or heart disease. The Fort Worth newspapers followed his final illness right through to his funeral. He was 72 years of age, hardly old by modern standards, but this was a man who had lived a full life as a soldier, outlaw, and celebrity. Despite one of the most spectacular careers in American criminal history, he was never convicted of anything, never served a day in prison, and died with his boots off. He had been a nonpracticing member of the Methodist church for years, but at his request it was a secular funeral held on the James farm. The service was conducted by Judge John F. Phillips, who praised the deceased as a godly, Bible-reading man. Afterward the body was sent to St. Louis for cremation and the ashes placed in an unnamed vault in Kansas City. James had explained his reason for wanting it this way was that he did not want his grave to attract the kind of morbid crowds that desecrated Jesse's grave in Kearney's Mount Olivet Cemetery.[36]

The public, including Fort Worthers, still have a certain fascination with Frank James, reformed outlaw. He was once a celebrity living among us, and for good reason. In the late nineteenth century Missouri was known as the Outlaw State because of the likes of the James brothers, the Younger brothers, Belle Starr, and "Bloody Bill" Anderson, who all hailed from there. Frank James was the only one to go straight. And he landed in Fort Worth. Seven years before his death a curious *Fort Worth Record and Register* reader asked the newspaper's "Question & Answer" column, "Is the outlaw Frank James still living and where?" The stumped columnist could only answer, "I do not know what has become of him." After Frank James's death in 1915, Fort Worth moved on to World War I, the Roaring Twenties, and the Great Depression, all world-shaking events. Only a vague memory of Frank James remained as a footnote in Fort Worth history. Let's breathe a little life into that ghost.[37]

Chapter 3

Will McLaury Goes to Tombstone to Bury His Brothers

Fort Worth has a family connection to the famous OK Corral gunfight of October 26, 1881. Two brothers of Fort Worth lawyer William R. McLaury were on the wrong end of the shootout when the three Earp brothers (Wyatt, Virgil, Morgan) and Doc Holliday squared off against Ike and Billy Clanton, Billy Claiborne, and Tom and Frank McLaury. Accounts differ about who started it, but the Earp-Holliday faction were faster on the draw and better shots. On the other side, Billy Clanton and Frank McLaury were the only ones armed. The shootout lasted less than twenty-five seconds, with most of the twenty-five or more shots fired coming from the Earp-Holliday faction. Morgan Earp and Doc Holliday grievously wounded Frank McLaury and Billy Clanton with their six-guns, then Holliday used a shotgun to take down Tom McLaury. Frank and Billy fought on, dying "game." With Tom that made three dead at the OK Corral. (Ike Clanton and Billy Claiborne fled; Virgil and Morgan Earp were wounded.) Thus ended the most famous gunfight in Western history.[1]

The next day the *Tombstone Epitaph* headlined the story: "Yesterday's Tragedy. Three Men Hurled into Eternity in the Duration of a Moment." A day after that came the coroner's inquest, a standard proceeding after any suspicious death, or in this case several deaths. It took testimony for two days but in the end assigned no blame. On October 29 Ike Clanton filed murder charges against the Earp faction. Virgil and Morgan were still recuperating from their wounds, so only Wyatt and Doc were arrested by Sheriff John Behan. They were hauled before Justice of the Peace Wells Spicer for an examination hearing and freed pending grand jury action on ten thousand dollars bond each, pledged by their friends. It was the responsibility of the examination hearing to make a recommendation to the grand jury if it found evidence of criminal action, so its conclusion carried a lot of weight.[2]

For friends of the McLaurys and Clantons, there was no doubt that the Earps and Holliday had committed murder, starting with the fact that four armed men against two was no fair fight. Furthermore, Sheriff Behan testified that he was on his way to disarm the "Cowboys" when the Earps and Holliday brushed by him and provoked the confrontation. By Tombstone standards the McLaurys were rowdies but not hard cases. They were part of a disreputable group dubbed the Cowboys who were known for wrangling other people's cattle. The term itself was Western shorthand for rootless men who were not much tamer than the cattle they worked. The McLaury brothers stood out from the others because they owned what one author describes as an "extensive ranch" on the San Pedro River.[3]

Whatever their feeling about the Cowboys' extracurricular activities, more than a few Tombstone residents considered the killings unjustified. The examination hearing was supposed to get to the bottom of what happened.

The locals knew much about the McLaury brothers. They did not live in town or socialize with the respectable townspeople. One of many mysteries after the shootout was that Tom McLaury had three to four hundred dollars in cash on him plus another three thousand dollars in checks and certificates of deposit. While the Hollywood version portrays him and brother Frank as ne'er-do-wells, Tombstone contemporary Billy Breckenridge considered them his steadfast friends, no better and no worse than others around town. Reportedly, at the time of their death they were planning to leave Tombstone to visit brother Will in Fort Worth. The money on Tom may have been for that purpose or some legitimate business venture. That was never learned.[4]

By some accounts there was a more personal element to the hard feelings between the Earp-Holliday faction and the Cowboys than simple male bravado. Historian Frank Waters relates a story about how the young daughter of Virgil Earp sneaked out one night to meet "one of the brothers" (Tom?). When she returned home her uncles thrashed her soundly for taking up with one of the Cowboys.[5]

The county prosecutor at the examination hearing was Lyttleton Price, but the anti-Earp faction did not have any confidence in him, so they hired Ben Goodrich to be co-counsel. The hearing stretched into three days and was still going on when Will McLaury arrived in town. Someone had sent him a telegram the day after the shootout notifying him of his brothers' death and of the large sum of money found on Tom's body. It took him a week by train and stagecoach to reach Tombstone, and the situation was not encouraging when he arrived. His brothers had already been buried in a single grave in Boot Hill (later two markers were put up), and the prosecution's case was not going well. Will was more than just a grieving brother; he was a practicing lawyer, highly respected in Fort Worth. He immediately took a seat at the prosecution table.[6]

The McLaury connection to Fort Worth involves all three brothers. They came from a family of eleven children. William Rowland "Will" McLaury, the oldest of the three brothers, was born on December 6, 1844. Frank was born on March 3, 1849, and Tom was born June 30, 1853. In 1855 the family moved to Iowa. Will served in the Civil War as a member of the Iowa 47th Infantry. After the war he settled in Sioux Falls, Dakota Territory, and read the law, which was the quickest route to becoming a lawyer. He passed the bar, though he later admitted he was not much good at drawing up legal documents. That was no problem so long as he could find a "fair son of Harvard Law School" and buy him a few drinks to draft any documents he needed. Mostly he handled small civil lawsuits and routine divorces.

He married Malona Dewitt, a dark-haired beauty, in 1872 and started a family. Four years later, because her frail health was unsuited to the harsh Dakota climate, they came to Texas. Frank and Tom were already in Texas in the cattle business. Will preferred town life and after passing the Texas bar opened a practice in Fort Worth, partnering with B. G. Johnson.

The McLaury brothers, Frank (*left*) and Tom (*right*). Their images as they appear here on cabinet cards were reproduced from photographs taken in Fort Worth, ca. 1876–1877. New York Historical Society, New York, NY.

They promised to "give prompt attention to all business placed in our hands in the courts of Tarrant and adjoining counties." Will's unfamiliarity with the finer points of the law suggests that he depended on his partner to do the heavy lifting. On the side they also sold real estate, which was not an unusual sideline for ambitious men on the frontier.

They advertised heavily in the newspaper, but their partnership did not last long. What happened is unknown, but Will soon found a new partner in Samuel P. Greene, who was the senior partner in the firm by virtue of being a Confederate veteran, Freemason, and pioneer resident of the city. Greene also went on to serve on the bench of the 48th District Court. Will saw lawyering and the real estate business as necessary steps toward a career in politics. He added "Esquire" to the end of his name and in 1878 threw his hat into the ring for elected office. He lost, but it would not be his last foray into politics.[7]

Will McLaury and wife, Malona, joined together through the magic of computer artistry. Photo by Paul Lee Johnson; artistic rendering by Deran Wright.

Frank and Tom spent some time with their brother in Fort Worth in the mid-1870s. They had been working as cowboys since this is what they knew best. Their trip included a visit to August R. Mignon's photography studio just off the public square. The resulting cabinet cards would eventually become cherished family heirlooms. They did not hang around Fort Worth for long because by 1878 they were in Arizona Territory, where they fell in with the Clantons. The McLaury boys did not pick their friends well.[8]

Back in Fort Worth, Will's life fell on hard times. In 1878 Lona gave birth to their third child, a daughter, who fell from a swing on July 28, 1880. Though "badly jarred," according to the newspaper, she was not seriously injured. Meanwhile, Lona's health had not been improved by the move to Texas. Chronically ill, she died at home on August 13, 1881, attended by Fort Worth's most respected doctors, W. P. Burts and E. J. Beall, who were helpless to save her. A grief-stricken Will was left a widower with three young children. He was just 36 years old.[9]

Less than three months later, Will McLaury was on his way to Tombstone on a personal mission to get justice for his murdered brothers. On November 4 he secured a temporary license with the Arizona bar to act as an "associate counsel" in the examination hearing. That afternoon he took his place at the prosecution table. An armed Wyatt Earp and Doc Holliday were in the courtroom as spectators. Will did not like the way things were going so he brought a fourth lawyer onto the team, James Robinson, and introduced a motion to have Wyatt and Doc returned to jail pending what he hoped would be an indictment for murder. Their lawyer, Thomas Fitch, filed a writ of habeas corpus forcing Spicer to set a high bail, $4,200 for the two of them, which they quickly raised and were back on the street again. Still, Will expected the examination hearing would lead to an indictment and jury trial ending in a guilty verdict. In spite of his abiding interest in the proceedings, his personal involvement in the prosecution was minor. He located one witness and had him subpoenaed, and he conducted a lengthy examination of Ike Clanton. Though it wasn't the prosecution's finest moment, he wrote to Sam Greene back in Fort Worth saying, "I think we can hang them." He called the deaths of his brothers, "as cold-blooded and foul a murder as has been recorded." However, believing that and proving it were two different things. He also misread the royal welcome to town he had received from the anti-Earp faction. Bent on his own "vendetta" (cf. Wyatt Earp's "Vendetta Ride"), Will made it his holy crusade to "see that these brutes do not go unwhipped of justice" and planned to stay in town until the grand jury convened in December.[10]

Justice Spicer gave his ruling on November 29, saying in effect that he had not heard enough evidence to refer the case to the grand jury. Instead, he found that Virgil Earp had acted "injudiciously" in deputizing his Wyatt and Holliday but attached no "criminality" to his actions. All four of the accused were "discharging their official duty," and there was a lack of the refuting evidence necessary to convict them in a jury trial. The verdict outraged Tombstone's anti-Earp faction in general and Will McLaury specifically. He not only objected to the verdict but also believed the Earp faction had prejudiced the news accounts of the shootout in their favor. History agrees that the Earps won the PR battle. Will also wrote his sister in Iowa denouncing the defense's testimony as perjury, adding, "I do not intend that these men

Top: Tombstone, Arizona Territory, rebuilt after the devastating fire of June 22, 1881. Author's collection.

Bottom: Boot Hill graves of Frank and Tom McLaury, marked for tourists. Author's collection.

shall escape. . . . I find a large number of my Texas friends here are ready and willing to stand by me with Winchesters if necessary."[11]

After the hearing Will did not leave town immediately. He stayed around to settle the affairs of his late brothers. Forgotten in history's obsession with the OK Corral is that in town at the same time was George Hearst (1820–1891), the mining-king capitalist and patriarch of the Hearst family (William Randolph, Patti, et al.). Hearst was looking for mining opportunities and hired Wyatt Earp as his bodyguard while he roamed the territory. Reportedly, the Cowboys planned to waylay Hearst and hold him for ransom, another black mark on their reputation in history.[12]

Will paid off his brothers' debts and closed the books with those who owed them money. He lost money in those arrangements, and his health suffered from the stress and frontier living conditions. Reportedly he gave legal advice to Ike Clanton and Ike's pal Sheriff Johnny Behan in their civil lawsuits against the Earps. His obsession with making a criminal case against the Earps kept him tied up for two months. His Iowa sister chided him in a letter for being away from his children that long. He finally headed home the day after Christmas. Thus, he missed the payback the Cowboys visited on two of the Earps. On December 29, 1882, Virgil Earp was bushwhacked and severely wounded by unknown parties. Two months later Morgan Earp was assassinated by a shotgun blast through a pool room window on a dark night. Some in town speculated that Will McLaury had been one of Virgil's bushwhackers, but there was no evidence to that effect apart from his outspoken threats against them.[13]

Back in Fort Worth, Will's fiery temperament cost him another law partner. Sam Greene had taken on an additional partner, Jonathan Hogsett. When Will and Hogsett got into a heated confrontation in court—not unheard of in frontier courtrooms—they had to be separated by a deputy sheriff. No blood was spilled, but the little dustup brought a twenty-five-dollar fine from Judge M. D. Priest and an end to the McLaury-Green partnership. For whatever reason, Will obviously preferred working in tandem, so within a month he had formed another partnership with respected lawyer (and Confederate veteran) C. C. Cummings. He also resumed his political career. It was much easier for an Iowa boy (and Union veteran) to get elected in

Fort Worth if he had a Confederate connection. Will won an appointment as city recorder (i.e., police court judge), which got him the right to be called "judge" thereafter. He ran unsuccessfully for city attorney in 1885.[14]

Eleven months after returning from Tombstone, Will took a second wife, Lenora Trimble, daughter of successful Fort Worth grocer Leonard A. Trimble. She became mother to his three children by Lona, and they had five children of their own. Between his law practice and working a farm just outside of town, Will was able to become a "very well-to-do" citizen of Fort Worth, though misfortune continued to plague him. His oldest, John, became the black sheep of the family, getting into trouble with the law in New Orleans in 1893. Will told a reporter in less than complete honesty, "The family name as far back as could be traced has never before been tainted by wrongdoing." He was either deluding himself or hoped no one remembered Tombstone.[15]

Will must have vented his spleen about town after his return from Tombstone, and as an upstanding citizen his word carried a lot of weight, especially since there was no one with the same passion defending the Earps. In the years that followed, Fort Worth newspapers had nothing good to say about any of the Earps, Wyatt in particular. In relating a garbled account of Tombstone events in 1894, the *Daily Gazette* accused the Earps and Holliday of gunning down the unsuspecting McLaury brothers as they emerged from putting away their horses in the OK Corral. Six years later the *Record and Register* described the Earps as "a famous family of border desperadoes . . . once the terror of Tombstone." The same newspaper described Wyatt Earp as "the notorious Arizona gun fighter and bad man." This was the Will McLaury version of history.[16]

In 1904 Will retired from his Fort Worth law practice and moved the family to Snyder, Oklahoma Territory, where he bought a nine-hundred-acre ranch that he operated until his death. Perhaps after all, the McLaurys were better at ranching than anything else. He died peacefully at home on February 16, 1913, at age 68. The funeral was a private affair, attended by Lenora and the children and a few family members from Fort Worth. He is buried in Fairlawn Cemetery in Snyder, Oklahoma. Lenora lived until 1931, dying at the age of 74, survived by three of her own children and three stepchildren.[17]

Chapter 4

Would You Like Egg Roll with Your Steak and Fries?

In 1961 longtime Fort Worth resident Jow Ming Dip opened Jimmie Dip's restaurant on the "strip" that was S. University Drive, the same area as the Farmer's Daughter, Kip's Big Boy, and Ol' South Pancake House. Jimmie Dip's, specializing in Cantonese cuisine, was not Fort Worth's first Chinese food restaurant. He was preceded by Joe Foo's Blue Star Inn in 1942 on Camp Bowie, and they were both preceded by Ng Wing's Bamboo Inn downtown in 1918. All three men were from the Canton district of China, so their cuisine was Cantonese Chinese, but they also served excellent steaks because this was still Cowtown.[1]

Dip, Foo, and Wing were not blazing new Cowtown culinary trails; they were simply carrying on a long tradition. The small Chinese population in Fort Worth, as elsewhere in the country, was known for three things: restaurants, laundries, and opium. Entrepreneurs only had to focus on one to be successful. As the smallest of the ethnic communities in Fort Worth (cf. African Americans and Latinos), they had to create their niche in the city, and these were occupations they knew from back in China and, equally important, translated well to their new home.

Jow Ming "Jimmie" Dip posing proudly holding a menu in front of his University Drive restaurant in July 1961. It was a westside dining landmark for over a decade. *Fort Worth Star-Telegram* Collection, Special Collections, University of Texas at Arlington Library.

The Chinese first came into this country through California and were put to work building railroads across the West in the second half of the nineteenth century. They did the brutal, back-breaking work of laying track, and wherever the rail lines were pushed into new areas they settled in all-male communities because they left the women back in China. Only as time passed, and they grew comfortable in their new communities did they bring in the women. Chinese men virtually never set up housekeeping with women outside their own race. This was one big difference between them and African Americans and Latinos. Chinese immigrants could enter the country legally until 1882.

Chinese immigrants during passage to America, ca. 1876. Author's collection.

While some hoped to make a home and start a family, the majority only wanted to make enough money to return home and live comfortably.

Even before settling in North Texas, the Chinese were an object of ridicule and contempt. The *Dallas Herald* referred to them as "the heathen Chinee." Polite whites called them "Chinamen" and barely tolerated them—only slightly better than they treated Blacks and about the same as Mexicans. At that, they were only tolerated because they performed useful jobs that no one else would do. In Fort Worth it was easy to tell the racial pecking order by whose heads the police busted when trouble arose between different minority groups. This was in part a legacy of slavery and the history of conflict between Texas and Mexico.[2]

Chinese businesses—laundries, restaurants, and opium dens—were patronized by Chinese and whites both. The free market did not care about racial stereotypes. Of the three, washing clothes and cooking were respectable, if demeaning, occupations, while rightly or wrongly, the Chinese were also blamed for introducing opium—and causing its related addiction—to America.

A Chinese laundry, late nineteenth century, the kind that was a family business, not a commercial operation (not Fort Worth). Laura E. Swan, Alberta, Canada.

The first Chinese persons of record in Fort Worth, Hong Wah and Hong Lee, arrived together about 1874, only a year after the town was incorporated. The record does not show where they came from. They were welcomed, however, as laundrymen in a community that sorely lacked clean clothes and bathing facilities. At the time Fort Worth was a struggling frontier community of a few hundred souls hoping and praying for the railroad to get here. The most numerous establishments in town were saloons, followed by churches. Later, Hong Wah and Hong Lee were conflated in public memory into a single Chinese laundryman. Their home and workplace were one and the same—a tent on the edge of town. They were not exiled; on the contrary, they had a lot of company. At this time the town's population had outstripped available housing. A "large number of families" were living in tents "in the suburbs." What happened to Hong Lee is unknown, but Hong Wah was eventually joined by other countrymen, forming a small male "colony" on the prairie outside the town center. They kept to themselves, seldom venturing onto the streets to mingle with the Anglo population.

Old-timers would recall many years later, "The people of Fort Worth never had any serious trouble with the Chinese." If true, it was not because whites were more tolerant than Americans in California, where riots and mob action were common, but because the local Chinese community was so small as to be practically invisible and therefore nonthreatening.[3]

The historical record is not quite as benign as old-timers' memories. By the 1880s there were several opium dens in the lower end of the city, which the Chinese called "clubs." Most were in the back of or above a store or other business. Opium dens were not illegal, just stigmatized. They were patronized by whites and Chinese alike, who paid anywhere from fifty cents to one dollar for a pipeful of languid dreams. The slang for indulging was "cracking a joint," remarkably similar to modern drug slang. The typical opium joint was anything but exotic or alluring. Usually, it was a single room with one or two rows of curtained-off bunks where the user could have some privacy and sleep it off afterward. The visitor found most of the bunks occupied by Chinese workers relaxing after work. Between day workers and night workers, the beds were occupied around the clock.[4]

While the authorities deplored opium for both racist and public health reasons, it was not illegal under either state law or local ordinance. Pharmacists sold opium over the counter in both gum and powder form ($3.80 to $4.80 a lb.), and purchasers did not have to explain whether they wanted it for medicinal or recreational use. What opium dens provided was a quiet place to indulge the habit with other users but away from prying eyes, like later crack cocaine houses. Still, police raided such dens regularly on general principle, charging the owners and sometimes the customers with "vagrancy" or running a "disorderly house." The fine for such minor crimes in police court could be as high as $100. The size of the fine depended on whether the accused was white or Chinese. One of those busted in such a police raid was Yo Lee, who knew enough about American law to hire a lawyer and appeal his fine. For that he got off with a slap on the wrist and a warning.[5]

In 1883 the *Fort Worth Gazette* editorialized that "nearly all" cities in the country had made opium smoking a misdemeanor for both the smoker and the keeper of the den. "Our city fathers should at once take hold of the growing evil and pass an ordinance to suppress it." However, legal prohibition of the

drug was still decades in the future. In the meantime, it was seen largely as a
Chinese problem, or as the *Fort Worth Telegram* put it later, "It is a rare thing
to find a Chinaman that does not 'hit the pipe.'"[6]

Some Fort Worth police were less interested in busting opium dens
than in running a protection racket on their "Celestial" proprietors, extorting
payoffs for looking the other way. In 1888 three veteran officers were caught
extorting payoffs from Jim Wy, who operated an "opium joint" on Houston
Street. Before they could be indicted, however, they skipped town, saving the
police department the embarrassment of a trial. The case was symptomatic of
a corrupt police force more than effective law enforcement.[7]

While opium got a mixed reception in Fort Worth, Chinese laundries
and restaurants were quite welcome, even if they were often fronts for opium
dens. They were also the butt of snide newspaper reporting. The *Fort Worth
Star-Telegram* years later described the city's laundrymen as a "Washee-
Wshee Tong," an oblique reference to the notorious Chinese gangs (tongs)
of San Francisco.[8]

By the turn of the century, Chinese hand laundries were a highly
successful business. They comprised six of the city's fifteen commercial
laundries. The tools of the hand-laundry trade were simple and inexpensive:
a wash tub, an iron wringer, and a flatiron. Besides offering lower prices,
some of them also offered free pick-up and delivery. For those who dropped
off their dirty laundry and picked it up, the standard Chinese owner's line,
according to amused reporters, was, "No bling monee, no get shirtee; can
savvy?" Racist humor aside, Chinese laundry standards were much appreciated by their customers whose shirts were always clean and white with all
the buttons still attached. Such attention to detail was a hallmark of Chinese
business practice.[9]

Chinese restaurants were only slightly less ubiquitous than hand
laundries. They offered whites welcome break from the familiar fare of
beefsteak and fried potatoes or pork and beans. Popular thinking was that
Chinese kitchens specialized in "eggs foo-young" and "chop suey," which
was ironic because the latter dish was not a traditional Chinese dish; it was
invented in the United States by unnamed Chinese Americans around the
turn of the century.[10]

Further growth of the Chinese population dried up after 1882, the year Congress passed the Chinese Exclusion Act. That was the first anti-immigration law in US history. Not only did it bar almost all immigration from China, but it also prohibited those already living here from becoming naturalized US citizens. Thereafter, the Chinese population grew mostly by natural increase augmented by illegal arrivals smuggled into the country.

By the turn of the century, Fort Worth's Chinese community numbered somewhere between 60 and 200, depending on who was doing the counting. They slipped between the cracks in census counts and did not always show up in city directories or other public records. No one really knew accurately how many Chinese there were because they were so clannish. Census records in the early twentieth century show a very small population in Fort Worth: 59 in 1910, 86 in 1920, 40 in 1930. By World War I the newspaper estimated the number to be fewer than 100 with no explanation of how that number was derived. Only about half were native-born; the rest were American-born and therefore US citizens by law.[11]

The Chinese congregated—both living and working—in Little Chinatown on the south end of town, the area formerly known as Hell's Half-Acre. The name was more impressive sounding than the reality. In size and numbers Little Chinatown did not compare to Little Africa in the first decades of the twentieth century, or to Little Mexico in the 1920s, both located in the same area. Having most of the city's minorities in one district (the Third Ward) eased the minds of whites and made it easier for police to keep an eye on them. However, it did not prevent white Fort Worthers of a more daring nature from taking sightseeing tours through the district, guided by off-duty members of the police department showing them all the hot spots. The sightseers could safely gawk at the "strange" residents without interacting with them personally.

Part of the fascination is that unlike with Blacks and Mexicans, whites were totally unfamiliar with Chinese culture. They knew the Chinese only as stereotypes: "the bland, childlike countenance" giving no inkling of the feelings "concealed under the placid mask of immobility." That mask was the usual reaction to rude questions directed at them by clueless sightseers. The Chinese were alternately characterized as either "heathen" or "inscrutable," depending on the context.[12]

One reason the Chinese population was concentrated in just a few blocks was because multiple residents shared the same house and often the same floor of a two-story building. Sightseeing whites pushed their way into living quarters to gawk at how these "strange" people lived. Sometimes the distinctive odor of opium wafted out the windows, adding to the exotic allure of the neighborhood. Oftentimes, visitors were invited by the resident to take a drag on the opium pipe, considered an act of hospitality.

As the years passed, Little Chinatown expanded beyond its unofficial boundaries, though still kept at arm's length by polite white society. There were Chinese residences on Fourteenth just east of Houston, restaurants on lower Main, a general store at Rusk (Commerce) and Thirteenth, and the lodge for Chinese Free Masons at Calhoun and Fourteenth. There was less resistance to the spread of this community than to the spread of the Black community. A well-established system of segregation known as Jim Crow kept Blacks and whites apart, a legacy of slavery.[13]

By 1919 there was only one Chinese laundryman still in business in Fort Worth, 75-year-old Hop Lee, who had arrived illegally in 1884 from his home in Beijing and started his business. Thirty-five years later he was still washing and ironing in the same location. Hop Lee was the last independent laundryman. All the other Chinese hand laundries had been forced out of business by modern steam laundries, like the sprawling Natatorium Laundry on East Belknap.

As small as the Chinese community was and as far from home, they still upheld their traditions. Most men still wore the queue (pigtail), they still ate a rice-heavy diet, and they still celebrated Chinese New Year on the last week in January. That celebration was especially significant in 1909, marking the first year of the reign of Manchu child emperor, Hsuan Tung. These were occasions for many Fort Worthers to be introduced for the first time to the Chinese calendar, Chinese culinary specialties, fireworks, and the languid pleasures of the opium pipe—entirely legal and no worse really than the rotgut whiskey served up by the local saloons year-round. Just as Fort Worthers celebrate Cinco de Mayo and Maifest today, in the early years they celebrated the Chinese New Year—and for the same reason: any excuse to party.[14]

Culture shock hit the Chinese like every other immigrant group when they had to deal with American criminal law, marriage and divorce practices, and gun violence. None of those were the same where they came from. These things could be either liberating or frightening.

Over the years, the Chinese were subsumed in the population boom that turned Fort Worth into a mighty metropolis. The old hand laundries disappeared first, then in 1914 Congress made opium illegal (the Harrison Narcotics Act). The only interaction law-abiding Fort Worthers had with the Chinese community was eating at a Chinese restaurant like Blue Star Inn or Jimmie Dip's. A Chinese restaurant was incorporated into Fort Worth's Frontier Centennial in 1936, which celebrated a hundred years of Texas history. In Billy Rose's plan for the grounds, it was part of the Mexican Village, a mashup of ethnic minorities in the exposition's mythic depiction of the Old West. In the global village of the twenty-first century, the Chinese are no longer an exotic species to be gawked at like freaks in a sideshow. They are part of the social fabric of the much larger, diverse community that is Fort Worth.[15]

Chapter 5

Booger Red Privett
The Man and the Saloon

The horse was as essential to Western life as the six-gun, and breaking them was a necessary skill, even a business for some enterprising young cowpokes. Eventually it became a rodeo event where cowboys pitted their skill against untamed horses—and each other. The king of the bronc-busters was a diminutive fellow names Samuel Privett Jr., better known to history as "Booger Red." While the main outlines of his life are familiar, some details and dates differ significantly from what is known. Memories and even the records do not always agree. It's all part of the legend of Booger Red.

Samuel Thomas Privett was born on the TP ranch in Williamson County, Texas, on December 29, 1858, or maybe it was 1862 or 1864. The record is not clear. He grew up on ranches riding and roping. Even as a young boy of barely 12 Sam was already breaking horses. He had a shock of red hair that got him attention as "that redheaded bronc-riding kid." He was either 13 or perhaps 15 when he got his lifelong nickname "Booger Red." He and a pal were attempting to make a homemade firecracker when it blew up on them, killing the pal and mauling Sam's face. Another kid, catching sight of him, commented how "boogered up" Red's face was. Thus was born a nickname that followed Privett the rest of his life, though friends called him Sam and business associates knew him as Tom.[1]

Though the nickname sounds funny, his injuries were anything but. The blast burned off his eyebrows and part of his nose. His eyes were reduced to slits, and he lost most of the sight in one eye. It took six months and multiple skin-grafting surgeries to save what was left of his face.[2] Anyone else would have retreated into seclusion, but Sam was made of sterner stuff. For the rest of his life, while he was understandably camera shy and wore his big cowboy hat pulled low over his face, still he embraced the nickname and even joked about it. His boogered-up face was just one of the curves life threw at him. In his teen years both parents died, forcing the orphan to strike out on his own.

Privett enjoyed steady work breaking horses for ranchers who knew him by his reputation. He made enough money to buy a wagon yard and stable in San Angelo, but he officed out of a pool room above a saloon, doing that for three or four years.[3] He also broke horses for the US Army, which needed plenty of animals to keep the cavalry mounted. On his bowed legs he stood about five feet, five inches tall and weighed little more than 150 pounds soaking wet, plus he was soft-spoken, leading some to misjudge him. The army offered him a deal: fifty dollars a month or one dollar a horse. He took the second offer, and by the end of his first day he was owed at least seventy-five dollars by the army. After that they withdrew their dollar-a-horse offer. He could make more freelancing for ranchers.[4]

He found more lucrative and more entertaining work performing in small-town fairs and stock shows. Ranchers brought their wildest horses to the events and offered a prize to anyone who could "gentle" them. What passed for an arena was a patch of open prairie surrounded by poles stuck in the ground with rope strung between them. Spectators sat in buggies or on camp stools. The "box seats" were those who watched from horseback. The crowd made bets on the horse or its rider. The contest ended when the rider went sailing or the horse quit bucking. Either way, the odds were about even unless Booger Red was the rider. He took on any animal, even those known as "man-killers." Mounting the horse was a challenge by itself. As there were no chutes—the side-opening chute came along years later—a rider had to get on while his fellows held the animal by its ears and covered its eyes. As soon as he was in the saddle, they let go and scattered. Sam rode one notorious man-killer that pitched and bucked all over several acres before finally coming to a halt, its sides heaving, its head low and mouth flecked with foam. Rider and animal were both exhausted, but Booger Red walked away with a nice purse.

Eventually these impromptu, open-air events were organized into rodeos that charged admission for a program of recognized events: bronc riding, bulldogging, roping, and trick riding. As the Old West died, rodeos and Wild West shows sprang up to keep the best parts of it alive. The shows were a combination of nostalgia and genuine cowboy skills.

In 1895 Sam Privett found love. He was about 37 and the girl was Mary Frances "Mollie" Webb, reportedly just 15 years old. Accounts vary on their ages and other details, but all agree it was a May-December romance.[5] They met at a church social, where he was providing harmonica accompaniment to the singing. She hailed from the little town of Bronte in Coke County, Texas, and was the prettiest thing he had ever seen. To his surprise she was taken with him, too. He soon discovered that Mollie was an accomplished rider, and apparently her parents had no problem with their teenage daughter dating a man nearly twice her age. The couple tied the knot before the year was out and lived happily ever after.[6]

They settled down in San Angelo, where he ran his wagon yard-stable and broke horses on the side. They eventually had seven children, starting with Roy in 1896, then came Ella, the twins, Tommy, Bill, and finally Alta in 1909. Only one of the twins, Luther, survived. The other they buried as "Baby Girl." None of the children ever got past the eleventh grade in school.[7] Growing parental responsibilities did not prevent Sam and Mollie from launching a new business. The settled life had never been for him, and Mollie was game for anything. He sold the wagon yard-stable business and used the money to start Booger Red's Wild West Show.[8] At the turn of the century, Wild West shows were all the rage, with Buffalo Bill's as the gold standard. But there was always room for another. Americans could not get enough of the Old West as re-created in arenas and coliseums.

Sam was the star attraction and business manager of the show. Though sometimes misidentified in newspapers as Tom Preuett, he was always

Left: Samuel Privett and his wife, Mollie. Partners in love and business both. Undated photo. Author's collection.

Right: Rare photo of Booger Red on his horse, Montana Gyp, his face hidden by his hat and the distance between him and the photographer. Author's collection.

Booger Red to his fans. A natural promoter, he called himself the Champion Bronco Rider of the World, insisting, "It ain't bragging if it's true." It was a family business. Mollie and all the kids old enough to perform were featured in the show. Mollie sewed all their costumes. Besides being the seamstress, she was an accomplished trick rider. The kids did trick riding and roping, and the older boys did bareback and saddle bronc riding. Ella was good enough as a trick rider to later get on with Ringling Brothers Circus. So was Tommy, who performed as a "fancy roper," and Bill was almost as good as his pa atop a horse. Sam could not have been prouder of all of them. He had taught them well.[9]

But the crowd came to see the man known as Booger Red. He displayed his riding skills on horses, steers, and a bull named Andy that was a regular part of the show. Sam bragged that he could ride anything on four legs and had a standing offer of a hundred dollars to anyone who could bring him a horse he could not stay on. Reportedly he never had to pay off any challenger, though many took him up on his offer. The family traveled between towns by wagon and horseback. No comfortable train rides for the Privetts. They camped under the stars and tended their own animals.[10]

Sam and Mollie were not the only performing couple on the Wild West circuit and not the best known either. Annie Oakley and Frank Butler were the married costars of Buffalo Bill's Wild West show. May and Gordon William "Pawnee Bill" Lillie toured together as the featured stars of Pawnee Bill's Wild West Show, as did Kitty Wilkes and future movie stuntman Yakima Canutt. Though Mollie was never as famous as Kitty or May, Booger Red's own star shone brightly.[11]

The real costar of the show was Sam's horse, Montana Gyp, whose former owner had once brought his "outlaw horse" to San Angelo and offered $1,500 to anyone who could stay on him. Sam took him up on his bet and rode the horse to a standstill. Then he used the prize money to buy Montana Gyp. Horse and man were inseparable for the next twenty-three years, as much a team as Roy Rogers and Trigger or Gene Autry and Champion.

Foghorn Clancy, one of the earliest rodeo announcers, helped make Booger Red a celebrity of one-name fame, like Buffalo Bill or Hopalong Cassidy. Privett typically entered events under his given name, Samuel Thomas Privett or Sam Privett, and that was how most announcers identified him until one particularly impressive ride. Clancy in the announcer's booth declared the winner to be Booger Red, using no other name. Asked about it afterward, Clancy explained that if he had used Privett's real name, "nobody would have known whom I meant." And that was how a legend was born. At least that's the accepted story.[12]

Wild West shows, like circuses, had to hunker down somewhere in the winter months. The Privett show wintered on a ranch just north of San Angelo. In time, however, the show got to be too much of a business, so he sold out to the 101 Ranch, a big-time Wild West show started by the Miller brothers, Joseph, Zachary, and George, in 1907. Even before that Sam performed in shows big and small, like "The Stockmen's and Cow Boys' [sic] Roping and Riding Contest." He was a celebrity wherever he appeared, performing with Clay McGonagill, "Champion Roper of the

World"; Jim Hooker, "Champion Trick Rider"; and Bill Pickett, the Black bulldogger famous for "bringing wild steers to the ground with his teeth." Sometimes Sam performed with his kids, appearing with the 101 Ranch and with the Ringling Brothers, Al G. Barnes, and Hagenbeck-Wallace circuses. The latter, like Wild West shows, were just another paying gig. Some competitive contests offered five thousand dollars or more in prize money. Sam faithfully sent his earnings home to Mollie, who as the years passed took to calling him Old Man, always in a loving way.[13]

Eventually the gypsy life on the road far from home, performing his dangerous act day after day, became too much. Sam decided to retire, and he was not alone. Many old-timers on the rodeo circuit were hanging it up around the time of World War I. He had no regrets. He was still the best at what he did; it gave him pleasure and paid the bills. But he had passed the half-century mark, which made him practically a dinosaur in the world of rodeo. He had experienced bright lights and big times, performing at the 1904 St. Louis World's Fair and the 1915 San Francisco Panama-Pacific Exposition, where he won the World Champion Bronc Rider title. As he saw it, there were no more worlds to conquer.[14]

In 1915 Sam moved the family to Oklahoma, buying a spread where he could relax and raise stock. He continued to spend a good part of every year on the road, but at least he had a place to call home. Mollie had long been retired from performing, preferring to stay home and raise the kids.

There were still world fairs and circuses, but Wild West shows were dying. In 1916 the 101 Ranch Show stopped touring independently and joined forces with Buffalo Bill's show. The following year Cody died and with him the Wild West show. People could sit in darkened theaters and see the Wild West on the screen free of the flies and smells of the real thing. Performers like Sam had to find different showcases to display their talents. Local fat-stock shows filled the void. Performers could still spend time on the road going from show to show, but appearing in fewer shows was a way to slide gently into retirement. San could pick and choose a few fat-stock shows a year. Mollie appreciated having him at home more, and so did his body, beat up from years of wrestling ornery steers and broncs.

One of Sam's favorite stops was the annual Southwestern Exposition and Fat Stock Show at Fort Worth. In March 1916 he arrived in town on a train at the Santa Fe Station. When he left a grip in the baggage room, the attendant offered him a claim ticket to present when he returned. Sam said he did not need one, telling the man, "This grip belongs to the ugliest man in Texas—in the world. If anybody uglier than Booger Red of Tom Green County shows up, give him the grip. He's welcome to it." Booger Red's face as well as his riding skill were his claim to fame.[15]

In 1918 the Fort Worth stock show moved indoors and added rodeo events to the program. That year's event in the Stockyards Coliseum was the world's first indoor rodeo. The competitive performances quickly became the main draw of the annual stock show, drawing huge crowds to see bull-dogging and bronc-busting and the other rodeo elements. Booger Red was one of the stars that year, his name and face well-known to the locals. He was Fort Worth's first rodeo celebrity.[16]

Some fifteen years earlier he had ridden half-wild broncs on the old stock-show grounds, a patch of prairie surrounded by a rope fence with a few bleachers knocked together for seating. Now thousands crowded into the Stockyards Coliseum paying twenty-five cents a head to see perfor-mances that were once put on for free. At least 54 years old now, he was the oldest performer competing for the three thousand dollars in prize money, but he could still outride all challengers on four legs or two. He continued to come to Fort Worth for the annual event for the next three years. Though he loved performing, he had an aversion to being photographed, pulling his hat down low over his face if he saw a camera being aimed in his direction. For this reason he also missed out on the dawn of the motion picture age. When movie companies came calling wanting to make him a star of the silver screen, he refused, though he could have made a lot of money if he had accepted their offers. No shrinking violet, he nonetheless did not consider the camera his friend for good reason.[17]

As a rodeo performer Sam was unusual not just for his advanced years and scarred face. He had never touched liquor, reportedly to keep a promise made to his mother on her deathbed. A cowboy who did not drink was like a musician who does not read music or a dog that does not bark, and abstinence was not easy. In the early years there was not much else besides liquor to drink, and later, men in his line of work used liquor to ease their aches and pains and pass the down time. (No one ever explained whether his vow covered beer or not.) This is not to say he was completely saddle-broke and curried when around polite folks. He smoked a corncob pipe and chewed tobacco most of his life. He could spit a stream of tobacco juice through his front teeth and hit whatever he aimed at.[18]

Riding half-wild animals was punishing to the body. It was also exceedingly dangerous, no matter how good you were. He suffered his share of broken bones over the years. Once a horse fell on him and broke his leg, but he refused to crawl away. He was still in the saddle when the horse got back up. No injury ever kept him from riding, not even a broken arm. This was part of what made him so admired by his fellow cowboys. He was the real McCoy, not some fancy-pants trick rider.[19]

A forgotten part of Sam Privett's story is the young protégé he mentored, a fellow known as Booger Red Jr. Despite the same name, Junior was no relation, though it was Privett who gave him that name. "That's the only kid I've ever seen that has the makin's of as ugly a man as I am," he declared the first time he laid eyes on the young man. Junior, whose real name is unknown, was an "all-round product of the Texas range" just like his mentor, and also a top rider who appeared on numerous programs with the real Booger.[20]

Booger Red Privett officially retired in 1921 but found he could not stay away from the arena, like an actor drawn back to the footlights. He returned to Fort Worth in 1924 for the annual Southwestern Exposition and Fat Stock Show as a spectator with no intention of performing. He considered all that behind him as he took a seat in the top of the stands on Monday, March 10, watching the matinee performance. He had a cap pulled low over his face, hoping no one would recognize him, and no one did until a horse from hell named Romeo electrified the sparse crowd by throwing his rider right after coming out of the gate. Someone in the stands hollered that Booger Red could ride him, and a woman sitting behind him spoke up and said, "He's right here!" The crowd started hollering for him, and Sam's blood started racing as in past days. The nearly bald old bronc rider stood and made his way down the steps to the arena floor, where he traded his cap for a Stetson. Then he climbed aboard the defiant horse and told the men to turn 'em loose. Romeo broke out of the gate furiously bucking, with Sam hanging on with one hand and waving his hat with the other. For Booger Red it wasn't the old "smell of the greasepaint, roar of the crowd" that motivated theater performers; it was the smell of horseflesh and the roar of the arena that made him feel young again. His ride on Romeo ended with him still tall in the saddle, keeping alive the Booger Red legend that no horse ever threw him. It was his last ride, and what a way to go out.[21]

Two weeks later, back home in his own bed, Booger Red Privett died of Bright's disease, the same disease that had taken his father. He was 66 years old—or maybe 64 or even 62. Again, the record is not clear. His last words to his family gathered around the bed began with, "Boys, I'm leaving it with you," and ended with, "Have all the fun you can while you live 'cause when you are dead you are a long time dead." He was buried in the Miami, Oklahoma, cemetery. It was not a pauper's grave, but Mollie reportedly could not afford a marker, so the grave remained unmarked until Ella put up a headstone in 1980. Mollie lived another forty-five years, dying on September 26, 1969.[22]

Booger Red was gone but hardly forgotten. He lived on in Western lore with old-timers telling stories of his exploits for many years. It seems like everybody witnessed his last ride in Fort Worth. Poets like Whitney Montgomery wrote poems about him. He was written up in the *Southwest Review* literary journal in 1944, and that story was picked up by *Reader's Digest* in 1946. Famed folklorist J. Frank Dobie also kept his story alive, and even seventy years after his death, Fort Worth journalists were still relating the story of "Booger Red's Last Ride" to new audiences. In 1991 all this public interest finally resulted in a biography, but the author, Charlise Poe, who was a Booger Red contemporary, ran into the same problems as all chroniclers of Western characters: memories are faulty, legends are inflated, and first-hand sources can contradict each other. Sam and Mollie's last surviving child, Alta, was still living in 1991 when her father's biographer came calling, and she filled in some of the details as she remembered them.[23]

More than a few Western characters ended their days performing in Wild West shows, rodeos, and the like, among them Buffalo Bill Cody, Annie Oakley, and Frank James (see chap. 2). Booger Red Privett was also a member of this exclusive fraternity. When the real West was gone, they kept the memory alive.

Booger Red lives on today in the Historic Fort Worth Stockyards. His 1924 ride on Romeo was the biggest thing in the coliseum until "Live, Main Event Wrestling" arrived in the 1960s and Major League Baseball

Booger Red's Saloon, Fort Worth, Texas, with its iconic buffalo-butt backbar and saddle stools. A favorite night spot in the historic Stockyards. Author's collection.

held their player draft there in 2024. When the 1907 Stockyards Hotel was remodeled in 1984, the owners named the bar-restaurant "Booger Red's Saloon." Instead of bellying up to the bar for "tanglefoot," patrons can sit on saddle-topped barstools. They may ask, "Who or what the heck is 'Booger Red'?"

The answer, of course, is he was a real person, a genuine cowboy and rodeo performer who rode his last ride right here in Fort Worth. Few recognize the irony of naming a saloon after a man who was a teetotaler. Tourists leaving the bar can walk half a block down Exchange Avenue to Cowtown Coliseum, as it is now known, looking the same as it did over a hundred-plus years ago when Booger Red performed there. The man and his legend were inducted into the Rodeo Hall of Fame (Oklahoma City, Oklahoma) in 1975, and as someone said many years before, "There will only be one Booger Red."[24]

Chapter 6

Fort Worth Abortion Doctor Goes to Prison

There is nothing new under the sun, as they say, which applies to the hot-button topic of abortion. While polite folks may not have talked about it, the law has always had plenty to say about it. Abortion has been illegal in Texas since 1857. The same law that made it illegal to perform the procedure also made it illegal to assist in the procedure. Anyone doing so was an "accomplice" in a crime. Paradoxically, the same law said a woman who "performed an abortion upon herself" was not guilty of a crime.[1]

Abortion did not come before the law very often, or at least it was not reported in family newspapers. It took a particularly sensational case or notably important defendant to get into the newspaper. In Dallas in 1894 a man was charged with being an accomplice for helping his girlfriend, Violet Lepert, abort a pregnancy. The report does not say how they did it. What made the case more sensational is that when the prosecutor asserted that the accused was the only man with whom she had engaged in sexual relations, Violet took exception, saying she had also been intimate with a Dallas police officer. The officer, William T. Farmer, was a respected veteran of the force, but that did not keep him from being fired the next day for "immoral intimacy."[2]

In San Antonio that same year, Dr. James M. Hayes, a "well-known physician," was charged with "malpractice" for performing an abortion on Annie Kreuger at the behest of James Thorp, who employed the girl in his laundry. To abort Annie's pregnancy, Dr. Hayes used a surgical knife, leaving the girl in critical condition.[3]

Nearly a decade later, abortion was still not a subject respectable folks talked about—at least until it became a headline story. On May 9, 1912, Mary Walker Piner died seven days after having an abortion. She died in horrible pain, attended only by a nurse until rushed to a hospital at the end. Charged with murder were O. W. Sayers, a male friend who skipped town; Della King, the nurse; and Drs. J. B. Norris and W. Collier. Additionally, the two doctors were also charged with performing a "criminal abortion." Charges against Nurse King and Mr. Sayers were dismissed, but the state proceeded with the charges against the doctors, pushed by both county and state medical associations who were "determined to break up such alleged practices," meaning abortions. Both doctors were released on bail and separate trials set on the district court docket. Typical of trials in those days, the juries were composed solely of men. Both defendants offered the same defense—namely, that the girl's abortion had been "self-performed," and they had only been called in afterward in their professional capacity to "relieve the patient [and] restore her to health." Most of the medical establishment of Dallas testified for the prosecution. Juries acquitted both men, Collier on July 11 and Norris two days later. Collier was a witness for the defense at Norris's trial. His jury came back with an innocent verdict in just six minutes. The *Fort Worth Record and Register* called it "one of the hardest fought cases" in Dallas history.[4]

Mary Piner's death and the subsequent trials were news all over the state, but for sheer sensationalism, that was nothing compared to what happened in Fort Worth in 1913 with Daisy Moore. She was another girl in a delicate condition who had an abortion, but unlike Mary Piner, Daisy did not die as a result. And in Daisy's case there were also accusations of incest and evidence that the procedure was not voluntary.

Dr. William A. Link was a Fort Worth resident for many years. He moved to town in 1890 from Robertson County, Tennessee, when he was 40 years old. He brought with him a wife, Elizabeth Payne Link, and two sons, Joseph and Charles.[5]

He was a general practitioner but was also an entrepreneur and something of a renaissance man. He marketed a variety of potions and ointments, including his own brand-name "kidney pills," "nerve and blood tonic," "digestive tablets," "pile suppositories," "anti-malarial tablets," and "complexion cream." He was no gynecologist, but his practice served women in particular. Among the medical products he sold were a "bust developer" (fifty cents), "ladies liniment" (twenty-five cents), and something called a "female regulator" (one dollar). He advertised extensively, saying his products were "guaranteed under the pure food and drugs act" of 1906, and everything was manufactured in his own laboratory. He even offered home delivery. Nor did the good doctor's entrepreneurial spirit stop with medical products. In 1913 he secured a US patent for an "animal trap" that would kill the animal by drowning it.[6]

In 1912 he moved into an upstairs office at Second and Main, next door to Stripling's Department Store. His Main Street office and membership in the Fort Worth Medical Association meant he was no quack. He was a respected member of the medical community with a side business performing abortions on demand. Word got around, and women with a delicate problem—with or without their male partners knowing—came to him for help taking care of it. The enterprising doctor saw an untapped market in the medical field and stepped in to serve it. He performed his procedures in his office not just for the sake of convenience but also because no hospital would let him do it on their premises.[7]

His side business finally got him into trouble in February 1911, when he was arrested by Tarrant County Deputy Sheriff Dick Bates. The charge was performing a "criminal operation" on Mrs. Minta Vogel. Her husband, John Vogel, was charged with being an accomplice. It is unknown who informed the authorities. The case was not a high priority for County Attorney John W. Baskin, who eventually got an indictment, and Link seemed headed to trial. But Link had a top-flight lawyer who filed a motion in 1913 to get the charge dismissed on the grounds that the indictment did not specifically say the criminal act was performed "designedly." While most

Fort Worthers scratched their head over what that meant, Judge Raymond Buck "quashed" the indictment, letting Link off the hook. Since he had been out on bail the whole time, nothing really changed for him except the county attorney's office now had the good doctor in their sights should he continue his criminal ways.[8]

It took him less than three months to get into the same hot water again. In May 1913 Dr. Link was arrested and charged with performing an abortion on Daisy Moore of Peaster, Texas, whose age was variously given in the newspapers as 17, 18, or 19. Daisy was the stepdaughter of William E. Fondren, a banker and gentleman farmer in the same town. Fondren was charged with being "an accomplice" plus committing incest with the girl. The evidence would show that he had been molesting Daisy for years before she became pregnant, since she was 8 or 9. The case was so ugly, the newspapers had a hard time finding the words to describe the crime without violating traditional community standards of decency.[9]

Daisy's mother, Rachel, had been married to Fondren since 1901. By 1913 they had brought an additional five children into the world. The youngest was an infant that Daisy helped take care of. As a banker, a husband, and a father several times over, William Fondren could not have been more respectable, but something very despicable was going on behind closed doors.[10]

When he found out Daisy was pregnant, Fondren instructed his wife to "get the operation performed and get it done as cheap as you can." She brought the girl to Fort Worth on May 1 to find a doctor who would do the procedure on the QT. They could not go to the city's Emergency Hospital because the procedure was illegal, not to mention the embarrassment of being identified publicly. A trustworthy doctor in private practice was the only possibility. Two doctors turned her down but referred her to Dr. Link, who was not too sure until Rachel offered him two hundred dollars to do it. She told him that Daisy was only 14 and "in a family way" because of a "Peaster boy." Her husband, she insisted, was not guilty of anything except taking care of his stepdaughter's condition. Link performed the procedure in his office immediately while Daisy's mother held her hand. Afterward, mother and daughter paid the bill and left the same way they came in.[11]

Only known photograph of Fort Worth Emergency Hospital (Fourth and Jones). It opened in 1913 with beds for eighty-five patients and was subsequently renamed City-County Hospital. It was not the place for a woman to come seeking an abortion since the procedure was against the law in Texas. Author's collection.

Rachel placed the girl with a Fort Worth friend so that she could catch the train home to Peaster. Fondren himself came to town a few days later to take the girl home, but her sister Pansy Kriby had learned what was going on in the meantime. She intercepted him and told him he was not going to take Daisy back to "use her as you please." It was Pansy who went to the authorities, while they, as it turned out, might have preferred not to know about the Fondren family's problems.[12]

The police arrested Dr. Link, and he was charged with performing a "criminal act." He did not spend any time in jail, as he was allowed to bond out the same day as his arrest. County Attorney John Baskin also intended to charge Fondren with incest, but that charge had to be dropped when it was pointed out that Daisy was his stepdaughter, not his daughter, and besides it was finally established that she was 19 and therefore legally of the age of consent. That left only the charge of being an accomplice in the abortion because he had paid for it and directed his wife to get it done. The doctor and the banker were tried separately, with Fondren going first in Judge Marvin

Brown's Seventeenth District Court. His lead attorney was Albert Baskin, the brother of prosecuting attorney John W. Baskin. That was just one of the unusual aspects of the trial. Thirty "prominent" Parker County men came to Fort Worth to serve as character witnesses for the defendant. They included a district judge, a district attorney, county commissioner, and sheriff. Link's lawyers got a continuance from Judge Brown for their client's case, so the public's attention was focused solely on the Fondren proceedings.[13]

The courtroom was packed for the trial. It was the best show in town. Daisy was on the stand from 11:00 a.m. until 5:00 p.m. the first day. She frequently broke down crying as she told her story. Judge Brown stopped her testimony at one point when he caught sight of a Black man sitting in the back of the courtroom. He told the bailiff to throw the man out, referring to him specifically by his race ("Throw that damned n—— out!") It was unnecessary to explain the reason to the gallery. No white person in the room wanted a Black man listening to the shameful testimony of a white girl.[14]

Fondren's three-day trial ended in a conviction and a five-year sentence. His lawyers promptly appealed the verdict, but Judge Brown denied their motion for a new trial. They appealed that, too, all the way to the state court of criminal appeals. Meanwhile, Fondren's brother and other prominent citizens of Peaster posted a five-thousand-dollar bond to get him out of jail while his case was being appealed. Nearly a year later the verdict was affirmed, and William E. Fondren was headed to the penitentiary.[15]

Daisy was the principal state's witness in Dr. Link's trial, too, forcing her to repeat her story before another courtroom of strangers. She testified that her stepfather had first molested her as a child in a cotton field and continued to do so secretly for years thereafter. She further testified in detail about the abortion procedure and the pain it had caused. She frequently broke down sobbing during her lengthy testimony. The defense argued that Daisy had not been pregnant, and even if she were, the fetus was already dead by the time the procedure was performed. They called in their own doctor to examine Daisy, and he concurred that she had indeed undergone an abortion. The defense argued, however, that Dr. Link had not performed a "criminal operation" since Daisy had walked in before the procedure and walked out again afterward; therefore, this was no surgical procedure that fit the definition of an "abortion." The prosecution scored points by getting into evidence that this was not the first time Dr. Link had performed the procedure, which was illegal whether the patient was confined to bed or not. But the shocker came when Daisy's mother took the stand for the defense. She testified that her husband was completely innocent. In fact, she said, she could think of "one hundred reasons" why he was innocent though she did not enumerate them. Dr. Link did not take the stand. The four-day trial ended on July 4 with Link being convicted. The jury took just two hours to reach its verdict, and it came out afterward that it was never in doubt. They sentenced him to four years in prison. His lawyers made a motion for a new trial, which Judge Brown denied. They then announced their intention to appeal the verdict on the grounds that "much of the evidence had no bearing on the case other than to inflame the minds of the jurors against the defendant." Like Fondren, Link was released on bail while his appeal wound its way through the courts.[16]

In February 1914 Dr. Link's sentence was affirmed by the court of appeals in Austin. His lawyers continued to battle for a new hearing until the court finally slammed the door in early March. Tarrant County Sheriff Bill Rea was prepared to take him into custody but held up while Link cared for his sick wife ("nervous prostration") and put his affairs in order. Then, instead of turning himself in to the sheriff, he announced that he would go to Huntsville on his own and turn himself in there.[17]

Neither Fondren nor Link spent much time behind bars. They were both pardoned without fanfare by Governor Oscar Colquitt on the recommendation of the pardon board in time to be home for Christmas 1914. Dr. Link's "conditional pardon" was helped along by a petition signed by 1,500 Fort Worth citizens, including eleven of the twelve jurors who convicted him. In 1921 he received a full pardon from Governor William R. Hobby. He returned to Fort Worth in 1914 and tried to put his life back together. His wife, "Lizzie," and two grown sons welcomed him home. Barred by state law from resuming his medical practice, he found work as the head of a medical supply company in Dallas and continued to list himself as a physician, no matter what the courts and state medical association said.

Texas Governor Oscar Colquitt at his desk in the capitol, 1913. He was willing
to pardon an abortion doctor as soon as the heat died down. No. c0031a,
Austin History Center, Austin Public Library.

Fondren went home to Rachel and the rest of his family (not counting
Daisy), devoting the rest of his active years to farming full-time. He lived a
quiet life until dying in 1950.[18]

In September 1928 the 78-year-old doctor took sick and was confined to
bed at home (933 Hemphill). He seemed to be improving in October but died

peacefully on November 20. He left an estate valued at nineteen thousand dollars to his widow and two sons.[19]

As for poor Daisy, she left the state soon after the trial, moving to Utah, where she married in 1918. With her new name she started a new life far from the scene of her humiliation. She had two children. Many years later and long after her brush with shame had been forgotten, she returned to Fort Worth, joining a Church of Christ congregation on the south side of town. She was still a member there when she died in 1977 at the age of 84. It is highly doubtful any of her fellow congregants knew of her part in a scandalous news story more than half a century earlier.[20]

As for the issue that caused so much grief, abortion, Texans continued to take the law into their own hands when it came to expressing their opinion. In 1921 Sam Ward of Hillsboro, Texas, emptied his revolver in the general direction of Sam Tonnahill at "closing school exercises." Ward believed Tonnahill had seduced his daughter and then convinced her to get an abortion when she became pregnant. Tonnahill had been convicted of both crimes, but the verdict was overturned on a technicality. Four of Ward's shots hit his intended target, killing him. The fifth struck a young schoolgirl in the leg.[21]

Chapter 7

Cato Sells
"Godfather of the Red Man"

Cato Sells (1859–1948) was one of Fort Worth's biggest boosters in the twentieth century, behind only Amon Carter and B. B. Paddock.[1] That remarkable claim is supported by considering what he did for our city for more than four decades. He put Fort Worth on the national map, brought in federal dollars, and fought to make it the First City of Texas. Much of that he did while commissioner of the Bureau of Indian Affairs in Woodrow Wilson's administration (1913–1921). He was the most important person to hold that post since Ely S. Parker, the first commissioner of Indian Affairs (1869–1871), who was forced to resign in disgrace. Sells left the office with the universal respect of the nation. As commissioner he worked so tirelessly for Native Americans that the newspapers dubbed him Godfather of the Red Man and, more dramatically, the Father of All the Indians, both politically incorrect but bestowed on him by admirers with only the best motives. A better term, if less colorful, would be Friend of Native Americans. Never a desk-bound bureaucrat, Sells put the Bureau of Indian Affairs (BIA) at the forefront of the federal government when it had long been an afterthought.[2]

Cato Hedden Sells was born in Vinton, Iowa, on October 6, 1859, to George W. and Elizabeth (Seddon) Sells. At that time Iowa was part of the

Left: Cato the Elder, second-century Roman literary figure and namesake for Cato Sells. Author's collection.

Right: Mayor Cato Sells of La Porte, Iowa, ca. 1882. Author's collection.

western frontier. His father was well-read in the classics and gave him the name Cato after the Roman literary giant Marcus Porcius Cato (a.k.a. Cato the Elder). George Sells died when his son was just 13, forcing Cato to go to work to support the family. While working in a hardware store, he attended school and learned enough to be admitted to Cornell College in 1875. He worked to pay tuition, room, and board until graduating in 1878. He studied law under Judge Charles A. Bishop for two years to gain admission to the Iowa State Bar Association at the age of 21. He settled in La Porte City and two years later was elected mayor, the youngest in the state's history.[3]

His rapid rise was attributable to his brains and energy. He had a simple, one-word motto, "work," and claimed to have never taken a vacation in his life. He joined the Democratic party and rose quickly in the ranks. He was a delegate to the Democratic National Convention in 1888 and again in 1892, and in 1893 served as president of the Iowa Democratic State Convention. By this time he had achieved national recognition in the party. The next year

President Grover Cleveland appointed him United States Attorney for the Northern District of Iowa. At 35 he was the youngest district attorney in the United States. He won acclaim among Republicans and Democrats alike for prosecuting pension fraud cases among Union veterans of the Civil War.[4]

He was touted as Democratic candidate for governor of Iowa in 1899, and though he had the endorsement of many of the state's newspapers, he was opposed by the Populists, who considered him too pro-business. He lost the nomination to Fred White, who lost the election to Republican Albert B. Cummins. Even though Iowa remained strongly a Republican state for years to come, Sells was still regarded as "the greatest of all Iowa Democrats" by his admirers. He presided over the state Democratic Convention again in 1899 and the next year chaired the Iowa delegation to the National Democratic Convention in Kansas City.[5]

In 1891 he married Lola A. McDaniel, a Wellesley College graduate who gave up a career in mathematics to become Mrs. Cato Sells. They were married for fifty-seven years and had three children: Dorothy (b. 1892), Donald Douglas (b. 1894), and Barbara (b. 1895). All three got college degrees and went on to successful careers in the professions. Cato and Lola proved to be a perfectly matched couple. She was as devoted to public service as her husband, and besides supporting him at his public events, she had her own causes. She was an early advocate of women's suffrage and organized the public affairs division of the Fort Worth Woman's Club. Another of her pet causes was building a federal prison for women, who historically had served their time in a separate section of the men's prison.[6]

With Iowa firmly in the hands of Republicans, Sells decided to relocate to Southern climes where Democrats ruled. It was a combination of politics and financial opportunity that brought him to Texas in 1906. Lawyer Sells came to Cleburne to represent a client in the sale of a piece of property. After collecting his one-thousand-dollar fee, he decided to stay on and hang out his shingle. It proved to be an excellent move because he was soon recognized as a "lawyer of reputation," and better yet, he got in on the ground floor when Texas State Bank and Trust of Cleburne was organized, becoming the bank's first president when it opened in 1907. He gave his brother D. G. Sells a job as a cashier. Sells served as president of the bank for three years.[7]

Sometime after coming to Cleburne, he was elevated to "judge," though the record does not show he was ever appointed or elected to any judiciary position. The title "judge," like "colonel," was widely used in the South as a sign of respect that was bestowed, not earned. The first mention of Judge Cato Sells in the newspapers appears in 1908 without explanation. He took an active part in the civic life of Cleburne. His bank sponsored a countywide spelling bee, which was promoted as "the greatest contest in the history of Texas." That claim is impossible to verify, but what is true is that more than one thousand people jammed into the high school auditorium, and Judge Sells judged the contest. His reputation for getting things done and in a big way spread beyond Johnson County. He was a member of a committee formed in Dallas to build an interurban rail line between Dallas and Cleburne. He also began to acquire admirers in Fort Worth, just forty-two miles away as the crow flies.[8]

Sells was just as active in party politics in Texas as he had been in Iowa. In 1912 he was a delegate to the Democratic National Convention when it met in Baltimore and nominated Woodrow Wilson. Though he supported William Jennings Bryan in the beginning, he quickly jumped on the Wilson bandwagon, winning fame as one of the Immortal 40 who battled successfully to get Wilson nominated. Then he campaigned vigorously for him in Texas against William Howard Taft and Theodore Roosevelt.[9]

When Wilson won the election, he recognized Sells's contribution to his victory in ways large and small. First, he allowed him to name the new postmaster for Vinton, Iowa, because that had been Sells's birthplace. He also supported him as the Texas representative on the Democratic National Committee, then in May Wilson named him commissioner of the Bureau of Indian Affairs, an agency in the Department of the Interior. Indians were considered wards of the federal government, and the commissioner's job had long been considered a political sinecure. It paid $7,500 a year, which was probably less than Sells was making as a bank president. The inside joke in the administration was that if Wilson had not won the election, "a whole lot of people would never have known there had ever been more than one Democrat in Iowa." The joke was on detractors of the BIA. Although it had long been treated as an afterthought, with six thousand employees, it was the largest agency in the federal government, and it became Cato Sells's fiefdom.[10]

Sells embarked on his new job with all the determination and focus he had brought to every job he ever held. Leaving his family in Cleburne, he moved to Washington, DC, which became home away from home for the next eight years. He was determined to raise up the Native American from poverty and backwardness, or, as he put it, to "help the Indian help himself." In 1910 there were on 265,700 Native Americans by census count in the United States, a number than had declined to 244,400 by 1920, but Sells wanted to debunk what he thought of as the prevailing myth of the "Vanishing Indian." It only seemed that they were a dying race because the public barely took notice of them. Sells was not about to be just another Washington bureaucrat. He made himself not just the most visible commissioner of Indian Affairs in history, but the "busiest man in Washington." In his first two years he visited every Indian reservation in the country—spread out across twenty-six states—traveling thousands of miles by train, automobile, and horseback. At every stop he worked to win the hearts of his "wards," referring to "myself and the other Indians here." Just as important, he garnered positive reviews for the Wilson administration everywhere he went.[11]

Wilson served two terms, and Sells was right there the whole time. He adopted a tough love approach toward his charges. Even before National Prohibition was adopted in 1919, he banned the sale of alcohol on reservations, holding himself up as an example as a teetotaler. He started reservation schools to teach practical skills to boys and "home crafts" to girls because he thought that would help them succeed in the modern world. His ultimate goal was to make Indians "self-sufficient" so that they no longer had to be dependent on government handouts. Besides schooling, "self-sufficiency" meant learning how to raise wheat and livestock and sell them on the open market. Sells also ordered the first hospitals and maternity wards to be built on reservations where hygiene and medical care were virtually unknown before he came along. He took a strong stand against polygamy, which was a standard practice by several tribes, including the Comanche. Instead, he said the Indian male should have just one wife as God ordained and "be good" to her and their children. He also encouraged the adoption of Indian children by nonwhites because he felt it gave them a better chance at life than growing up on a reservation.[12]

He considered the American Indian a unique race, which is why in 1914 he banished any book from reservation schools that said Indigenous Americans originally came from Asia. He was convinced that aboriginal Americans were descended from the Lost Tribes of Israel.[13]

Despite his travels about the country and punishing workload, Sells still found time to visit North Texas, in particular Fort Worth. He made speeches to civic groups and hobnobbed with local officials. He was the guest of honor at the 1918 Exposition and Fat Stock Show. As a faithful Christian and accomplished speaker, he found an appreciative audience wherever he went. His most popular speech was "The Trial of Christ from a Lawyer's Standpoint."[14]

His popularity in his adopted state was so great he was urged to make a run for Congress in 1916. Even Iowans recognized how much he had done for Texas. Said one Republican newspaper presciently in 1910, "Judge Sells will in our opinion grow steadily in influence and usefulness in the affairs of Texas." The rumors of a run for Congress were persistent enough that he issued a public statement disavowing any political ambitions, stating that he was completely committed to the "protection and progress of the Indian race." He also devoted himself to Woodrow Wilson's reelection campaign in Texas. That did not stop Sells's supporters from continuing to float his name for state office. In 1917 he was touted for governor, another honor that he declined, and though he chose not to run for political office, that did not stop him from offering his considered opinions on foreign policy (expansionist) and national prohibition (pro).[15]

He took a particular fondness for Fort Worth, whether because of its warm-hearted hospitality or its nearness to his Cleburne home is unclear. And that fondness was reciprocated. Whenever he came to town, city fathers rolled out the red carpet. Depending on how long he was in town, the chamber of commerce would hold a luncheon or banquet for him, selling tickets that were always snapped up quickly. Sells had a lifelong habit of printing up copies of his speeches and distributing them to those who bought tickets to his appearances. He was always guaranteed a large audience in Fort Worth.

In turn, he was the city's man in Washington. In 1915 he went to work getting a new federal building for Fort Worth. The existing structure was nearly twenty years old, since which time the city's population had more than quadrupled. City fathers had been lobbying Washington for a new building for the post office and other federal functions since 1913 but had gotten little sympathy. Sells's involvement was a definite plus, although ultimately the city did not get a new federal building (post office) until 1931. Ironically, at the same time Fort Worth leaders and Sells were campaigning for a new federal building for Fort Worth, Cleburne was also lobbying for a new federal building, albeit without Cato Sells in their corner.[16]

He also went to bat to get Fort Worth the southwestern headquarters of the Federal Farm Loan Bank. The *Star-Telegram*, one of his biggest fans, felt obliged to explain why this Cleburne resident was such a big Fort Worth booster: "He has long identified himself with Fort Worth interests and is regarded as a resident of [our] city in the discussion of matters pertaining to [our] material development." So, take that, Cleburne.[17]

In the run-up to the election of 1916, he urged President Wilson to come to Fort Worth, assuring him that his visit would bring out "the largest [political] gathering ever held in Texas." Sells's voice was not the only Texas voice in the president's ear. He was part of a Texas contingent in the administration that included Colonel Edward House (advisor), Albert Burleson (postmaster general), Thomas Gregory (attorney general), and David Houston (secretary of agriculture).[18]

Sells's proudest accomplishment as Indian commissioner may have been getting six thousand Native Americans from all over the country to enlist in World War I. Native Americans were not subject to the draft and they had no reason to love the United States, so getting them to enlist was a signal accomplishment. He focused most of his highly persuasive talents on the Oklahoma Cherokee, who signed up in large numbers. Indian volunteers from all over the country trained at Camp Travis (San Antonio) and Camp Bowie (Fort Worth). Sells could take personal credit for bringing three hundred Native Americans to Camp Bowie from Oklahoma. In March 1918, while attending the Fat Stock Show, he paid a visit to Camp Bowie, posing for pictures that appeared both in the newspapers and in army recruiting literature. A month later he

US Commissioner of Indian Affairs Cato Sells with Oklahoma trainees at Camp Bowie, 1917. A wartime photo opportunity intended to show the patriotism of Native Americans. Byron C. Utecht Papers, Special Collections, University of Texas at Arlington Library.

came back and "inspected" the Oklahoma recruits training there. It was his personal campaign to integrate Indians fully into American society, and part of that was seeing them train alongside other (meaning white) recruits. Fourteen different tribes were represented in the 142nd and 144th Infantry regiments training at Camp Bowie. The *Star-Telegram* tagged along on his April trip to take pictures that were carried in the national news. It is doubtful there would have been a Native American contingent training at Camp Bowie and Camp Travis if not for Cato Sells.[19]

Seven months after his second visit to Camp Bowie, he was back in Fort Worth, only this time not representing Uncle Sam or Native Americans. While touring West Texas oil fields he came down with influenza, which at the time was sweeping the country. He was brought to Fort Worth and put in isolation at the Westbrook Hotel. Because of who he was, he got personal doctor's visits and was waited on round the clock until he recovered. While he was battling the flu, World War I ended in an armistice. In the months to come, his Oklahoma boys would come home, but he would not be there to welcome them back.[20]

As the Wilson administration wound down, Sells prepared to return to Texas. He took pride in his accomplishments as Indian commissioner, and most of those he had served lamented his departure from the office he had held for eight years. The only sour note to be heard came from a Native American publication in Minnesota that blasted the BIA in general but went easy on "the Hon. Cato Sells" personally. It did, however, state that he ruled over his wards "with greater power than the Kaiser or Czar over their subjects."[21]

It was not just Commissioner Sells but also Mrs. Sells that won the hearts of most observers. Both with and without her husband she visited reservations around the country. A Wyoming newspaper described her as "a most charming personality." She called her husband their "friend" and told her Indian audience she hoped they would be "as good to their wives and children as her husband had been to her and their children." They in turn gave her an Indian name, "Mrs. Spotted Rabbit," with no explanation of just what it meant exactly. She took it as a compliment.[22]

The end of Cato Sells's tenure as Indian commissioner came in April 1921. In one of his final speeches, he repeated the message he had consistently asserted for eight years: "The Indian race is not a dying race but a living race with a glorious future. . . . I have faith in the Indian people, and I have reason for that faith. I believe in the policy that I have followed—a policy that allowed me to give to the Indian people better health, education, and industrial prosperity and thereby secure to the race the opportunities its pristine qualities and power deserve."[23] As much as any outgoing member of the Wilson administration, his departure from office was news all over the country. His employees recognized his service by giving him a handsome silver chest as a going-away gift. He announced that his and Mrs. Sells's future home would be Texas, without specifying exactly where that would be. Many suspected that he had outgrown Cleburne, and if Fort Worth was not already at the top of the list as a future home, it didn't hurt that one of their daughters was "educational director" for W. C. Stripling Department Store in Fort Worth. They traveled some to see their other children before coming back to settle permanently in Fort Worth. They bought a house at 2016 Windsor Place and joined the First Presbyterian Church. Later they moved to 2831 Princeton, their final Fort Worth residence.[24]

Sells may have retired from government service, but he was not ready for the rocking chair. He continued to work for Native Americans in the 1920s, representing them in court battles for their rights after oil was discovered on reservation land. He also kept an active hand in the Democratic party and in Texas boosterism. He joined a Rotary Club offshoot composed of "progressive businessmen" calling themselves the All Texas Special. They took as their mission "selling Texas to the North and East," a goal at least as old as the Texas Spring Palace (1889–1890). He was the only Fort Worther on the organization's executive committee.[25]

Three years later he was named chairman of the Texas Centennial Celebration (1836–1936) committee in charge of planning an extravagant 1936 event. Also on the committee were fellow Fort Worthers J. T. Pemberton, Van Zandt Jarvis, I. H. Burney, and Joseph S. Myers. Their job was to create a Centennial Exposition that would "Texanize Texas," whatever that meant, and in the process create something that would "rival the great expositions previously held in the United States." The committee did indeed plan a grand event, though it could not keep Dallas and Fort Worth from going their separate ways. The Fort Worthers on the committee may have secretly been glad that Fort Worth did its own "Frontier Centennial."[26]

He enjoyed a solid relationship with *Star-Telegram* publisher Amon Carter, who sought an appointment for him to the State Highway Commission. Sells had a long record of supporting transportation, including road and interurban rail construction, but Governor Dan Moody blocked it. That veto did not particularly bother Sells, but it produced a permanent rift between the publisher and the governor.[27]

In 1941 Cato and Lola celebrated fifty years of marriage with their golden wedding anniversary. The *Star-Telegram* carried the story of the loving couple along with an accompanying photograph. The photo almost certainly shows a man who had suffered a stroke at some point previously. Medical records are not available, but his complete absence from party and civic affairs in his final years is further evidence. If true, this was a sad fate for a man who had a been such a dynamo and workaholic all his life.[28]

Cato Sells died peacefully in a Fort Worth hospital on December 30, 1948. He had suffered physical problems for at least five years. The funeral

Cato and Lola Sells celebrate fiftieth wedding anniversary, June 30, 1941.
Cato's physical appearance shows the telltale signs of having suffered a stroke.
Fort Worth Star-Telegram Collection, Special Collections, University of Texas at
Arlington Library.

was from First Presbyterian Church two days later. He was buried in Cleburne
Memorial Cemetery.[29]

Cato Sells's legacy is enormous. He rightly considered his time at the
head of the BIA his "greatest achievement." When he left the agency, the
superintendent of the Five Civilized Tribes noted that during his tenure, he had
handled hundreds of millions of dollars, "more money than has ever passed
through [the agency's] hands before," adding, "It is the only seven [*sic*] years
in our history in which there has not been a scandal in that department."[30]

A further testimony to his influence was that in the years that followed,
"many" young Indian men adopted the name Cato Sells. It was a widespread

practice among Native American tribes for boys to choose a lifetime name for themselves when they reached their majority. One report claimed at least a hundred such decisions were made in the next six years. Though a white man himself, it is amazing how much of an inspiration Sells was to Native American males who grew up during his tenure at the BIA.[31]

It took a Democratic president, Woodrow Wilson, to appoint him to that office as a reward for his invaluable support. Most scholars give credit to Edward M. House for carrying Texas for candidate Wilson in 1912, but some contemporary Texas insiders asserted the credit rightly belonged to Sells. Said one, "It might truthfully be said that Cato Sells put Wilson in the White House." That was why when Sells came out in favor of William G. McAdoo for the Democratic nomination in 1924, many thought history would repeat itself. That did not happen, but the Sells name was still one to contend with in Democratic party politics.[32]

Sells was also an early advocate of bringing higher education to West Texas, a vast territory without a single institution of higher learning. He was part of a group that included Amon Carter and others who favored legislation creating "a coeducational institution for white children which shall emphasize instruction in agriculture and home economics." That dream eventually became Texas Tech University.[33]

Finally, when he left Washington Sells took with him back to Texas a large collection of Native American artifacts and craftwork, acquired over eight years on the job. Some of it was displayed in their home. Other pieces went into storage. In his last days he indicated a desire to donate it to an appropriate institution. After his death Mrs. Sells donated most of the items to the Fort Worth Children's Museum, providing the basis of their enviable Native American collection. Sells, along with Weatherford's G. A. Holland, were two of the biggest if not the biggest collectors of Native American artifacts (a.k.a. "relics") in Texas, and both were major benefactors of the Children's Museum collections (now the Fort Worth Museum of Science and History).[34]

Chapter 8

Manet Harrison and James Fowler
America's First Black "Power Couple"

Power couple" is a term applied today to a married or romantically linked couple where each partner is accomplished in his/her own right. It has been applied to Eleanor and Franklin Roosevelt and Barrack and Michelle Obama, among others, but Fort Worth arguably gave the nation its first Black power couple, Manette (also Manet, pronounced Man-ā′) Harrison and Stephen Hamilton Fowler. In their day she was more famous than him, which makes them even more remarkable. Today they are largely unknown.[1]

Both were born and grew up in Fort Worth, children of the Black middle class. She began life in 1895 as Minnia Helen Harrison. As a young woman she Gallicized her given name to Manette, which she considered more suitable for a cultured lady of French Creole heritage. Some newspapers had trouble with that name, writing it as the reporter heard it or translated it: Minnie or Banet. She traced her family roots back through Louisiana to the Caribbean diaspora of Africans and came to consider Yoruba, not English, her mother tongue. When she finally had her own school, she insisted that her Black students learn the difficult Yoruba language. In the racial distinctions of the time, both Manet and Stephen were described as "mulatto" in the 1920 census.[2]

Stephen was born in 1881 and, like Manet, came through the segregated Fort Worth school system, which until 1910 stopped at the primary level. That was the year the Colored High School opened. The accepted version of Manet's story says she graduated "with highest honors" and went on to Tuskegee Agricultural and Normal School (Alabama) in 1912, graduating a year later, this time with "highest honors in music and art." Reportedly, she got to know both George Washington Carver and Booker T. Washington, two icons of Black education, at Tuskegee. Likewise, Stephen also went on to college, graduating from Prairie View Normal and Industrial College in 1901 after just two years, which was the standard course of study at teaching (normal) schools then. There is no indication that he graduated with "highest honors." The record is clear, however, that he returned to Fort Worth to teach high school as "Professor Fowler," an honorary title bestowed on Black men with college degrees who took up a career in education.[3]

Manet was a child prodigy, giving piano recitals at age 6. She started formal piano lessons at age 7 with Jeanie Marie Roe, daughter of wealthy (white) Fort Worth lumberman A. J. Roe. At the going rate of twenty-five cents a lesson, this was something of a sacrifice for her father, an employee of the US Post Office. According to someone who knew her personally, she actually left Tuskegee with a degree in "domestic science," which she never used, then joined the faculty at Prairie View, where she put her true talents to work teaching music. Fort Worth drew her back to teach in her hometown, although her options were extremely limited. As a Black woman she could only teach in one of the three "colored" schools, but even with a college education there was no guarantee she would be hired. White women also taught in the "colored" schools, which led the city's Black leaders in 1901 to petition the city council to hire not just white teachers but "the best teachers our [own] race affords."[4]

It was a love of music and church that brought them together, though their paths probably crossed earlier as middle-class Blacks on the fast track to success. Both were also members of Mount Gilead Baptist Church, the "mother church" of Fort Worth's Black Baptist congregations. He was on the staff teaching Bible classes. She was director of the choir and the organist. In 1915 they tied the knot at Mount Gilead in one of the biggest

Manet Harrison and Stephen Fowler wedding photos, 1915. Manet's photo from Linda Jo & Scott Barker Collection. Stephen's photo courtesy of Nilah "Peaches" Davis.

social events of the year in the Black community (unnoticed in the white community). In the next ten years they would have five children (two girls and three boys), whom they raised to value education and make their way in the professional world.[5]

It was as professionals that Stephen and Manet made their mark. Within two years of taking a position in the Fort Worth public schools, she was promoted to "director of music" for the three "negro schools." In that role she put on choral programs ("festivals") of African American folk music for audiences around the city, building bridges between the Black and white communities that broke down the era's Jim Crow conventions. Meanwhile, after eighteen years teaching in Tarrant County schools, Stephen resigned in 1919 to become the first general secretary of Fort Worth's "Negro YMCA," a position he would occupy for the next twenty years. One of his goals was "promoting cooperation" between the white and Black communities.[6]

Both were talented, ambitious, and entrepreneurial. Like many creative prodigies, Manet refused to be defined by conventional categories. She
played piano and pipe organ, sang, and painted in more than one medium.
Stephen turned the Negro YMCA into a virtual settlement house, offering a
variety of community-based services that the city's Black residents could get
nowhere else. Those included, most notably, a trade school and an employment "bureau." Thus, Stephen Fowler was associated with the city's Black
community centers, Mount Gilead Baptist Church, and the Negro YMCA.
On his own time, he organized a male quartet that performed African
American folk songs and spirituals for both Black and white audiences while
Manet made an impact beyond performing and teaching. She was elected
president of the Women's Federated Missionary Society of the Black Baptist
church and a founder of the Texas Association of Negro Musicians. Their
first collaborative effort was a musical pageant, "Up from Slavery," to raise
money for Fort Worth's Negro YMCA. It played two nights at the North Side
Coliseum, one night for a Black audience and the next for a white audience.
A decade later they took another original pageant, "The Voice," to Chicago
for the golden jubilee of the National (Black) Baptist Convention of America.
A cast of two thousand depicted "the birth, growth and achievements of the
Baptists of the world," focusing on Black Baptists, naturally.[7]

In 1925 she organized the Negro Music Institute of Fort Worth, which
was an integral part of the Texas Association of Negro Musicians (TANM),
which was affiliated with the National Association of Negro Musicians
(NANM). She was the first president of the Texas branch, headquartered
in Fort Worth. Her mission as an educator went beyond teaching music to
promoting education among African American youth. At the time most Black
children did not go on beyond grade school, much less all the way to college.
To change that she used children's natural love of music to spark a love of
education in general. Stephen joined her in this pursuit. Both were on the
institute's board and taught there. They enrolled two hundred children in their
first class in 1926, setting a remarkable number of young African Americans
on the path to break out of the prison of Jim Crow segregation.[8]

They expanded the institute two years later to create a "master summer
school of music" under the auspices of the TANM, the first of its kind

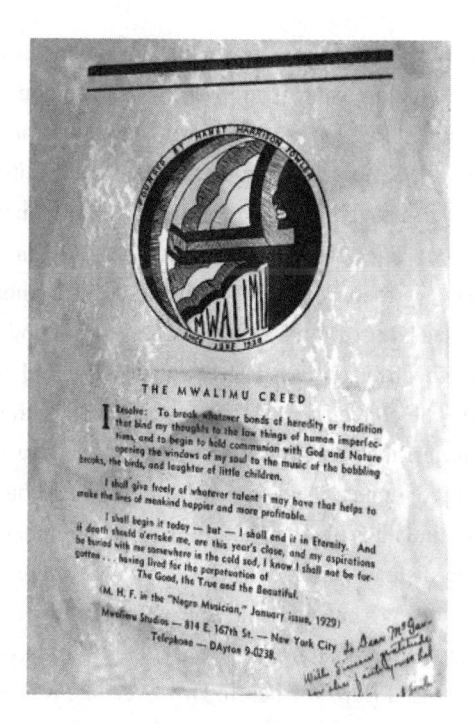

The Mwalimu Creed, this one signed by Manet Harrison Fowler herself, ca. 1928. Courtesy of Nilah "Peaches" Davis.

anywhere in the state. Students came from all over Texas and Oklahoma to attend a week of classes. Stephen was vice president and treasurer of the school while Manet organized the classes. It kicked off with a music program at St. James Baptist Church. The city opened James E. Guinn Elementary for the classes.[9]

The master summer school was a remarkable accomplishment. It drew faculty from all over the state, and not just African Americans. Among the white teachers was E. Clyde Whitlock, longtime arts and music critic for the *Record-Telegram* and later the *Star-Telegram*. Whitlock would closely follow Manet's career long after that summer, serving as a very public advocate for the woman. The school was about more than just music. It amounted to a deep dive into African culture for American-born children and proved such a success that they offered it during several successive summers, splitting the classes between Zion Baptist and Mount Olivet Baptist Churches. In the following summers it grew from one week to six weeks. It must have been successful to draw children into stuffy summer classrooms day after day, week after week, when freedom and the out of doors beckoned.[10]

The summer of 1929 was a busy time for Manet. In addition to the master summer school, she persuaded NANM to hold their annual convention in Fort Worth. The *Star-Telegram*, which generally ignored the Black community, covered the event, reporting three hundred delegates among the thousand people who attended. Out-of-town visitors had to be put up in private homes and the handful of boarding houses because Fort Worth did not have a Black hotel at the time. The convention ended on August 30 with a concert in the North Side Coliseum that brought out both Blacks and whites—sitting in segregated seating, of course. And somehow during these busy years, Manet found time to continue her own education. Her professional training was in "church music," a distinct genre from classical, contemporary, or what was widely known as "Negro music," and she performed as a concert pianist. It was her skill at the keyboards that got her the job right out of college as pianist at Mount Gilead Baptist Church. However, she was not content to be a church pianist. She began studying voice at the Chicago Musical College and the American Conservatory of Music, winning plaudits as a soprano who possessed "a natural voice of great beauty, range, and dramatic quality." Subsequently known as a "dramatic soprano," after 1929 she was more in demand as a vocalist than a concert pianist.[11]

By 1930 she was a "national figure" in the fields of both music and education. That did not mean she had outgrown her hometown, because that same year she held a vocal recital at Allen Chapel, a smallish Black church on the edge of downtown. The *Star-Telegram* called her "the first individual of her race" to be honored with a solo performance anywhere in Fort Worth. As usual, her audience included both Blacks and whites. She started with a selection of classical pieces—"material that can be heard at any vocal recital," said Clyde Whitlock—followed by Black spirituals before finishing with "genuine African melodies sung in native languages." An admiring Whitlock wrote, "Despite long association with European [i.e., classical] music, she retains the feeling for these songs which is inherited."[12]

While she performed at various venues across Fort Worth, her favorite place to perform was where it all started, Mount Gilead Baptist Church. The congregation was her extended family. Her recitals always brought out a racially mixed audience, the only time most of the whites had ever been in the place. Manet's performances in the city paved the way for the most famous Black vocalist of the day, opera star Marian Anderson, to come to Fort Worth twice, first in 1939, then again in 1941. Anderson came as the guest of the all-white Civic Music Association, performing at Will Rogers and Mount Gilead. The warm reception Anderson received, in particular performing highbrow opera music for a church audience at Mount Gilead, was because of Manet.[13]

Manet never thought of herself as simply a musical artist, and her stage was bigger than Fort Worth. She dreamed of transforming her summer masters' school into a year-round program of "African civilization, art and culture." (She disdained the name "Negro" as a demeaning relic of slavery.) Stephen supported her in this dream, but it was always her dream. She needed not just a building but financing, and those were not going to happen in Fort Worth. It took a few years, but in 1932 her dream became a reality when she moved the master summer school to the Bronx, where she expanded the curriculum to include all things African: history, art, culture, geography.

One source suggests that what brought her to the Bronx was staying close to her eldest daughter, Manet Helen, who had enrolled in New York University. Manet and Stephen raised their children to pursue the path of higher education, not just for the financial rewards but also to help lift their race out of servitude, and Manet Helen was on that path. However, attributing the move to New York as merely an expression of a mother's love is to discount Manet's driving ambition to change the world. New York at the time, Harlem in particular, was the mecca for Black intellectuals and artists. It was home to Langston Hughes, W. E. B. DuBois, Marcus Garvey, Duke Ellington, and Bessie Smith. Nowhere else in America could she rub shoulders with such a glittering assemblage of stars of her own race, collectively dubbed the Harlem Renaissance. She set up shop in the Bronx and in 1933 renamed her school the Mwalimu School of Music and Creative Art. (*Mwalimu* is Swahili for "noble or distinguished teacher.") Before moving she had visited to talk up the school and gauge the receptiveness of the Black community. In New York she would be more than just another Black musical performer. She could pursue her dreams as an educator and be judged by her accomplishments, not the color of her skin. Still, New York was the big leagues, home to millions of people of diverse backgrounds. It took the Black community a while to find her. As usual, she turned creative to get the word out, offering free voice lessons to all comers.[14]

Music training was not her ultimate goal, however. That was expressed in the "Mwalimu Creed," a statement of personal commitment that she had composed years earlier, combining Christian piety with nineteenth century naturalism and a dash of Emile Coué's philosophy of self-improvement:

> I resolve: To break whatever bonds of heredity or tradition that bind my thoughts to the low things of human imperfections, and to begin to hold communion with God and Nature opening the windows of my soul to the music or the babbling brooks, the birds, and laughter of little children.
>
> I shall give freely of whatever talent I may have that helps to make the lives of mankind happier and more profitable.
>
> I shall begin it today—but—I shall end it in Eternity. And if death should o'ertake me, ere this year's close, and my aspirations be buried with me somewhere in the cold sod, I know I shall not be forgotten . . . having lived for the perpetuation of
> The Good, The True and the Beautiful.[15]

She aimed to impart that philosophy to all her students. The school was a gamble that there existed in the Black community a desire to rediscover their African roots. Africa was not a place to escape from but a homeland, possessed of all that was "good and true and beautiful" for the African diaspora. She designed the school's curriculum to include, besides music instruction, such creative and practical subjects as interpretive dancing, "artistic photography," African history, "elementary journalism," and cosmetology. With financial success she was able to move the school to Harlem (76 Edgecombe Ave. at 138th), in the heart of the Harlem Renaissance.[16]

The school might have been just another Black enterprise in a neighborhood famous for such pioneering enterprises if not for the Mwalimu

Festival Chorus, a vocal group she formed expressly to promote the school. The chorus first performed in public in May 1933, directed by Manet. They sang in English and Yoruba as well as other "African dialects." (Yoruba was taught at the school.) By performing numbers from across the musical spectrum—including classical, African, contemporary, and even opera—they showed the "Negro contributions to [world] culture." The chorus was not well received at first. About one early performance, the critic of the *New York Age* said, "The voices often sounded harsh . . . [and] the singing in general was not flexible." He added more generously, "The chorus may in time become one of our leading groups." His prediction turned out to be correct. Within a year they were appearing in some of New York's finest concert halls and also performing in Boston and Chicago to effusive reviews. She built on that success, introducing audiences to "African music" oratorios. Their performances were a riposte to popular white misperceptions of African music as nothing but "jungle rhythms." When not directing the chorus and teaching, Manet continued to make "professional appearances" herself. She also continued her own education by enrolling in Columbia University. Besides her studies, she added her voice to the school's "choral club."[17]

In June 1938 Mwalimu School celebrated its tenth anniversary, dating back to its Fort Worth beginnings. The public was invited to view "authentic African articles" that included art objects and artifacts. The occasion was also a fundraiser to build up the endowment, expand the campus, and offer more courses in the liberal arts. Among her most ambitious plans was building a full-size African village on the school grounds. Though now a resident of New York, for years she continued to regard Fort Worth as her "home base" because Stephen still lived there.[18]

Since leaving Fort Worth Manet had been on her own. Stephen stayed behind, working for the YMCA and, through that organization, for the city's growing Black community. He was a member of the Texas Commission on Inter-Racial Cooperation, a forerunner in Texas of the National Association for the Advancement of Colored People. He was also a member of the State Public Health Board ("Colored Dept.") and the National Baptist Convention. In 1925 he chaired the "Colored Division" of Fort Worth's Diamond Jubilee event celebrating the 75 years since Fort Worth's founding. The fact that Blacks were even included in the celebration was thanks to men like Reverend Lacey K. Williams of Mount Gilead Church, William M. "Gooseneck Bill" McDonald of the Fraternal Bank and Trust, and Stephen Fowler.[19]

In 1932 what was now known in polite circles as the "Colored" YMCA hosted the annual convention of the Negro State Teachers' Association. Three years later Stephen presided over the opening of a new, expanded Colored YMCA branch. In 1938 he resigned from the Y to move to Harlem and become "director" of the Mwalimu School, relieving Manet of many of her administrative duties. Two of their adult children also went to work for the school, making it a family business. The faculty was 100 percent African American, including famed Black historian Carter Woodson, with distinguished visiting professors from historically Black colleges. With the school on a firm footing, Manet and Stephen began performing together again, putting on recitals with him singing and her accompanying him on the piano. They performed in a variety of musical styles that crossed racial and cultural boundaries. As lifelong Baptists they also continued to be active in church work.[20]

They spent their final years as residents of Manhattan. For three decades she split her time between performing publicly, being the face of the school, and serving an active role in NANM. She also found time to launch a booking agency for Black musicians. Occasionally she came back to Fort Worth to visit family and keep in touch with her hometown admirers. In 1962 she attended the fiftieth anniversary of I. M. Terrell High School's 1912 graduating class. (The school was not named for Isaiah Milligan Terrell until 1921.) The school had earlier recognized Stephen's contributions by inviting him to be the commencement speaker at their 1953 graduation exercises. At the time of Manet's 1962 visit, there was talk of reopening the Mwalimu School in Fort Worth, which would have fit in with the rising spirit of Black nationalism in the late 1960s, but nothing came of it.[21]

The five Fowler children—Manet Helen, George, Carrol, Rose Marie, and Stephen Jr.—were a credit to their parents. Manet Helen graduated as valedictorian of her class at I. M. Terrell High school, and all five went on to get college degrees. Two received advanced degrees. Stephen Jr. died

Mount Gilead Baptist Church, where Manet Harrison and Stephen Fowler were married in 1915. A bastion of the Black community. *Fort Worth Star-Telegram* Collection, Special Collections, University of Texas at Arlington Library.

soon after graduating from Tuskegee. The other four went on to distinguished careers: Manet Helen, still a teenager, had helped break down racial barriers at New York University. She went on to become the first African American woman to earn a PhD at Cornell (1952). George held a master's degree from Columbia University and later served in the cabinet of New York Governor Nelson Rockefeller. Carrol attended Columbia too, and the Juilliard School of Music. Rose Marie attended Harvard and made a career in civil service. One of the reasons their parents moved to New York was to give their children better educational and career opportunities than Fort Worth could offer.[22]

Stephen Fowler died in 1965 at the age of 84, alone in a hotel room while attending the Empire State Baptist Convention in Syracuse, New York. Services were held at Mt. Olivet Baptist Church of New York City, where he had been a member for the last twenty-seven years of his life. He was buried in Rose Hill Cemetery in New Jersey. His obituary in the *Chicago Defender* said, "He was once voted 'The Most Valuable Citizen of Fort Worth, Tex.' his native city." If so, no one remembered it in 1965, because his passing was not noted. His memory flickered briefly in 1989 when the Fort Worth school board was casting about for a name for the new Crenshaw Avenue elementary school. One name with some support was that of Stephen H. Fowler. School trustees rejected it, however, because "Fowler's name is hardly a household word in the community and would promote little neighborhood identification with the school." So today, though he was an educator whose name bears mentioning in the same breath with James Guinn and Isaiah Milligan Terrell, Fowler is largely forgotten by whites and Blacks alike.[23]

Manet died in New York on February 16, 1976, at the age of 80. She was buried three days later with Stephen in Rose Hill Cemetery—reportedly in the same grave, following the custom of burying close family members together. Sadly, she did not rate an obituary in the *Fort Worth Star-Telegram*, the newspaper that had described her years earlier as "the most capable negro musician of the city."[24]

No sooner was she dead than she was forgotten. Even her gravesite was a mystery until a recent inquiry discovered her final resting place. She is remembered (barely) with a brief entry in the *Handbook of Texas Online* and even briefer mention in the 2008 anthology *Grace & Gumption: Stories of Fort Worth Women* (TCU Press). Her papers wound up at Yale and Emory Universities, while her worldly goods attracted little interest when they came up for auction. Even the historical record gets it wrong. She is called "Margaret Harris" in a 1972 newspaper story, and the name of her school is misspelled "Nawlimu" in another source. Stephen is, if anything, even less remembered. He does not rate an entry in either the *Handbook of Texas Online* or any known encyclopedia of black history.[25]

A better indication of Manet's and Stephen's significance is not how many pages they rate in the history books but the recognition they received during their lifetime. Before Manet, no Black woman had been written up as much in the nation's newspapers since Harriet Tubman—not

Madam C. J. Walker, not Ida B. Wells, not Mary McLeod Bethune. The first New York concert of the Mwalimu Chorus was hailed as the first American concert to be performed in "African dialect" (not the same as traditional Black spirituals). The concerts that followed got them an illustrated write-up in *Newsweek* magazine. She was an early proponent of what came to be known as Black nationalism, and though a latecomer to the Harlem Renaissance, she was an important contributor to the broader acceptance of African culture. She embraced the Harlem initiative, naming one of her musical pageants "The Voice" after the pioneering Harlem newspaper of the "New Negro movement."[26]

Manet's other accomplishments are equally impressive. Her pageants, "The Voice" and "Up From Slavery," used music and sweeping themes to teach Black history, and they were magnificent productions that played before large audiences. She was both the writer and director of those productions, as well as a symphonic poem, "Come Let Us Sing," that she wrote and directed for I. M. Terrell High School. She was the first African American to be featured on Fort Worth radio, a WBAP Christmas program in 1930. Four decades later she was honored along with Duke Ellington and Ramsey Lewis at the 1972 awards dinner of the NANM at the Commodore Hotel in New York City. And her creative talents were not limited to music. Her artwork is considered collectible today. Some of it is held by the Yale Library.[27]

Manet and Stephen may not have been the most distinguished Fort Worth African Americans of their time; that honor belongs to William "Gooseneck Bill" McDonald. But they did as much as anyone to change traditional white perceptions of Blacks, quietly challenging the status quo with their music and community work. And they were arguably the first power couple to emerge in the national Black community. As a branch executive Stephen began changing the Fort Worth YMCA from the lily-white organization it was to the ethnically and racially diverse organization it is today. He was able to sit down with white business and civic leaders to create the range of "Y" activities we know today. Manet amazed audiences of whites and Blacks alike with her musical talents. Together, they broke down walls and blazed a trail in education and the arts that stretched from Fort Worth to New York City, in the process bringing a bit of the Harlem Renaissance to Texas.

What makes Manet and Stephen's story so remarkable is that they were able to break out of their segregated hometown and achieve national recognition. Sadly, the recognition they achieved in their day has been largely forgotten by Fort Worth. The pair deserve monuments and plaques in their honor. Instead, they are still relegated to the back of history's bus.

Chapter 9

B. H. Carroll
The Man and the Legend

B. H. Carroll is a patriarchal figure in Baptist church history, known by his initials rather than his full name, Benajah Harvey Carroll. He was a practitioner of the Old Time Religion who preached the Word with the zeal of the true believer. The familiar photo we have of him shows Carroll with a long flowing beard looking like he just came down from the mountain with God's commandments. As an evangelist he had the full package: an encyclopedic knowledge of scripture, charisma to spare, and a remarkable talent for raising oodles of money. But he also had a very human side; Carroll was no saint.[1]

He made his home in Fort Worth for only five years (1909–1914) but left an enduring imprint on the city that ranks up there with fellow Baptist pastor J. Frank Norris. Together they are remembered by churchgoers and nonchurchgoers alike.

Carroll was born on December 27, 1843, in Carroll County, Mississippi, to Benajah Sr. and Mary Eliza Mallard Carroll. Theirs was a large family with twelve children. Father was a Methodist minister, and it was his church work that brought the family to Burleson County, Texas, in 1848.[2]

Benajah Harvey Carroll, president of Southwestern Baptist Seminary, looking like an Old Testament patriarch. B. H. Carroll Presidential Papers, Southwestern Baptist Theological Seminary Archives, Fort Worth, TX.

The unusual given name has caused problems for researchers and historians. For instance, the records of his Confederate service were filed under both "Benajah Harvey" and "Harvey Benajah." For most of his life he simply went by his initials. Even at the end, newspapers were still referring to him as "Benjamin." His given name is practically unknown today even in Fort Worth.[3]

Carroll's life even before answering "the Macedonian Call" is the stuff of legend. At different times he was a Texas Ranger, Indian fighter, self-taught scholar, soldier, and avowed "infidel." When the Civil War came in 1861, he joined the Confederacy, enlisting at San Antonio in Henry McCullough's First Texas Cavalry regiment.

He signed up for three years, but poor health and bad luck ended his service after just two years. He was an indifferent soldier. Three months after enlisting he was listed on the roster as "absent without leave." He came back, but in December 1862 he was sick in the hospital. Though he recovered, he was listed as "sick" again in December 1864, this time sick enough to get a medical discharge. In between he was seriously wounded at the Battle of Mansfield (April 18, 1864). He had entered Confederate service as a 19-year-old private and left the army with the same rank two years later. Preaching, not soldiering, was his passion, and he exercised it around many a campfire during those two years. A firm believer in the gospel of love, after the war he took a lead in bringing blue and gray together again in worship.[4]

In 1865 at a Methodist camp meeting in Texas, he heard the calling to become a born-again Christian and preach the gospel. He had given his life to Christ, but not as a Methodist as his father had been. He joined the Baptist church and was still just 22 years old when he was hired as pastor of the little church at Caldwell, Texas. He had found his life's work; all he needed was a wife to share it with him.[5]

Young Pastor Carroll was a strapping six feet, one inch tall with fair complexion and piercing blue eyes. An educated man and accomplished orator, he would have been quite a catch for any girl. He had married in 1861 just before going off to war. When he found out she was unfaithful, he divorced her in 1863. In 1866 he remarried, this time to Ellen Virginia Bell, a transplant from Starkville, Mississippi. Ellen Carroll died in 1897.

She had been a true helpmeet. According to her obituary, like her husband she was "distinguished in religious circles." Two years later the 56-year-old Carroll married for the third time, to Miss Hallie Harrison, eighteen years his junior. She came from a distinguished family of military and naval officers. Together they had one child, making him a father five times over, counting the four he had with Ellen. All of his children grew up to be successful and God-fearing.[6]

In 1870 Carroll took the pulpit of First Baptist Church of Waco, where he pastored for the next twenty-eight years. A pastor's success is measured by the size of his congregation. During Carroll's time in Waco, First Baptist's membership grew to more than a thousand, the first congregation in Texas to count that many members. He was also deeply involved with Waco University (the future Baylor), retiring from the pulpit to raise money and serve on the board of trustees. During his lifetime he raised more than $1 million for his church and school. He was equally committed to teaching and preaching, which led him in 1905 to found Baylor Theological Seminary to train future preachers.[7]

He was also a leader for many years in the prohibition movement in Texas. In 1887 he chaired the statewide campaign to get it adopted as law. As part of that campaign, he eagerly debated prominent anti-prohibitionists like Sul Ross and Richard Coke. They lost the fight, but the movement continued to grow until finally achieving national success in 1918.

The Southwestern Baptist Theological Seminary is considered Carroll's crowning achievement, his "greatest piece of work." He single-handedly raised $500,000 to start it and set up a permanent endowment. He was the seminary's founder and first president. In its first four years it was part of Baylor University. Then in 1909 he secured three hundred acres just south of Fort Worth to build its own campus. Based largely on his name and reputation, it attracted religious-minded students from all over the southwest, rivaling the Southern Baptist Theological Seminary at Louisville, Kentucky, as a center of Baptist learning. When he died in 1914, it had grown from an original enrollment of 100 students to 250.[8]

Seventy-year-old Benajah Harvey Carroll died on November 11, 1914. He had been in failing health for more than two years, but family and friends had held out hope for his recovery until the last six months. His passing caused not only Baptists but also the entire state of Texas to mourn. The funeral service was held in the chapel at the seminary with a who's who of Fort Worth and Dallas Baptist leaders in attendance. The widow and four children were present, with only B. H. Carroll Jr. missing. He was in Venice at the time serving as a US consul to war-torn Italy (after World War I). After the service the body was sent to Waco for a memorial service at First Baptist of Waco, followed by interment in Waco's Oakwood Cemetery.[9]

Four days after his passing, the Reverend J. Frank Norris preached his Sunday morning sermon on "The Life and Work of Dr. B. H. Carroll." First Baptist Church was packed even more than usual. Ironically, Norris later separated himself and his congregation from Southwestern Baptist Theological Seminary, declaring it and the Southern Baptist Association it was part of to be too liberal. Hallie Carroll returned to Waco after burying her husband but soon thereafter moved to California to live with her son Harrison Carroll. She died in Los Angeles in 1938. About her one biographer said marrying her "reinvigorated" B. H. Carroll at a time when he was "just about ready to collapse." It was her inspiration that gave him "the heart" to create the seminary.[10]

B. H. Carroll left an estate valued at $20,000, which included a house in Fort Worth, extensive property in McLennan County, a vast library, and future royalties from a book of his lectures on the Bible. But his most valuable legacy was his name and his record of service, which continued to exert influence long after his death. His children and his brother carried on the family tradition of service to community and church for years to come, and though B. H. Carroll only lived in Fort Worth for five years, that name carried a lot of weight. In 1921 B. H. Carroll Jr. floated his name as a candidate for US senator from Texas. In the press announcement it was stated that he was "the son of the late Dr. B. H. Carroll, the leader of the Baptist churches in Texas for a half century." In 1947 J. B. Cranfill published seventeen volumes of Carroll's lectures, entitled *Interpretation of the English Bible*, that is still used in the seminary today.[11]

In 1922 the Fort Worth Independent School District paid the ultimate compliment to Carroll by naming a school after him. B. H. Carroll

Elementary School (3908 McCart Avenue) is unique because it is the only public school in Fort Worth named for a religious leader. By tradition, name proposals for new schools were submitted to the school board by residents of the area, with the board having the final say. The fact that there were no complaints when the decision was announced in 1922 shows how much Fort Worthers of all religious persuasions still admired a man who had been dead and buried for eight years at that point. Masonic Lodge No. 1164 laid the cornerstone of the building, and Reverend Jefferson Davis Ray of the seminary gave the dedication address that recognized the school as "the first monument ever erected to Dr. B. H. Carroll in recognition of his services to schools." However, thereafter some confusion arose over just who the school was named for, because B. H. Carroll Jr. had died that same year in Cadiz, Spain, where he was consul. The body was brought home by the US government for burial at Waco. The real B. H. Carroll connection to Fort Worth is the father, not the son. In 1941, when the school board was ready to close B. H. Carroll Elementary because of small enrollment, the neighborhood rose up in protest to keep it open. The FWISD finally closed B. H. Carroll Elementary for good in 1984 amid much hand-wringing and neighborhood protest. It reopened a year later as the B. H. Carroll Center for New Lives, keeping the great man's name alive in the FWISD lexicon. It is still open today.[12]

The Carroll name continued to carry weight years after the great man's death. In 1918 one "B. Carroll" was appointed superintendent of Tarrant County Schools. He had a distinguished, eight-year tenure (1918–1926), so much so that years later some sources claimed he was B. H. Carroll Jr. But there was no family connection between Burl Carroll and B. H. Carroll. The superintendent may have been encouraging the deception by the fact that he always went by B. Carroll publicly and emphasized his strong Baptist and prohibitionist roots. The people of Fort Worth could be excused if they mistook him for a member of the B. H. Carroll family.[13]

In 1946 B. H. Carroll Memorial Baptist Church was organized, and the next year they dedicated their building at 3801 McCart. While many seminary students attended church there, it has no formal connection to either the

Top: B. H. Carroll Memorial Baptist Church, ca. 1956. Author's collection.

Bottom: Students at B. H. Carroll Elementary, 1929. Author's collection.

seminary or B. H. Carroll Elementary except the admiration of its members for the man who had such a great influence on Fort Worth.[14]

From the beginning Carroll's story was ripe for legend-making, repeated by the faithful in almost reverent tones. For instance, it was said that he could quote every word of the Bible verbatim, from Genesis through Revelation. It was also said that he could recite every event in the Bible in chronological order. Whether he could actually do those things is irrelevant, because his parishioners believed he could. At memorial services in later years, he was hailed as not just a "great religious leader" but also a "great statesman." He was reputedly approached by leaders of the Democratic Party at one time to run for governor of Texas but turned them down, saying he had "a higher calling." He was called "a giant, physically and spiritually, which was true as far as it went. Although he was six feet, three inches tall, he was sickly much of his life. It was also part of the legend that he was a self-proclaimed "infidel" before being called by God, when the truth was he was raised in the Methodist church and attended Baylor University before going off to war in 1861. Carroll could also be overbearing and manipulative. He was absolutely convinced of the rightness of his views and did not brook opposition graciously. He constantly battled with the *Texas Baptist Herald*, the denomination's official state organ.[15]

There was also a darker side to the man. His three marriages might raise eyebrows among the faithful today, in particular number one. He was also a Son of the Old South who may not have owned slaves himself but had fought on the side of the Confederacy for two years to keep the institution alive. Years later, after answering the call to the ministry, he retained his Old South thinking. During his tenure the seminary never admitted a Black student. His stand at the time was not questioned because Fort Worth was as much a part of the Old South as the Wild West.

Ironically, while the Carroll name carried great influence in Fort Worth at large, it was not so honored at the seminary he founded. For many years, according to the *Star-Telegram*, there was not "a stone on the campus that bears his name." The school eventually made up for that slight by putting a life-size, oil portrait of him in the main hall. His legacy in his adopted city is safe.[16]

Chapter 10

Charles L. Stowe
A Legend in His Own Mind

ort Worth's Opal Lee was in the news in 2021 when Congress officially made Juneteenth a national holiday, something for which she had led a solo personal crusade for many years. The nonagenarian civil rights icon's story has been oft told, how as a 12-year-old girl in 1939 little Opal Flake's Morningside home was targeted by white segregationists opposing "negro encroachment" in the neighborhood. That little girl grew up to be Opal Lee, a force for change, first in Fort Worth then on the national scene.[1]

One of the leaders of that 1939 violent opposition to desegregating the neighborhood was Charles L. Stowe Jr., no longer remembered today because he placed himself on the wrong side of history. Stowe lived on E. Morphy, just a few streets over from 940 E. Annie where Otis Flake and his family lived. Morphy and Annie Streets were both in the Fifth Ward, which in 1939 was entirely white. Charles Stowe was much better known than Otis Flake in the spring of 1939 as a longtime resident of the city, a self-styled war veteran, newspaper publisher, would-be politician, and all-round gadfly.

He was the son of Charles Lucius Stowe Sr. and Maggie Fitch Stowe of Gaston County, North Carolina, who came to Texas just after the Civil War and settled in Grayson County. He was born in 1874. His brothers were John and LeRoy. Stowe Sr. was successively a farmer, then a grocer at Sherman before being appointed US marshal for the Southern District of Indian Territory by President Grover Cleveland. After his service as US marshal, he returned to Sherman, where he engaged in the "oil mill" business and became a big booster of Sherman as a member of the chamber of commerce. In 1916 Governor James Ferguson appointed him superintendent of Public Buildings and Grounds in Austin.[2]

Papa Stowe was a hard act to follow. Respectfully addressed as Colonel for his active involvement in the Sons of Confederate Veterans, prominent for many years in the political and business life of Texas, when he died in 1923 his obituary was carried in newspapers from Texas to the Carolinas. On top of that, Junior carried the weight of family history on his shoulders. He would later claim to be an eighth-generation descendant of English historian John S. Stowe, who was a friend and colleague of famous Puritan poet John Milton.[3]

Charles Jr. was driven to succeed from a young age. He was a child prodigy, reading Latin at age 11. In 1890 his parents moved the family to Austin to take advantage of the "superb schools." He entered the University of Texas at 16 and worked his way through school as a printer and occasional correspondent for the *Austin Statesman*. At the time W. C. Brann was editor of the paper and became a major influence in Stowe's life. The fiery newspaper editor left the *Statesman* in 1892 to start his own newspaper, *The Iconoclast*, which combined eloquent writing with strong opinions that attracted as many opponents as readers. Young Charles had God-given writing talent and practical skills to go with it. He joined the Austin Typographical Union, and a few years later, not yet 25, parlayed his writing and printing talents into the editorship of the *Austin Evening Tribune*.[4]

His other interests besides journalism were the military, music, and patriotism. While still a student at university, he joined the Texas Volunteer Guard (forerunner of the National Guard). He loved wearing the uniform and marching in parades, two loves that never left him. He enlisted in the army to fight in the Spanish-American War in 1898, but the war ended before he saw action. It did not matter; he could say he was a war veteran, something he never let anyone forget for the rest of his life. He regaled youngsters with stories of the Rough Riders and claimed to have a "letter of commendation" from Theodore Roosevelt himself that was lost in a house fire in 1943. The same fire touched off his old .45-70 Springfield rifle ammunition, which sent firemen diving for cover. It was all part of the legend of Charlie Stowe.[5]

He was also a fine singer and self-taught musician who could play several musical instruments, nothing ordinary like brass or woodwinds but the xylophone and something called the tubyphone. He could also play the piano, but he was mostly known for performing as a one-man band where he played and sang at the same time. He favored the songs of the Old South, and even after jazz and big band became popular, he continued to perform oldies like "Carry Me Back to Old Virginny" and "Swing Low, Sweet Chariot." His whole life followed Henry David Thoreau's advice about traveling to the beat of a different drum. The musical performances that he did for many years were one part of that journey.[6]

After visiting Fort Worth on several occasions, in 1903 he moved here, taking a job on the production line of the *Fort Worth Record*, operating the linotype machine, then moving to the *Fort Worth Star*. While his interests ran in many directions, typesetting remained his main source of income in the coming years. He joined the Typographers' Union and rose to be vice president. A devout man, he was a faithful member of First Presbyterian Church of Fort Worth for many years. He had a curiosity about many subjects, which led him to the St. Louis World's Fair in 1904.[7]

He jumped into local politics uninvited. He attended Fort Worth city council meetings every week as if he were an elected member, and he was not shy about speaking up. He freely offered his opinions on business before the council, peppering his orations with biblical and literary quotes. He boasted that if he ran for office, he could beat any current member of the council. Perhaps recalling the fate of W. C. Brann, who was severely beaten and eventually assassinated by critics of his editorial stands, Stowe never went anywhere unarmed. Once while delivering one of his diatribes at a city council meeting, his pistol fell out of his pocket twice. Curiously, he also carried a slingshot, though he never explained why. When he was not bloviating at council meetings, he was writing heartfelt letters to the newspaper. He was not picky; the *Fort Worth Star-Telegram* and *Fort Worth Record* were equally favored with his compositions. A surprising number were printed in full, either because of his status as the town's gadfly or because the subject of his letter touched a nerve. Those letters included a Christmas wish to his fellow citizens on Christmas day, 1918.[8]

Being a thorn in the side to high-ranking people was following in the footsteps of his idol, W. C. Brann. Charles Stowe was Fort Worth's iconoclast, a person who was always at war with somebody over something. His choice of issues to take a stand on was often quirky. He complained loudly that the US flag was not raised daily over city hall as it was over the courthouse. He also embarked on a personal mission to punish speeding automobile drivers in town by taking a baseball bat to their windshields as they whizzed by.[9]

While Stowe had many admirable qualities, his ideas on race were definitely old-fashioned. He was a son of the Old South who had no use for African Americans. He enjoyed putting his musical talents to work in blackface minstrel shows that were very popular with white audiences.

Stowe found a new cause to take up in 1916, honoring an unrecognized military hero. On March 9, 1916, after Pancho Villa crossed the border from Mexico to hit Columbus, New Mexico, US Army Colonel Herbert J. Slocum organized the pursuit that chased Villa back across the border. To Stowe, Slocum was a hero deserving of public recognition. He launched a drive to raise the $200 or $250 he estimated it would cost to purchase a "jeweled sword" to present to Slocum. The old letter-to-the-editor writer enlisted the assistance of the *Star-Telegram* to kick off a fundraising drive, donating the first dollar to the drive. He followed that up with an open letter to the newspaper calling on his fellow citizens to come up with the rest of the money. While he was at it, he deplored the "outrage after outrage" committed against Americans worldwide, citing great Americans in history like Daniel Webster and Andrew Jackson who stood up for the country. There is no record that his sword drive achieved its goal, but it kept him in the public eye.[10]

Returning to his first love, the newspaper business, he launched his own publication, which he modestly called *Stowe's Chronicle*. He was editor, publisher, and chief reporter. It started out as an occasional newsletter in

1918 that offered his opinions and observations on a variety of subjects. In 1920 he took it to a monthly "magazine," though in truth it was never more than a three- or four-page tabloid. It cost a modest two cents an issue, or two dollars a year for a subscription. Most interesting was its mission statement: "devoted to the betterment of Fort Worth and humanity in general." He also promised it would be "mental food for meat eaters" and "have enough cayenne" to interest readers. Unlike any of the city's other newspaper that came before *Stowe's Chronicle*, it featured a photo of the publisher on the front page. He worked on a shoestring budget out of an office at 108 E. Weatherford.[11]

The paper was a mix of local news, human interest stories, and opinion pieces about anything that caught his attention, all mixed willy-nilly on the pages. Both the *Star-Telegram* and the *Record* carried the announcement of the paper's launch. Neither viewed *Stowe's Chronicle* as serious competition for their readership. He published the paper for a few years, then shut it down. In September 1934 he revived it. The announcement in the *Star-Telegram* revealed the main problem with keeping the presses rolling: "*Stowe's Chronicle* is not run as a money-making institution but in an effort to make America safe for Americans and for the upbuilding of our community, State and Nation." Stowe's "America" was clearly an America that did not include people of color, be they Native Americans, African Americans, or Latinos. He was not out of step with the majority of his countrymen, just more outspoken. There is no record of what his readership was during either run of the paper because he never shared those numbers. A very few copies of the newspaper exist today in library collections.[12]

Charles Stowe remained a bachelor until the age of 45. As such, he lived in a succession of boarding houses. In 1910 he was living in the boarding house of Mabel C. Curtis, a divorcee who at 16 in 1888 had married Leslie "Tobe" McKinney. After divorcing him in 1899 she reclaimed her maiden name, so she was Mrs. Mabel C. Curtis when Charles met her. She and her daughter Fannie were running a boarding house, and she had a side business as a "masseur." After marrying off Fannie to J. C. Hooper in 1916, she lived alone until taking up with Charles, who had been a boarder all this time. Disaster struck them in January 1919 when a gas stove caught her clothes

(*Left*) Young Charles Stowe (1918) and wife, Mabel Curtis Stowe (*right*), whom he married in 1919. Author's collection.

on fire. Fortunately, Charles was there and quickly smothered her "blazing garments." Both were "slightly burned," but the accident had a happy ending because they married less than a month later. They honeymooned in Sherman before taking up residence in her house. Eventually, they moved to Avenue H and were living there when Mabel died in August 1937 of pulmonary tuberculosis (myocarditis). She was buried in Greenwood Cemetery.[13]

Since he was making scarcely any money from his newspaper and had a family to support, he had to find some other source of income. Days before Christmas 1918 he joined the Texas oil boom after gushers came in in Eastland County. Oil companies were hitting black gold all over the state, and fortunes were being made. Stowe resigned his $2,000-a-year linotype job and went to work as a "sales agent" for Union Oil & Refining Company out of California. They were new in Texas but already had nearly seven thousand acres in oil leases in nine counties. Like everything else he did, Stowe jumped in with both feet, setting up an office in the Texas State Bank building, pushing the stock as a surefire thing and promoting the company shamelessly in the pages of his newspaper. *Stowe's Chronicle* became a virtual organ of the company, urging readers to buy the stock before it went up. "It's no longer a question of do you want to invest in Union Oil & Refining Company," he declared, but "how much do you want to invest?" As always, each ad and story came with a picture of Stowe himself.[14]

Stowe did more than just sit in an office writing copy and selling stock; he went on the road to look over the company's holdings in North Texas and Oklahoma. The *Wichita Times* called him a former member of the "print fraternity" now a member of the "oil fraternity." He was one of the most successful salesmen of oil stocks in Fort Worth. Stowe was a born salesman; his knowledge of the oil business was strictly self-taught. Oil stocks practically sold themselves. After three or four years he lost interest in the oil industry. For virtually the last thirty years of his life he was "retired."[15]

Stowe was either a thorn in the side of city officials or a champion of reform, depending on your point of view. In 1933, finally following through on his boast that he could beat any current council member he ran against, he threw his hat in the ring against E. T. Renfro, a popular incumbent who owned a chain of namesake drugstores. Stowe hoped to ride the coattails of the reformist Citizens' Ticket into office. His impressive platform consisted of investigating the police department, regulating public utilities, property-tax relief, and "municipal economy," but he never got a chance to test any of his ideas with voters. As a write-in candidate, he failed to get enough signatures to get on the ballot, which did not keep him from showing up at the first meeting of the new council to offer his opinions on various matters, including who should be city manager. (He denounced both the current officeholder and his predecessor.) He was interrupted mid-speech by councilman D. W. Carlton, who told him to "bring your blood pressure down." Four years later he led a one-man boycott of city hall, calling for recall of the entire council for corruption and mismanagement.[16]

He never gave up his ambition for public office. In 1941, 1943, and 1949 he announced himself as a candidate for city council, but each time something happened. In 1941 he was a write-in candidate on a Roosevelt-like platform of a "square deal" for everyone "union and nonunion, banker and ditch digger." The voters weren't buying a Roosevelt wannabe. In 1943 and '49, he withdrew before formally filing. In 1941 he phoned on the last night to file asking the city secretary to keep his office open for him. He phoned back at 11:30 p.m. to say his "jalopy" had broken down and he could not get there.[17]

He saw no contradiction between being a thorn in the side of city officials and a big Fort Worth booster. For the Frontier Centennial in 1936 he published a souvenir edition of *Stowe's Chronicle* that he titled the *Frontier City Weekly Star* and distributed for free on the exposition grounds. Readers were informed on page one that the editor was "Charles L. Stowe, Jr." He also posed for a photo op with a member of the exposition's Indian Village, with what intended message is anybody's guess. His other public-spirited activities included speaking frequently to civic and school groups, where he was never less than colorful in a Jed Clampett sort of way. He wore his politics on his sleeve: white supremacy, racial separation, states' rights, patriotism, and a strong nation. He campaigned for Strom Thurmond and the States Rights faction of the Democratic party in 1948, telling a Fort Worth audience, "My granddaddy was on General Lee's staff, and I'm fighting for him again. And I'm going to win this time!" Evidence that his grandfather was on Lee's staff is as unproven as it is that an earlier ancestor was friends with seventeenth-century English poet John Milton. His talent for weaving a good tale was recognized in 1946 when the Fort Worth Anglers Club gave him the Albert Woods Medal "for telling the biggest lie"—all in fun, of course.[18]

Stowe's closest brush with fame came in 1939, a time of racial strife in Fort Worth. That spring he was living at 1456 E. Hattie in the Morningside neighborhood on the east side of Fort Worth. The old neighborhood was changing as Black families began to move in. B. L. Manley, who lived at 1124 E. Hattie, was one of a small group of neighbors willing to sell to Blacks—not out of any sense of magnanimity but with the intention to moving to an all-white neighborhood. Stowe was a vocal opponent of selling to Blacks, heading up the Anglo-Saxon Committee of the Fifth Ward Civic League. They publicly spoke in euphemistic terms about the "Negro Question" while putting up signs warning Blacks not to move into the area. On the other side of the question, Manley spoke for many white residents, perhaps a majority, when he said, "the neighborhood is becoming mostly colored anyway," so why not sell.[19]

Left: Rare copy of *Stowe's Chronicle* (1934). Dolph Briscoe Center for American History, University of Texas at Austin.

Right: Carefully posed picture from Stowe's other publication, the *Daily Star* (1936 Frontier Centennial). Stowe, who was no progressive when it came to race relations, is seen here making nice with an unnamed Native American. He does not look comfortable. *Fort Worth Star-Telegram Collection*, Special Collections, University of Texas at Arlington Library.

Things came to a head on Friday night, May 12. Stowe exchanged shots with Manley and his son. They fired thirteen shots in all. Thankfully no one was hit, and the next day the *Star-Telegram* ridiculed the shooters with a headline that said, "This Would Make Annie Oakley Cry," which proved to be ironic, considering what happened next. When police arrived on the scene that night, they got completely different stories from the participants about how the shooting started. The shootout at the "Morningside Corral" ended with no casualties and no one taken to jail. Stowe flashed a "constable courtesy card" given to him by H. W. "Dusty" Rhodes, so the police took no action beyond confiscating their guns and ordering them to report to District Attorney Jesse Brown the next morning. After sleeping on it, Stowe told the DA he was willing to make peace if the Manleys would apologize, which they refused to do. All three were finally persuaded to be nice and "leave each other alone." The only penalty paid was that Stowe lost his courtesy card, which did not solve the bigger problem. Trouble continued to brew in the neighborhood. Threats were issued and lawyers were consulted.[20]

It was about a month later that violence erupted again in Morningside. On Friday night, June 16, what the *Star-Telegram* generously described as "a crowd" gathered at the intersection of E. Annie and New York Ave. to protest a Black family that had just moved into the house at 940 Annie. Otis Flake was a railroad employee with a wife and three children. He was no civil rights activist, just a man looking to raise his family in a nice neighborhood. It was anything but a welcoming neighborhood. White residents had earlier organized the Fifth Ward Civic League, protested to the city council, and hired a lawyer to look into legal action. On Saturday night the mob was back, 150 "irate [white] residents." They filled Otis Flake's front yard and began throwing rocks at the house and shouting threats. The police showed up but did nothing, and after venting their anger for a couple of hours, the mob dispersed, but they were back for a third night on Monday, this time some 500 strong with bricks and baseball bats. They bombarded the house with bricks and anything else they could get their hands on, forcing Flake and his family to flee. Then they broke into the house and ransacked the place, carrying off what they didn't destroy. Contrary to much later accusations, however, they did not set the house on fire. The police and sheriff's deputies had both showed up to keep an eye on things but made no arrests. The good news was that no shots were fired, and the Flakes were not molested, but they got the message and moved shortly thereafter.[21]

What Fort Worth newspapers played down as a "protest" and as harmless "violence" was called out for what it was by other newspapers in the state— a "near riot." The police launched an investigation but claimed to be unable to identify any member of the mob. No charges were ever filed. Police patrolled the neighborhood on Tuesday as the Flakes packed up and moved out.[22]

There is no evidence that Charles Stowe was part of any mob. He was not a rock-throwing kind of person, but he was willing to serve as spokesman and even instigator of those who were. He had called the Fifth Ward Civic League to action and carried their story to various fraternal organizations where he described the problem as a "Negro Question." He claimed to be working with unnamed "Negro leaders" to keep "peace and harmony between the two races." In his mind that could only happen on white terms. As always, he was armed, ever ready to defend his person and principles against those who threatened either.[23]

Stowe followed the white flight out of the neighborhood, finding a small house to rent at 2712 Avenue C in the still-white Poly section not far from his previous residence. When that house burned down on September 3, 1943, he was left homeless. The irony of his own house mysteriously going up in flames could not have been lost on his critics.[24]

One is reminded of Stowe's statement that he never published his newspaper to make money. In fact, none of his causes ever put any money in his pocket. How he ever supported a family is a mystery. He spent his life tilting at windmills. He was Fort Worth's Don Quixote, his stooped, string-bean form a familiar sight on downtown streets. In his later years he lived on the edge of poverty, supported at least in part by gifts from unnamed friends. After the little house on Avenue C burned down, First Baptist Church hired him as night watchman, an easy job that came with living quarters in the church basement. It wasn't a simple matter of Christian charity. Stowe had history with Pastor J. Frank Norris. He was one of the men who had signed on as surety for Norris's $10,000 bond to keep the preacher out of jail while awaiting his 1926 murder trial. They were also kindred spirits because of Norris's close ties to the Ku Klux Klan. If the bond had been forfeited, there is no way Stowe could have come up with a realistic share of the money, but that was not going to happen—not just because Norris was unlikely to jump bail but because twenty-nine other men also signed on as sureties.[25]

Stowe's frail health was a constant concern to church members. One Sunday morning in 1951 they found him too ill to get out of bed and rushed him to City-County Hospital. Doctors gave him the usual battery of tests but could not discover the nature of his illness. When they released him, he was transferred to Elmwood Sanitarium, a "charity institution" maintained by the county. He suffered a debilitating stroke in 1952 but hung on until death finally took him on October 21, 1954, at the age of 80. He is buried in Greenwood Cemetery beside Mabel. Only a brother, John F. Stowe of Waco, was listed in the obituary as a "close survivor." What happened to daughter, Rubye, born in 1914 and married to Ben Lewis of San Antonio in 1936, is unknown.[26]

The man known as old Charlie Stowe was gone and soon forgotten. He had lived in Fort Worth for fifty-one years and considered himself a town booster in the mold of B. B. Paddock, John Peter Smith, and Amon G. Carter, even if he never achieved their level of wealth or respect. In his own mind

Photo of Charles Stowe that appeared in *Fort Worth Star-Telegram* with his obituary on October 22, 1954. Author's collection.

he was more than just a booster. He was the conscience of Fort Worth. City officials dubbed him "Place 10 Councilman" when the council only had nine members. His district was the entire metropolis, and he did not mind "raising a little hell" to be heard. He dedicated his life to what his obituary called "the social, commercial, and moral betterment" of Fort Worth. The fact that his fellow citizens never raised him to the elevated heights of Paddock, Smith, and Carter was not his fault as he saw things. Like Carter he started a newspaper, like Paddock he was a prolific writer, and like Smith he constantly promoted the city. But unlike them he was his own worst enemy.[27]

Chapter 11

Faye Cotton
The Frontier Centennial's "Sweetheart No. 1"

Faye Cotton was a small-town girl who captured Fort Worth hearts in 1936 with a big helping of Billy Rose showmanship. The wide-eyed girl from Borger, Texas, was the biggest thing to come out of her hometown since the oil strike of 1926. She grew up in the tough boomtown where crime was high and opportunities outside the oil industry were practically nonexistent. That is why the resident population was small. Most of the transient population were oil roughnecks and wildcatters looking to make as much money as possible before moving on to the next big oil field.

It was Fort Worth's Frontier Centennial that turned the Borger teenager into a star. In 1936 in the depths of the Great Depression, beauty contests were not passe as they are today; they were perfectly respectable and very popular events. Their contestants were shown off like prize livestock, which Fort Worth knew a lot about. The *Star-Telegram* was not a bit embarrassed about printing Faye's ample measurements: 5' 6", 120 pounds, and most important, 35–24½–35. And just for good measure, they threw in her thigh measurements (20"). Completing the picture, she had gray eyes and brown, "naturally wavy" hair. There is no indication that Faye was offended by being weighed, measured, and put on display. During Casa Mañana's four-month run, the newspaper described her as "the luscious Faye Cotton." And producer Billy Rose reportedly proclaimed her "the most beautiful woman I've ever seen."[1]

She was born Fay Ruby Cotton on August 22, 1918, to Guy and Ruby Cotton in Rush Springs, Oklahoma. Cotton was her mother's second husband. Before him she was married to Leonard "Bud" Osborne (1904), then in 1912 she married Cotton in Grady, Oklahoma. Fay became one of five daughters in the family. In 1930 Ruby was living with E. T. Brown in Borger, Texas, but sometime before 1936 she married Everett Benjamin King and remained Mrs. King until her death in 1947. Ruby's taste in men ran to those who worked with their hands: livery stablemen, farmers, oil roughnecks. Before coming to Fort Worth and becoming a star in the Frontier Centennial, Faye Cotton was Fay Cotton. The change in spelling is probably the same reason pop singer-composer Carol Klein became Carole King. Her future as an 18-year-old girl in Borger, Texas, in the spring of 1936 was most likely marriage and a family and perhaps a working-class job in town.[2]

A veteran showman, Billy Rose knew the appeal beautiful women added to any production. The bottom line for any show was simple: sex sells! After arriving in Fort Worth in March, Rose announced he would be holding a beauty contest to pick "Texas Sweetheart No. 1," inviting every town in the state to send the pride of their female population to participate. To sweeten the deal, he promised the winner would receive a starring role in the Frontier Centennial and a movie contract with a Hollywood studio. Fort Worth's entry, picked on May 26, was Alice McWhorter, a recent Paschal High School graduate.[3]

Rose could not have known it, but this was not the first time Texas beauties strutted their stuff on the big stage. In 1893 ten "Lone Star beauties" went to Chicago to represent Texas at the World's Columbian Exposition. Before they left Texas, Chicago promised to give them a "hearty welcome."[4]

One of the eighty-two beauties who descended on Fort Worth for the May 29, 1936, was Borger's Fay Cotton. It was a daring decision for the 19-year-old as the rules dictated contestants would have to "pass in review" wearing a bathing suit or dance costume before Rose and an audience of leering males. It was an intimidating prospect for the young, small-town girl. Fay made the 360-mile trip from Borger to Fort Worth by automobile over mostly unpaved roads, which shows how far Borger was off the beaten path. She packed light, not expecting to stay long, and her older sister Lillian came along to chaperone. They found a family in Fort Worth to put them up for a couple of nights.[5]

The contest was held in the Paschal High School auditorium, and it was packed. Most of the audience had not seen this much bare flesh on display outside of a burlesque show. Some even brought binoculars, the better to see the pulchritude parading across the stage. The girls wore swimwear in a variety of form-flattering styles, from old-fashioned, one-piece suits (maillots) to the latest styles of latex and cotton or flashy satin-and-sequin numbers. High heels were de rigueur. Fay wore a conservative black-and-white polka-dot suit belted at the waist, form-fitting but not racy. The *Star-Telegram* reported all the girls had painted nails and "soulful eyes," as if anyone was looking at their eyes. Audience participation was the key to the contest because they got to pick the winner by acclamation, indicated by the level of clapping and cheering each girl inspired. The contest came down to three girls with, Rose declaring Miss Borger the winner over a Miss Paris and Miss Fort Worth as Ed Lally's orchestra played "A Pretty Girl Is Like a Melody" from the MGM musical playing in theaters at the time. Margaret McLean, chairperson of the Woman's Division of the Frontier Centennial, was invited onto the stage by Rose to gush her approval.[6]

The selection of "Texas Sweetheart No. 1" was nothing more than another Billy Rose gimmick to drum up interest in the Frontier Centennial. It had nothing to do with staging a musical revue, much less a state-fair-type exposition. That explains why the evening's other activity was picking some of the dancers and chorus girls who would perform in what was being called "the follies" at this stage. In showbiz lingo this was known as a "cattle call." The applicants had to strut their stuff before a panel of four male judges: Billy Rose, John Murray Anderson (the Casa stage director), Lucius Beebe (a New York syndicated columnist), and Fort Worth's Dr. Webb Walker.[7]

Rose, a modern P. T. Barnum bringing his act to the provinces, gave so many interviews, he could not keep his stories straight. One time he said Fay was "the most beautiful girl I've ever seen." Another time he described his "Sweetheart No. 1" as "one of the most beautiful girls I've ever seen." No one seemed to notice the difference. According to subsequent Casa Mañana press releases, Fay was the representative Texas gal, enjoying "dancing, shooting, and reading her Bible every day." The only thing missing was drinking long-neck beers, but this was the 1930s, and ladies did not do such things.[8]

Fay would not be going back to Borger any time soon. She made arrangements to board with a Fort Worth family for the duration of the show and spent the next six weeks in rehearsal and being fitted. Lillian stayed on for a week to field phone calls and act as a mother hen for little sister. Fay had a tiny part in the show but proved a trooper. She caught on quickly to being a show girl, taking John Murray Anderson's blunt stage direction well. Rehearsals were in the Hotel Texas ballroom while workers built the open-air theater-café that would be Casa Mañana. The grueling, daily rehearsals left little free time, but that did not keep the newspapers from bird-dogging her whenever she came out. Small-town Fay became celebrity Faye, the arche-typical Texas gal. Mary Crutcher of the *Fort Worth Press* depicted her as the embodiment of "the new woman in show business," not a glamor doll or a seductress but a wholesome, natural beauty. She was also Texan through and through because she posed for photographs clutching a long gun.[9]

There were rumors of romance after she was seen holding hands across the dinner table with Tommy Gleason, a dancer in the "Peppers" act. They were on stage together every night during the "Toy Balloon" number, which had to be rehearsed. The talk in the Casa troupe was that Tommy was a lothario engaged to three different women in three different cities. Rumors of a romance were still being talked about a year later.[10]

Daily rehearsals moved to the theater as soon as the revolving stage was completed. The production had its share of problems. Everett Marshall, the "handsome headliner" brought in from the Metropolitan Opera, was supposed to escort Faye offstage, which was complicated because it was not a traditional proscenium with wings. Exiting the stage meant traversing the forty-foot "lagoon" via ramps while the platform revolved to bring the next scene around. At one rehearsal, as Marshall was escorting Faye offstage, it began revolving too soon, and he tumbled into the water. Fortunately, neither of them was in costume. The *Star-Telegram* jokingly referred to it as a "ducking," but such a mishap could not happen on show night with Marshall in a tuxedo and Faye in her gold costume.[11]

The Frontier Centennial opened on Saturday afternoon, July 18, with Casa's doors opening at 6:30 for dinner and dancing followed by the first performance at 8:00 and a second at 10:00. Rose kept the performers practicing until past midnight the night before the opening, and they had to be back for makeup and wardrobe the next morning. Opening day came off without a hitch. The critics were gushing in their praise. *Dallas Morning News*'s amusement editor John Rosenfield called the exhibition "a show of immensity, novelty and resourcefulness." The *Star-Telegram* called it "a type of [Broadway] entertainment the state has never seen before." Drama critics from all over the country struggled to describe a spectacle that "beggars description." The stars of the show, besides Everett Marshall, were dancer Ann Pennington and burlesque performer Sally Rand. Faye was not mentioned in the early reviews. The *Star-Telegram* admitted, "People from out of the State probably do not know who Miss Cotton is," but hastened to add that "Texans undoubtedly recognized the beauty contest winner." Little did anyone suspect, a star was born that night. The *Star-Telegram* described her foray downtown the next day as "Faye Cotton and Attendants."[12]

Her hometown was thrilled with their little girl. She pushed oil and crime news both off the front page of the *Borger Herald*, which reported, "Borger's glamorous Faye Cotton" is "Sweetheart No. 1" in the show at the Frontier Centennial. The newspaper was stretching the truth describing the former sandwich-stand cashier as "glamorous." For all the attention she got in Texas newspapers, she might have been mistaken for Ann Pennington or Sally Rand. Her appearance in the beginning was limited to coming out for the grand finale wearing a stunning, forty-pound, gold-mesh gown with an elaborate train. What the *Star-Telegram* called a "fairyland gown" had a value of $5,000 ($86,000 today). Faye's statuesque size had a lot to do with why she was tapped to be "Sweetheart No. 1." Rose liked statuesque women because they stood out on stage. Besides, the show-stopping gown would have swallowed up anyone smaller. It took three attendants to help her squeeze into it before every show and had to be stored in a "safety vault"

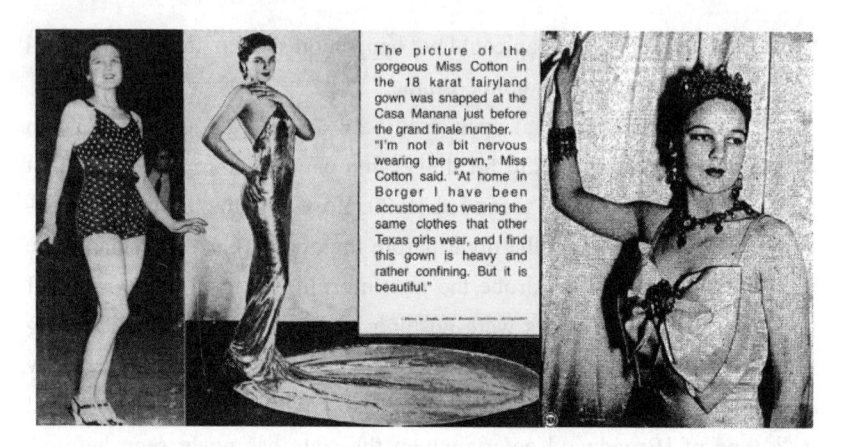

The picture of the gorgeous Miss Cotton in the 18 karat fairyland gown was snapped at the Casa Manana just before the grand finale number. "I'm not a bit nervous wearing the gown," Miss Cotton said. "At home in Borger I have been accustomed to wearing the same clothes that other Texas girls wear, and I find this gown is heavy and rather confining. But it is beautiful."

Left: Fay (or Faye) Cotton, Casa Mañana royalty, winning the first Sweetheart contest in a polka-dot swimsuit. Author's collection.

Center: Faye looking statuesque in the fabulous golden gown she wore for Casa. Author's collection.

Right: Faye wearing Empress Marie Louise's jewelry. Author's collection.

between shows. Photos of the two runners-up for "Sweetheart No. 1" show girls just as shapely but much more petite.[13]

Faye seemed to have a fairy godmother looking after her. The girl who had never been on the stage even in high school was suddenly in the big time. Rose's promise of a movie contract seemed to be coming true when Universal Studios executive Rufus LeMaire flew in from Los Angeles to see the show. The press release from Rose's office said that he planned to "take her to California" and she had signed a "term contract" to go right after the show closed for the season. The *Star-Telegram* even revealed the name of the show she would be in, "Hippodrome." If true, Faye would be following other Texans already under contract to Universal, including 19-year-old Russell Wade of Fort Worth. The question still to be answered was whether she could act.[14]

It was certainly true the camera loved her. She was photographed trying on shoes at Baker Shoe Store and clothes with Sally Rand at the National Fashion Exhibition, going on at the Hotel Texas. It was not just the camera that loved her; newspaper readers loved reading about her.[15]

She was turned into a fashion plate with the help of Amon Carter's *Star-Telegram* staff, and you did not need an agent when you had Amon Carter shilling for you. Her every appearance in public was reported across the state. She was photographed wearing $500,000 worth of jewels given to Empress Marie Louise by Napoleon Bonaparte, which came through Fort Worth while touring the country. Newspapers leaped at the chance to put two beautiful things together. According to reports, she was only the fourth woman ever to wear the jewels. She also modeled for a "morning coffee revue" at The Fair department store in September. But the *Star-Telegram*'s stroke of marketing genius was encouraging readers to send in clothing designs for Faye that were then turned into cutouts for paper dolls, a type of cheap plaything for Depression-era little girls. For weeks the newspaper carried "Faye Cotton Fashion Designs" submitted by readers. "Cut 'em out and color 'em!" young girls were advised, hooking the next generation of readers early. The series of cutouts eventually constituted a full Faye Cotton "wardrobe."[16]

"Sweetheart No. 1" became promotion gimmick no. 1 for Casa Mañana. She was on stage less than ten minutes twice a night, but she still generated endless stories in print. No one was more amazed at her notoriety than Faye herself. She was approachable and open with reporters. She was seen tucking into a "man-sized steak" just like an ordinary person, unconcerned with keeping a girlish figure. She chatted with reporters about life in Borger and did not bother to powder her nose in public before the flashbulbs went off. She even admitted, "There isn't a glamorous thing about me, and I still don't know why they picked me." She had to be reminded who Billy Rose was despite the maestro's gushing compliments.[17]

As Faye's fame spread, her role in the show was expanded. By early August she was coming out on stage to release 160 silver balloons "while the Varsity Eight serenaded her with 'Toy Balloon.'" She was still not part of the dance numbers, which might suggest John Murray Anderson's evaluation of her talent. The publicity folks had to find other ways to keep her in the news. Toward the end of the season, they had her selling Roosevelt-Garner souvenir campaign coins in the Hotel Texas lobby.[18]

In August her older sister, Lillian, came back to town to be chaperone and keep house for the budding star. Her mother also drove down to see her performance "opposite Everett Marshall." Faye told reporters Ruby Cotton "liked the show and had left it up to her whether to go into the movies."[19]

Despite early reports that Faye would be heading off to Universal Studios when the show closed, that is not what happened. There was interest from Hollywood, but no contract had been signed. The report in the *Star-Telegram* after the first night that she was "as good as in the movies" was more show boosting aimed at the local audience. A few weeks later the newspaper reported that Faye "and a number of other" show members were auditioned by an MGM scout in Rose's Sinclair Building office. The auditions consisted of "brief skits to demonstrate the quality of their voices." The scout offered no hint of his impressions. Eventually Faye did indeed sign a "long-term-option contract" with Universal, meaning they might or might not put her in a future movie. Friends and family envisioned their gal being on the silver screen as soon as 1937.[20]

The Frontier Centennial closed on Saturday, November 14. For the last week, the publicity boys promoted their homegrown star with words like "glamorous Faye" and "luscious Faye," none of which added a penny to her bank account. The weekend before that, she got a "farewell shower and auto-graph party" hosted by a sister-in-law, Mrs. V. P. Howell. The whole city was invited, or at least the part that read the entertainment section of the newspaper and wished to say farewell to "Sweetheart No. 1." Faye herself determined the menu: red beans, potato salad, onions, pickles, coleslaw, and cornbread—the kind of fare she had grown up eating. On the last night, described as a "gay mixup [*sic*]" of emotions and raucousness, Everett Marshall kissed Faye good-bye on stage, the first time he had been so forward. The day after the show closed, she went home to Borger for a few days' rest then packed and was off to Hollywood and the next chapter in her life. The town turned out to see her off, which took her back to Fort Worth to catch a plane to Los Ange-les. She had to be at Universal Studios on December 1.[21]

The ground crews were still cleaning up when William Monnig, chair-man of the Frontier Centennial's Board of Control "pledged" to do it again the following year. "It's been a wonderful show," he said, "and has brought Fort Worth millions of dollars' worth of advertising." He added that "it took us out of a rut." It put Dallas to shame in some ways, made Fort Worth the preeminent symbol of the Wild West, and created a new celebrity, the "Texas Sweetheart."[22]

That new celebrity did not fare so well in Hollywood, though the *Star-Telegram* tried to follow her budding screen career. Apparently, she passed her screen test with Universal, and the callow West Texas girl was turned over to trainers, makeup artists, and costume designers. Folks back in Texas read that her first role would be "a small part" in *When Love Is Young*, directed by Hal Mohr. She told a Fort Worth reporter that stars Virginia Bruce and Kent Taylor were very helpful and character actor Walter Brennan very "nice." All the work she put in paid off when she got a dance scene with Virginia Bruce. The film was released on March 28, 1937, but Faye's name appears nowhere in the credits.[23]

Her part may have ended up on the cutting-room floor. Her screen debut had to wait until *Top of the Town* came out in March 1937. It was the smallest of bit parts with only spoken words according to the *Star-Telegram*'s Mary Wynn. The film got to Fort Worth in April where it played the Worth theater. Mary Wynn reviewed the film, calling it "vast in settings, huge in noise . . . but puny in plot." There was not much to say about Faye's blink-and-you-miss-her scene where she "twirls a water goblet in her fingers." That did not keep Universal from issuing a press release hyping Faye as "destined for big things." They were wrong. The movie did nothing for anyone's career.[24]

Faye may have realized that her Hollywood career was going nowhere, or the small-town girl got lonesome for home, because not long after the film opened, she was back in Borger for a six-week vacation. While at home she announced her engagement to another local, a former Borger High School classmate and football star, Ralph Shelton. They reconnected in Los Angeles, where he had gone to study geology. He gave her not one but two diamond engagement rings, and they set a wedding date in three months— or maybe sooner, she explained cryptically. Faye had acquired a taste for the finer things in life, including diamonds and a Hollywood wedding. She told a reporter she had chosen marriage and family over career, though her sister Lillian may have come closer to the truth when she said that Faye's screen tests revealed a voice "a little too high" for a future in talkies, but

Faye appeared in two movies in 1937, *Top of the Town* (*left*) and *When Love Is Young* (*right*), neither of which launched a Hollywood career. She did not have the elusive "it" that turned starlets into stars. Author's collection.

she hastened to add defensively that it did not matter because little sister "doesn't like pictures at all."[25]

While Faye was home in Texas, she returned to the scene of her glory. Fort Worth and Billy Rose were working on a sequel to the Frontier Centennial for 1937, to be called the "Frontier Fiesta" (or alternatively "Frontier Festival"). Dear sweet Faye Cotton was still remembered as the star of the 1936 show. In March WBAP radio, looking down benignly on the city from atop the Blackstone Hotel, broadcast a musical program of Casa numbers from the 1936 "Frontier Centennial Revue" dedicated to "Miss Faye Cotton."[26]

Promising to hold another contest to pick another "Sweetheart No. 1," Billy Rose held Faye up as the role model for the bunch of entrants. As the *Star-Telegram* described her Cinderella story, she was "lifted from behind a cash register to find fame having Everett Marshall woo her with love songs."

It was truly a fairy-tale story, only with some big differences: In 1937 the production company paid round-trip rail or bus fare for the entrants to come to Fort Worth plus the cost of a hotel room for the night of the contest. And because of Faye's reported success in Hollywood, the participants had even bigger dreams of future fame. The small-town girls waited until they got to Fort Worth to "shop for the most bewitching bathing suits on the market"— tastefully revealing, of course. And the final difference: The gold mesh gown to be worn by the winner for the show would be even more spectacular, created out of five hundred yards of satin, described as "the biggest dress in the history of the theater." Rose & Co. predicted one million advance ticket sales.[27]

The 1937 "Sweetheart No. 1" contest was held on Saturday night, May 22, in the Hotel Texas Crystal Ballroom, a big step above the Paschal High School auditorium. The hundred fresh-faced beauties had primped and preened to a fare-thee-well for their big moment. All nonsense about audience "voting" aside, they only had to impress one judge—Billy Rose. That was the same as 1936. The winner was Grey Downs of Temple, a Texas beauty with "bronze" skin, perfect teeth, a wholesome appearance, and a visible confident air. Rose announced his choice while holding up her hand and proclaiming, "The winnah!" He was smart enough to make Fort Worth's entrant runner-up and announce he wanted her "in the show," too. Miss Downs's win came with the promise of "an opportunity in motion pictures."[28]

Faye was present in the audience that night because, as the *Star-Telegram* pointed out, "When it was announced last year that a Texas Sweetheart No. 1 would be selected, it was simply a 'title' as far as the public was concerned, but now everyone associates the distinction with [Faye] Cotton." Interviewed after the contest, Faye gave her successor her "stamp of approval," crying out, "Isn't she cute!" The admiration was mutual. Three weeks later they were photographed and interviewed together on opening night. They took turns complimenting each other for the clearly enchanted reporters. A couple of days later they sat down together for an interview on WBAP broadcast across the state from its studio atop the Blackstone Hotel. Apparently, Faye did not plan to return to Hollywood because she explained to the radio audience why she preferred "the role of housewife to the glamorous parts offered her in the film capital."[29]

Sweetheart Is Altar Bound

FAYE COTTON.

Faye Cotton's wedding announcement, 1937. Author's collection.

Being done with Hollywood did not mean Faye was ready to settle down in Texas. She gave some thought to getting married in Los Angeles since her fiancé was still living there. They turned down an invitation from Billy Rose to have the ceremony on the Casa stage with Paul Whiteman's band playing the wedding march and "I Love You Truly." Rose, ever the showman, argued, "No spot could be more fitting for the wedding ceremony of the Texas Sweetheart No. 1 of 1936 than the incomparable setting of Casa Mañana." Apparently, Borger, Texas, was never in consideration for the ceremony.[30]

In the end, Ralph Shelton and Faye Cotton said their vows in neither California nor Texas. They were married with no fanfare in Reno, Nevada, on September 5, 1937. It is not known why they chose Reno—unless they wanted to do a quickie marriage—or if any friends or family members were present.[31]

Fort Worth recreated Casa Mañana two more years before World War II shut them down. By 1938 it was a summer tradition put on by the Casa Mañana Association. Part of that tradition was continuing the contest to choose Texas's "Sweetheart No. 1." There were also some important differences. For one, Billy Rose was not present to announce "the winnah!" In his place was a panel of three distinguished "authorities on the subject of feminine beauty." And the contest was held on the Casa stage at intermission during the third night of the show. Invited to serve as "honorary judges" in 1938 were former sweethearts Faye Cotton and Grey Downs. Grey was now Mrs. Larry M. Baugh of Temple, Texas, while Faye (Mrs. Ralph Shelton) declined because, she said, she lived "too far away to accept the invitation."[32]

Faye would not make another official appearance in Fort Worth for another eight years. Her time was taken up being a full-time wife and mother, and she had no interest in revisiting her days as a beauty queen. (Grey Downs had her own issues. In December 1940 she was badly burned in an accident at home and forced to endure painful skin grafts for months thereafter.) Ralph and Faye left California in early 1940 and moved to Missouri. That summer they moved back to Texas, settling in Amarillo next door to her mother, Ruby, and stepfather, Everett King.[33]

After 1939 Fort Worth tried to keep up with its first and most beloved sweetheart but without much luck. In January 1946 Faye came to town with one of her sisters on the way from Oklahoma to Amarillo. She was headed back to her home in California. Ralph had served in the US Navy as a radar-man during World War II, leaving her to wait for him in Los Angeles as a war wife. To fill her time awaiting his return, she told a reporter she did some modeling (a "sideline career") and worked in a few movies, which she did not name. The couple had one child, a son, leaving her plenty of time to devote to her other love, fashion design, something she had been interested in since her Casa Mañana days. According to her interviewer, Ida Belle Hicks, Faye had "the same unspoiled, natural personality" she had when she first came to Fort Worth, and she looked "simply stunning in a black suit topped with a black Homberg" (borrowing a page from Marlene Dietrich's fashion wardrobe). She inquired about "all the Fort Worth friends she had made" and the girls she had performed with. Hicks could not stop gushing about Faye's unblemished beauty even ten years after her nights on the Casa stage.[34]

That same year Clyde Whitlock, arts and entertainment editor for the *Star-Telegram*, revisited the glory of the 1936 Frontier Centennial on its ten-year anniversary. All that remained of Casa at this point was the "rusty steel skeleton of the revolving stage." He mentioned Jumbo the elephant, Billy Rose, Paul Whiteman, and "oh yes," Sally Rand, but saved his most fond reminiscences for the "glamorous Faye Cotton."[35]

Three years later Fort Worth was feeling historic-minded on the one-hundredth anniversary of the city's founding. That included staging a small "re-enactment" of the original Frontier Centennial ("Fiesta-cade") at Farrington Field. As part of the celebration, *Star-Telegram* editors set out to find as many of the "Casa Mañana beauties" as possible, starting with "the beautiful Faye Cotton [*sic*]." They were able to report that most "are now housewives," still the ultimate dream of most of their female readers, so, therefore, life after Casa had turned out well. Some of the chorus girls, still looking quite fetching, agreed to strut their stuff for a newspaper photograph. And, of course, they had to have a glamour shot of Faye—showing more cleavage than she ever showed in 1936.[36]

Faye Cotton's "fifteen minutes of fame" lasted about twelve months. Forty years later, she might as well have dropped off the face of the earth. *Star-Telegram* entertainments editor Elston Brooks had no idea what happened to her. And in 1985 the newspaper's "Answer Man," Ed Brice, got an inquiry from an unidentified man who said he "had the privilege of dating Faye on several occasions that summer [of 1936]." He wondered what ever happened to her. All Bryce could say was, "After weeks of attempting to find

Enduring fame comes to Borger, Texas! *Boomtown*, an oil painting by Thomas Hart Benton, 1928. Author's collection.

out whatever became of Faye Cotton, we have to report we were unable to find anyone who knows." Two years later author Chris Evans ran classifieds notices in the *Star-Telegram* trying to find her for a book he was writing on Casa Mañana. No luck either.[37]

But Faye had not dropped off the face of the earth. She and Ralph were divorced after the war. He died in Arlington, Virginia, in 1954 and was buried in Arlington National Cemetery, Virginia. He had never remarried. It is not known whether Faye attended the funeral or not. Faye did not remarry either. She moved back to Texas and in 1966 was living in Lubbock. Eventually she moved back to California, returning to her small-town roots. She was living in Porterville, Tulare County, when she died on November 26, 1992, at the age of 74. Her neighbors did not know much about her. She was described as "an actress and model and a former Miss Texas [*sic*]." She is buried in Vandalia Cemetery in Porterville.[38]

Faye Cotton was the second thing to put Borger, Texas, on the national map. The first was "regional" artist Thomas Hart Benton's 1928 painting, *Boomtown*. Eight years later "glamorous Faye Cotton" blew into Fort Worth like a West Texas dust storm. One small-town newspaper declared that the triumph of dark-haired Faye "rang the death knell for blonde supremacy in Texas." That never happened. Years later, Benton's painting is still celebrated while Faye Cotton has been largely forgotten.[39]

But her legacy was so much bigger than the people of Borger or Porterville could ever have imagined. Reportedly, it was her scantily clad form riding a bucking bronco, which graced the advertising campaign for "The Last Frontier," that Casa inundated the state with in 1936. It is still the single most iconic image associated with the show even today.[40]

And though she was never Miss Texas, Faye had a huge impact on Texas beauty pageants. She was the very personification of Texas femininity: naturally beautiful, modest, and morally above reproach. The "Texas Sweetheart No. 1" contest and all the publicity surrounding Faye Cotton sparked an interest in beauty pageants that led to the state's first representative (Miss Corpus Christi) at the Miss America Pageant later that same year. The following year saw the beginning of a statewide Miss Texas pageant. One of two contestants Texas sent to the Miss America Pageant that year was a Fort Worth girl, Alice Emerick, first runner-up in Atlantic City. And Texas's obsession with beauty contests continued in 1940 when United Artists held the world premiere of *The Westerner* in Fort Worth. Part of the festivities was a contest to pick the "Most Typical Texas Girl," another way of saying most beautiful. Bob Hope joined the fun by having his picture taken ogling the winner, Ruth Evelyn Foote of Abilene. But it all started with Faye.[41]

Chapter 12

The Police Chief and the Showgirl

This is the story of another legendary Casa Mañana performer, but the chapter's suggestive title is not a teaser for a tale of illicit love between an older man and an ingenue in the chorus line. The show girl was Casa star Mary "Stuttering Sam" Dowell. And the police chief was her father, Arthur E. Dowell. In 1936 he was the better-known member of the family.[1]

Arthur Edwin Dowell was born September 11, 1877, in Pike County, Missouri, the fourth of nine children born to Nehemiah Dowell and Mary Francis Rinker Dowell, who at 26 was twenty years younger than her husband.

In 1914 Arthur went to work for the St. Louis–San Francisco Railroad (the Frisco) in the "law and police" division. He worked out of their Springfield, Missouri, headquarters until coming to Fort Worth in 1920. In 1921 he quit to take a job with the Fort Worth Police Dept. (FWPD) in the administration of newly elected Chief Harry Hamilton. His experience as a railroad detective stood him in good stead as he was hired straight to the detective division. For the rest of his career he never worked as a beat cop.[2]

While in Missouri in 1908 he met and married Martha Rea Logan. They had four daughters between 1911 and 1914. The fourth was Mary Louise

Dowell, born in North Platte, Nebraska, on December 14, 1914. Six years later the family moved to Fort Worth because of her father's job with the Frisco Railroad. After going to work for the FWPD he built a house on the North Side (2012 Market Street) with a little apartment in the back, spending just $3,100 total. Never a stay-at-home mother, Martha taught music classes at the Chestnut Avenue Disciples of Christ (a.k.a. Christian) Church. Arthur remained faithful to the First Church of Christ, Scientist. Under their mother's influence, performing came naturally to her daughters. Arthur and Martha Dowell quickly made friends in Fort Worth. They were close enough to Dr. B. U. L. Conner to frequently borrow his Cadillac (Arthur did not own a car) to "show the family a good time."[3]

Arthur Dowell was not a typical flatfoot. Besides never working as a patrolman, he was a Christian Scientist—so far as is known, the only member of the FWPD ever to practice that religion. The Church of Christ, Scientist, was on the liberal end of the theological spectrum, which may help explain how two of his daughters came to be show girls. By temperament and interests he was "mild-mannered" and an avid reader who favored philosophy and poetry. As a detective he considered himself "a student of human nature" more than a by-the-book lawman. He was as likely to try to understand a perp as to throw him in a cell. It did not hurt that Dowell was a physically imposing figure, standing nearly seven feet tall "with a physique that was in proportion." He passed his physical size on to daughter Mary.[4]

His rise through the ranks of the FWPD was swift. He became police inspector (the equivalent of lieutenant) after less than two years on the job. Chief Hamilton put him in charge of a drive to rid the city of "undesirables" during the annual Southwestern Exposition and Fat Stock Show. He was tough on his own men. In June of 1923 he suspended two officers for getting into a public fistfight. A year later, when police were called to a KKK women's auxiliary meeting at Klan Hall on N. Main, he was the officer in charge on the scene. It seems a dustup had occurred among the ladies that turned physical. Dowell decided there was no need for police and sent his men away, choosing to defuse the situation with talk rather than force. Later he led a drive to shut down illegal gambling in Fort Worth, raiding games at

Fort Worth Police Captain Arthur E. Dowell. Courtesy of retired FWPD
Sergeant Kevin Foster.

several locations. He knew all the big players and their favorite sites, which included private clubs and high-class hotels like the Texas.[5]

His work was satisfactory, and his politics attuned correctly because by 1927 he had risen to captain under Chief Henry Lee, in charge of the North Side substation. Lee's long tenure as chief (1922–1933) protected Captain Dowell from the usual turnover in the department that followed every election.[6]

In July 1933 he was promoted to captain of detectives. Four years later, in another department shakeup, he was appointed chief by City Manager L. W. Hoelscher, a position he held until October 1938. He got the promotion after Chief Henry Lewis was unceremoniously demoted. Dowell kept his predecessor's second in command, R. E. Dysart, and announced there would be no further shakeups "so long as every man does his duty diligently." At the same time, he took a get-tough approach to the criminal element. "We are serving notice on all law violators that their activities must cease," he said. "If they do not, we shall take the proper steps." The department he inherited was wrestling with illegal gambling going on right under the noses of the police, and more than a few officers were on the take. Dowell promised to address the problem of illegal gambling with a nuanced approach: "There will be no policy of raid, raid, raid, but if that becomes necessary, we can do that." He added, "We're not going to be fanatical about it." Then, in a burst of candor that would come back to haunt him, he admitted, "We are not so foolish as to think that we can stop every little dice or poker game . . . but we're going to stop all we can."[7]

Dowell's tenure as police chief lasted just over a year. All the tough talk proved to be empty rhetoric. On Wednesday, October 12, 1938, he tendered his resignation "at the request of City Manager Dudley Lewis." The announcement caught the city by surprise. He was demoted to captain of detectives to be replaced by Captain Karl Howard. City Manager Lewis offered a cryptic explanation of the move, saying it was "to preserve harmony in the Department." Dowell's firing was the biggest news in a general house-cleaning of the FWPD ordered by Mayor T. J. Harrell. A clue to the reason came from Councilman Ward B. Powell, who declared after coming out of a closed-door council meeting that the city was not going to "countenance gambling, slot machines, marble boards or any other character of lawlessness." Dowell took his demotion like a good soldier. House-cleanings, usually for political reasons, were standard operating procedure in the FWPD. His letter of resignation sounded like a desperate plea for his job: "At your request I am asking to be relieved of the duty of the chief's office. In doing so I wish to say I have enjoyed working with you, and too, that I have no bitterness against anyone. I want to continue in the service and promise my undivided loyal support to make the administration a success."[8]

Arthur Dowell lived another six years, working as captain in the Detective Bureau almost to the end. In April 1942 he returned to uniformed service but still retained his captain's rank. He died on Sunday, June 7, 1942, shortly after coming off duty. The cause was a fatal heart attack suffered while she was showing the Market Avenue apartment. Daughter Mary Louise had just left on Friday to go back to New York. He was 64 years old and a Christian Scientist to the end. The funeral service was conducted by a Christian Science "reader" before burial in Fort Worth's Greenwood Cemetery. His legacy as a man and a police officer was being an inveterate optimist, a kind soul, and a "conscientious" officer.[9]

Despite Arthur Dowell's rise to the top of the FWPD and his dramatic downfall, the most famous member of the Dowell family was daughter Mary Louise. By the time Arthur was demoted, she was a star performer on the stage with a bright future ahead of her.

If she had come along today, Amazonian-like Mary Louise Dowell would be recruited to play basketball, but in her day that was not an option for a young lady. Born on December 14, 1914, in Lincoln, Nebraska, the red-haired girl was already 6' 3" and easily 130 pounds by the time she was 17. She was also a daddy's girl with confidence and personality to spare. Her size she got from her father; her other talents were God-given. "Statuesque" and "Junoesque" were how newspaper reporters described her because she towered over men and women alike. But the compliments only came to her as an adult. She grew up on the North Side of Fort Worth, feeling like a "freak," she confessed to reporters, convinced she was "the unhappiest girl in Texas."[10]

Her feelings of inferiority probably caused her to stutter. She outgrew the former eventually and learned to live with the latter. It turned out she was a born performer who became quite the social butterfly. On return visits to Fort Worth from New York City years later, she asked friends to "get loads of photographers and reporters there to meet us," and after her night-club performances in the Big Apple, she would come out into the audience and take a seat at some VIP's table, striking up a spontaneous conversation. At such moments her stuttering made her that much more enchanting to the gentlemen at the table.[11]

Her show business career was launched in the spring of 1936 when she accompanied older sister Virginia, already a talented dancer, to auditions at the Texas Hotel for Billy Rose's Frontier Centennial, to be staged that summer in Fort Worth. Big little sister was standing quietly to one side in the Crystal Ballroom when the five feet, four inches Rose noticed the strik-ing young woman and called her over. When he quizzed her about who she was, she was so nervous she stammered out her replies. The next thing she knew she was auditioning for a role in the show. Rose hired both sisters, but it was producer John Murray Anderson who gave Mary Louise Dowell the name that followed her for the rest of her life, "Stutterin' Sam," usually shortened to just Sam. He was known for giving nicknames to all the girls in his shows. The curious thing was that her stuttering was a reflection of simple nervousness, never a lack of confidence. That was clear her whole life. She was a remarkably mature and clear-headed girl who knew her talents and her limitations.[12]

In the run-up to the 1936 Frontier Centennial, Casa Mañana costumer A. M. Blumberg had to make special allowances for Sam because she did not fit the typical show girl form. She endeared herself to both Rose and Anderson because she was a trouper willing to do whatever was asked of her without complaining. That included wearing skimpy costumes that scandalized churchgoing folks but were part of the show girl's life. Showmen like Billy Rose were selling sex as much as musical performances. What made her the star of the 1936 Casa show was the grand finale of "Stars and Stripes Forever," which required her to climb sixty feet of stairs and come back down again wearing an elaborate head-dress and wings and dragging a five-hundred-yard-long train behind her.

Top: Casa Mañana was the biggest thing on the grounds of the 1936 Frontier Centennial, subject of post cards like this one. Author's collection.

Bottom: The Casa revue and audience on show night. Author's collection.

It weighed so much she had to be outfitted with shoulder braces beneath her costume. Only someone of her size and strength could have done it, and it left her in tears at the end of every night's performance. She even mastered the trick of descending the stairs without looking down at her feet and with a big smile on her face.[13]

The season, which ran from July 18 through November 14, was a huge success. Two million people passing through the gates onto the grounds. The nightly Casa shows weren't for everybody, but they attracted more than their share of attention—of both hometown folks and talent scouts. Even before the season ended, Sam was making plans to take her act to New York City. The girl who had never been any farther from Fort Worth than Dallas—and then only with her mother—dreamed of making it on Broadway. After receiving permission from mom and dad, she made arrangements to leave the show early. Sam boarded a train on Monday morning, September 28, clutching a purse full of introductions to Broadway people.[14]

Less than a month later, she was "making shorts" for Warner Brothers and had been promised a place in a nightclub show. Plenty of local swells were willing to show her around the Big Apple. Her only complaint at the time, in letters home to mom and dad, was how "noisy" it was.[15]

In early 1937 she got on with Sally Rand's musical revue ("burlesque theater"). She knew Miss Rand, also a Billy Rose act, from Casa, and that connection helped get her a part in the show. Not as well-known was that Rand also had a speech impediment, a severe lisp, which made her simpatico with the callow girl from Texas. Observers said Sam strutted her stuff "as though she had clear title to the whole show." In April she left Rand's show to come back to Fort Worth. It was her first trip home since leaving for New York in September, and Fort Worth was thrilled to welcome its celebrity girl home. Life was also looking up for her father, who had just been promoted to police chief.[16]

She signed up for the second season of Casa Mañana in May and was part of the dance company working under Lauretta Jefferson, who had also trained the chorus line in 1936. Sam's limited talents may explain why the breakout star of 1936 was relegated to the second row for most of the evening. She appeared in two segments, a "Gone with the Wind" scene based on Margaret Mitchell's book and a "Lost Horizon" scene based on James Hilton's book, but according to the *Star-Telegram* there was no doubt she was the star of the show. "She was given a hand second only to the Stuart Morgan Dancers." For the second year in a row she was outfitted in a bizarre costume, if anything even more excessive than her headdress in 1936.

Left: Stutterin' Sam in oversized headdress, 1936. Author's collection.

Right: Sam in extravagant peacock costume for "Lost Horizon" scene, 1937. *Fort Worth Star-Telegram* Collection, Special Collections, University of Texas at Arlington Library.

This time it was a "peacock costume" that had her dragging a Brobding-nagian train behind her. What the audience loved, however, aroused the ire of moralists on the city council who only saw the amount of thigh she displayed. Several weeks into the show an order came down that a "tiny gold fringe skirt" be added to the costume.[17]

She ditched the peacock costume for her big scene in the grand finale, "It Can't Happen Here," taken from the Sinclair Lewis novel. Sam portrayed the "Symbol of Peace" in a white satin gown with a pair of ten-foot wings strapped to her back and a long train carried by twenty-four "trainbearers." She had to lug that costume up a four-story staircase. It was classic Billy Rose spectacle, and the audience ate it up. The *Star-Telegram* proclaimed her the "premier showgirl of the [1937] Casa Mañana Revue."[18]

She won the audience's sympathy by pushing through some physical problems that arose during the production. On the weekend of August 7–8, she was sidelined with a swollen black eye. (How she got it went unreported.) Her value to the show was demonstrated when her replacement for the

"Lost Horizon" segment did not have the strength to handle the big peacock train. A few weeks later an exhausted Dowell fainted on stage during an early scene. An ambulance rushed her to the hospital where her parents joined her. But Stutterin' Sam was a trouper. She was back on stage in time for the grand finale that night.[19]

As a celebrity no part of Mary's life was off-limits for public consumption. She was the subject of romantic pairings like any Hollywood starlet. During the 1937 show she was linked to Jimmy Brierly, a vocalist with the Paul Whiteman Orchestra. Professionally, their names were attached to a performance of Shakespeare's "Romeo and Juliet" on WBAP radio that August. A *Star-Telegram* reporter dared to wonder aloud how Sam would handle her lines with her well-known stuttering. It may have been curiosity about that very thing that drew listeners to tune in. Or it may have been curiosity about the budding romance. This was the first time Sam had been linked publicly to anyone, and the newspaper suggested it was serious by calling it "more than regular balcony baloney."[20]

She returned to New York after the 1937 Casa season, only to just make ends meet with a series of show girl jobs plus writing a regular newspaper column. Sam made enough to split the rent on a flat with two other show girls until she was finally able to get her own place. In a letter home she called her new digs "the first time I've ever lived alone."[21]

Any dreams Sam had of a career as a stage actress were doomed by three liabilities—her height, her speech impediment, and her broad Texas accent. She towered over every leading man, and there were no camera angles on a Broadway stage to cover that up. The accent could be trained out of her with work, but the stuttering, while charming in person, would be a killer on the stage. She eventually learned to control it to a certain extent but never completely overcame it. It also cost her a possible radio gig in New York.[22]

Sam acquired a press agent, Sidney Spears, laughingly promising him a job "on Dad's police force if he'd only give up Broadway for an honest living." She also sanded off some of the rough Texas edges that she came to New York with. Everett Marshall, the Casa star from 1936, saw her a year later and noted admiringly, "The big city has made her quite sophisticated looking." Still, under all the makeup and glitzy costumes, she was Mary Dowell from North Fort Worth who believed Texas was "God's own country." The folks back home were able to follow their girl through her regular reports to the *Star-Telegram* and frequent Jack Gordon's coverage for his columns in the *Press*. He considered Sam and Ginger Rogers the twin "Texas beauties" making it big on stage and screen. The fact that both had a Fort Worth connection made their stories even better.[23]

Sam stayed in touch with Billy Rose, and when he opened the Diamond Horseshoe nightclub in December 1938, he put her in the show. His musical revues were known for big production values and scantily clad girls. One of those revues was an adaptation of his Casa Mañana production only on a smaller stage. It ran for six months. She worked for Rose for the next five years and not just as a dancer. Apparently, her stuttering did not keep her from doing impersonations of famous people such as Greta Garbo. She branched out from her nightclub gig by writing a regular column for the *New York Times* about "the life of a New York showgirl." She was a natural writer and found writing more satisfying than being a show girl, though she admitted to being "a bit self-conscious about [my] writing ability as a professional." She grew her literary audience by sending "Tidbits on Broadway's Doings" three times a week to the *Star-Telegram*, which also kept her in the spotlight back home.[24]

The *New York Daily News* described her as "one of the highest paid night club and musical comedy decorations." That sort of empty praise did not keep her from wanting a "normal" life away from the stage, even if that meant working as a thirty-dollar-a-week typist. The same newspaper called the February 17, 1940, show at the Diamond Horseshoe "positively a farewell performance," a tip they could only have gotten from someone close to her. This was the sort of intrusive reporting that the tabloids thrived on, and this was mild compared to some other stories they ran on Sam. At different times she was linked to Fort Worth's most eligible bachelor, Bob Nicks, and to a "sheik" who reportedly dumped her to return home. She fed the public's curiosity by telling one reporter, "I won't marry anyone for his worldly possessions. . . . Of course, if I were in love with a rich man, and he with me, that would be Utopia." The Fort Worth newspapers picked up the stories on the wire and repeated them for the hometown folks. Her dream of love with a rich man seemed to come true in 1940 when she was linked to 27-year-old Benjamin Welles, son of FDR's undersecretary of state. They met while she was writing for the *New York Times*. She said it was true love and announced that they planned to get married. The romance must have been one-sided because Welles told the *Times'* Society columnist that he barely knew her and was "not engaged to anybody." Her humiliation made headlines in both New York and Fort Worth.[25]

Sam stretched her "fifteen minutes of fame" to the max. Though a New York show girl since 1937, her appeal was always more of a curiosity than a glamour doll or stage actress. Big Apple society embraced her because she was something fresh in their jaded lives. Elias Sugarman, tart-tongued editor of the trade magazine *Billboard*, described her as "easy on the eyes, but not quite beautiful enough to register on that score alone. It's her personality that does the trick." Her stutter could either be a charming eccentricity or a fatal flaw in a town obsessed with physical beauty. Stutterin' Sam, not Mary Dowell, was her New York moniker. It was immaterial that her speech impediment disappeared when she sang, became angry, or read lines. She was a six-foot, three-inch Amazon who stuttered. When fashion maven Helena Robinson did a runway show dedicated to "the [celebrity] Tall Girl," Mary was the tallest of the participants. All the others were between five feet, six inches and six feet tall.[26]

Mary was never comfortable with showbiz fame. Her unguarded personality and small-town values did not fit the big city. The real New York was not all bright lights and beautiful people. She found that out one night early in her time there after she was introduced to a Washington State US senator. As she related the story to Jack Gordon, he was a "nice-looking old gentleman" who squired her around the "night spots" one evening ending at the Stork Club. When they got back in the cab, he told the driver to take them to the Ritz hotel. She demurred sweetly at first, then more forcefully. As she described things, when she tried to get out of the cab, he "started beating my brains out. He popped me in the eye, hit me and kicked me. I had to wear dark glasses for two weeks." What she was describing was sexual assault, but any show girl could have told her it came with the territory.[27]

As Sam told anyone who would listen, she much preferred the life of the writer to strutting her stuff on the stage. Jack Gordon quoted her in the summer of 1938 when she was at the peak of her stage popularity: "I intend to be a newspaper woman." Small-town girls with big showbiz dreams might not have understood, but Sam was recalling the advice of Casa wardrobe mistress Jewel Carter in 1936: "Up to fourteen a girl needs good parents; from fourteen to forty, good looks; from forty to sixty, personality; and from sixty on, cash." Sam had the upbringing, the looks, and the personality. What she did not have was a husband, and the shelf life of a show girl was oh so short. She told another newspaper reporter in 1938, the show girl's life "is all so futile, phony and make-believe," adding for good measure, "I can't sing or act. I'll never be anything but a show girl," and that meant endless encounters with lotharios like the US senator. She said she could not get through an evening at the Diamond Horseshoe "without at least one proposition. Proposition, mind you, not marriage proposal." More than once she said she was heading home for good, calling New York "just a bad city."[28]

It took a couple of things to finally move her to act on those threats. The first was the passing of her beloved father. Arthur Dowell died in June 1942. At the funeral she shared the pain of losing him with a *Star-Telegram* reporter: "My happiness shall never be complete because my darling Dad isn't here to share it with me." Another two years would pass before she came back to Fort Worth again, although she kept in touch with her mother and sisters through her letters.[29]

What finally got her out of New York was not homesickness for Fort Worth but a career opportunity that fell in her lap. She met Hollywood studio mogul Jack Warner, who took an interest in her. She had met Hollywood types before, including Lew Wasserman when he was a talent agent for Music Corporation of America, but all they saw were her physical attributes, not her brains. She sent Warner a script she had been working on for a long time about the life of a Broadway chorus girl, titled *Here Comes the Girl*. What followed was, the *New York Times* reported on May 9, 1943, that she had signed a contract with Warner Brothers "to write for films, starting with one based on her show girl script." Reportedly, the studio had Ann Sheridan in mind to star. Sam was supposed to report to Warner by the end of the month. Her pending departure from the Big Apple was news in New York and back in Fort Worth and even carried in *Collier's Magazine*. She took the Twentieth Century Limited, a celebrity favorite, from New York to Chicago and the Santa Fe Chief from Chicago to Los Angeles, a forty-hour trip altogether to meet her new bosses.[30]

Whether there is any truth in Jack Warner's personal involvement is impossible to say. It could be another one of those fabulist show-biz stories. She had certainly demonstrated writing talent, but a newspaper columnist was a long way from a scriptwriter. It was not unusual for Hollywood studios to commission scripts on spec for possible future films, although nothing came of it 99 percent of the time. Sam's *Here Comes the Girl* script turned out to be one of those 99 percent times. She spent over a year writing and rewriting while working on other film projects. Two of her scripts were picked up by Warner Brothers, one of which became the Howard Hawks 1944 film *To Have or Have Not* with Humphrey Bogart and Lauren Bacall. Years later Hawks still remembered the novice screenwriter with the stutter because of the "beautiful dialogue" she wrote. Her Fort Worth family and friends believed she had three film scripts in the works when she finally left Hollywood for her ultimate dream.[31]

Mary Dowell was always at heart an old-fashioned gal who had always wanted someone to share her life with. She finally found that man, ironically, in New York. She was first introduced to Sigmund Henley by another show girl, Dorothy Bigbee, also of Fort Worth. He was a 42-year-old stockbroker and manufacturer with a "beautiful [estate] home" and a fortune estimated at $20 million. He was also a Princeton graduate and twelve years her senior. What sealed the deal was that he fell for her immediately and was not bothered by the fact that she towered over him. What kept them from the altar for nearly a year was that Mary was in Hollywood working on her script for *Here Comes the Girl* and wanted to finish it before starting her new life. It was no secret that Henley was not at all the kind of man Mary Dowell would have ended up with had she stayed in North Fort Worth. She would have ended up more like her sister, Virginia, who married a North Side boy and during World War II worked on the Globe Aircraft assembly line in the Stockyards. Society columnists trying to figure out the attraction described him as a "Texas cattle rancher," which he was not. He was willing to come to Fort Worth for the small wedding Mary desired as opposed to an extravagant New York ceremony. With her wedding announcement she said she was retiring from professional life to become "a good housewife." On March 31, 1944, she flew into town from California to make the arrangements for an April 11 wedding. Henley arrived two days later.[32]

The planned nuptials made the news in Texas and on both coasts. California newspapers called it the wedding of the "chorus-girl-turned-scenario-writer" to the rich socialite. The *Fresno Bee* even explained how the bride-to-be got her nickname: she "scrambled her words when she talked." The *Star-Telegram* offered more in-depth coverage of the nuptials but also more embarrassing: "Stutterin' Sam Will Be a B-B-Bride Before Long," said the headline. The full article was full of similar faux stuttering text.[33]

Mary turned her script in to Warner Brothers and waited expectantly. To her disappointment, *Here Comes the Girl* never got out of development, though everyone agreed a story about Broadway chorus girls had a lot of appeal. Paramount Pictures finally ran with the idea, making a small-budget movie in 1953 with the title *Here Come the Girls*. Instead of a behind-the-scenes look at the life of a show girl, it was a mystery with the show girls threatened by a slasher. The kind of movie Paramount wanted was evident from their choice for the lead, Bob Hope. Apart from the similarity in title and setting, it is difficult to tell how influential Mary's script was. The writer of record was Edmund L. Hartmann, and Mary Dowell's name appears nowhere in the credits. Any future Mary had in Hollywood was as a writer.

Mary and Sigmund said their vows in her mother's living room at 214 Market Avenue, the same house where she had grown up. Her two married sisters who stood up with her met the groom for the first time when he arrived on the big day. It was a simple ceremony with just thirteen guests present. Sister Virginia was her matron of honor, and Virginia's husband was Sigmund's best man. Some newspapers described the marriage as that of a former "bump-and-grind" girl to an East Coast sophisticate. The *Star-Telegram*'s society reporter pulled out all the stops to describe the ceremony in detail. The newlyweds announced they planned to make their home in Watertown, New York, where Sigmund's estate was.[34]

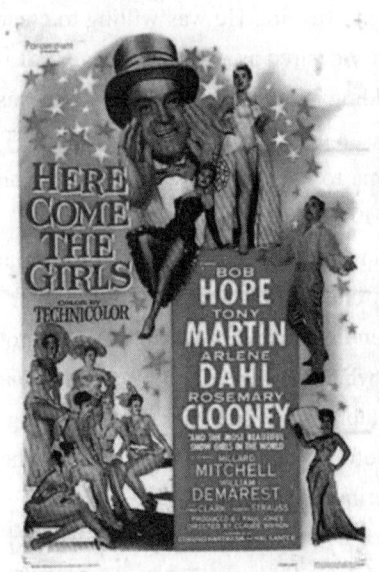 

Left: *Here Come the Girls*, 1953 Bob Hope movie derived from Mary Dowell's original script.

Right: Mary Dowell as Hollywood script writer, 1944. Author's collection.

Mary's marital happiness was short-lived. Henley died six years later on the date of their sixth wedding anniversary. Financially, she was not broke, but neither was she ready to retire from the working world, another reflection of her old-fashioned values. She took a job in the marketing department of Marx Toys in New York. More newsworthy, however, was that she remarried just four years later to the delightfully named Guild Copeland, a divorced New York bachelor gushingly described as a "Madison Ave. ad genius." They were living in New York when Mary Copeland died on April 9, 1963. For the last six years of her life, she suffered from a rare blood disease called porphyria. She was just 48 years old.[35]

Her passing was widely mourned, though not accurately reported. Newspapers and fan magazines had always embroidered her story, calling her "beautiful," saying she left college in 1936 to join Casa Mañana, and crediting her with being a hometown columnist for the *Star-Telegram*. Dorothy Kilgallen described her work after Sigmund's death as "a toy business

—*Star-Telegram* Photo.
Mr. and Mrs. Sigmund Hindley.
MR. AND MRS. SIGMUND HINDLEY.

Stutterin' Sam (Mary Dowell) and Sigmund Hindley's wedding photo, 1944. Author's collection.

executive," which the *Star-Telegram* repeated. The newspaper also interviewed longtime Fort Worth friends and family, asking them to share their memories of the girl who helped put the Frontier Centennial on the map. One sister was still living in the same house on Market Street that their father had built and where they had grown up. Mary had always thought of Fort Worth as her real home. Her mother (who died in 1949) and father were both buried in Greenwood Cemetery, and she wanted to be buried there, too, after being cremated. University Christian Church's Granville Walker conducted the small, private ceremony.[36]

Mary Dowell and her father make an interesting pair in Fort Worth public life. Had her father not been a Christian Scientist and her mother not musically inclined, it is doubtful Mary Dowell would ever have embarked on a stage career that took her to the Big Apple and Hollywood. Her father Arthur Dowell's life did not follow a traditional path either. For one thing, he is still the only Christian Scientist to serve as Fort Worth police chief. (His successor was a Southern Baptist.) In the end Mary owed her success to a sharp mind and irrepressible personality, not a stutter or impressive physical attributes. Author Jerry Flemmons was engaging in journalistic license when he described her as having "perfect legs and a pert face" and being a "model showgirl." Journalist Bill Fairley jumped on that bandwagon, crediting her with a "perfect figure" and "classically beautiful features." Truth be told, what she had was that indefinable quality known as "it."[37]

Many years after Stutterin' Sam's star turn on the Casa Mañana stage, old showman Billy Rose lamented that "the glamour girl has just about disappeared from the American scene," replaced by the fashion model and the Hollywood starlet. In reflecting back over his sixty-year career as a show-biz impresario, one girl stood out in his mind: "I had a six-foot beauty from Texas named Sammy Dowell [sic] whom we called 'Stutterin' Sam'." It was only after she got to Broadway that talent scouts rightly gauged her as a novelty act rather than a big-time show girl. Beneath the glamorous exterior she was a country girl who grew up on "mamma's chicken-fried steak and cornbread" (her own words). The society columns did not report that she had to battle weight gain her entire adult life. She was always a better writer than actress, but that, too, was unpolished when she got to New York. She showed one of her early short stories to syndicated newspaper columnist Louis Sobol, who bluntly advised her to "tear this carefully into small bits, chuck it in the wastebasket and try again." In the end she found her niche as a celebrity, the Zsa Zsa Gabor or Paris Hilton of her day.[38]

Chapter 13

Artie Glenn
Crying in a Fort Worth Chapel

F ort Worth has produced more than its share of musical talent: Euday Bowman, Van Cliburn, Bob Wills, Townes Van Zandt, Kirk Franklin, T-Bone Burnett, and Manet Harrison, to name just a few. We can also add another, little-known name to the homegrown talent: Artie Glenn.

Born Charles Arthur Glenn in McLennan County, Texas, in 1915, he took up music and moved to Fort Worth with his wife and son in 1950. He went to work on the assembly line at the Convair bomber plant as an upholsterer and was still working there when they were purchased by General Dynamics in 1953. The family settled on the North Side, which was just a short drive to work for him. The bomber plant was his day job, but his passion was music. He played (guitar and bass fiddle) with various Texas and Louisiana bands before joining Fort Worth's famous Light Crust Doughboys. He also formed his own country-western band, the Rhythm Riders. Glenn did more than just play music; he wrote it, too, though without much success before 1953.[1]

In 1953 Glenn was a dapper, 38-year-old with a receding hairline and the pencil mustache popular with artiste types going back many years. That was the year life threw him a curve as he faced spinal surgery for a chronic back problem. The surgery was performed at Harris Hospital, and while still

REV. LESLIE BELL AND FAMILY

THE LOVING AVE. BIBLE BAPTIST CHURCH

2806 LOVING AVE.   REV. LESLIE BELL, PASTOR

**WILL OBSERVE 6TH ANNUAL HOMECOMING AND FELLOWSHIP
SERVICE ALL DAY SUNDAY, MAY 18**

DINNER WILL BE SERVED BY THE LADIES OF THE CHURCH

PREACHING AND GOSPEL SINGING THROUGHOUT THE DAY

ALL PREACHERS PRESENT WILL BE RECOGNIZED

REV. LESLIE BELL

Top left: Reverend Leslie Bell and family for Loving Avenue Baptist Church, 1947.

Right: Reverend Bell, thirty-two years later. He was able to lend a sympathetic ear when Artie Glenn needed it the most. Author's collection.

recuperating in the hospital, he promised God he would be a better person if he were allowed to resume an active life. As soon as he was released from the hospital, he went to the Loving Avenue Baptist Church, one block from where he lived. He had not been a particularly religious man before, but now he sat in the chapel with tears pouring down his face. Reverend Leslie Bell came and sat down beside him. Bell had been pastoring at the church since 1941 and even led the move to rename it from Rosen Heights Fundamental Baptist Church to Loving Avenue Baptist. Together the two prayed, and when Glenn left, he felt uplifted. Back home he sat down and wrote out the music and the lyrics to the song he called "Crying in the Chapel." He would later say it came from a place of inspiration. Written as a country song, it had an appeal across the musical spectrum.[2]

He tapped his son Darrell, a junior at Technical High School and a budding country-western singer, to cut a demo with the Rhythm Riders backing him. Darrell had already recorded with Bob Wills as the prize for winning a talent contest, so this was not his first rodeo. Everyone who heard the song thought it would be a hit record—except publishers. He finally sold the song to Valley Records in Knoxville, Tennessee. They released the record that summer, and it raced up the country-western charts, breaking into the Top 10. It also made the jump to the pop charts. June Valli, discovered on the Arthur Godfrey talent show, had the biggest hit of her career, taking it to number four in August 1953. (She is mostly remembered today for inspiring teenager Francis Castelluccio to adopt the stage name Frankie Valli.) Meanwhile, in an era when sheet music was still an important revenue source, the sheet music for "Crying in the Chapel" featured young Darrell Glenn on the front in full Roy Rogers regalia in a fancy Western shirt and neck kerchief.[3]

On August 3, 1953, the Christophers, a gospel-music organization whose mission was spreading their faith through the media, gave an award to Darrell in New York City. The bronze "plaque" (medallion) they presented him was for a piece of music that showed how "God-given talent can be exerted by one individual in the literary and entertainment fields." The proud father (and composer) remarked, "Some of the fellows said I had to raise a son before my songs went over."[4] Even after his breakthrough in the music business, Artie Glenn remained just a Convair upholsterer in Fort Worth.

Either fortunately or unfortunately, depending on your viewpoint, "Crying in the Chapel" fell victim to a standard music industry business practice: releasing different versions of the same song to different markets—thus, the country-western and pop versions. It was a perfectly legal practice that allowed record companies to milk maximum profits out of a song, releasing it by different artists in different styles. A rhythm and blues (R&B) version of a song, for instance, earned a different stream of income than a pop version of the same song. Crossover hits like "Crying in the Chapel" were beloved by record companies who owned the rights to a song in any version in which it was recorded. That is how the doo-wop group the Moonglows scored in 1954 with an R&B version of Doris Day's pop hit "Secret Love," and how The Orioles took an R&B version of "Crying in the Chapel" up the charts all over again in 1959.[5]

Artie Glenn could not have realized when he wrote "Crying in the Chapel" that its crossover appeal would make it a hit on three different charts for years to come. Besides June Valli's, and The Orioles' cover versions, it was also recorded by cowboy singer Rex Allen and jazz singer Ella Fitzgerald.

Artie Glenn holding a 78 rpm phonograph record of his 1954 hit "Crying in the Chapel." *Fort Worth Star-Telegram Collection*, Special Collections, University of Texas at Arlington Library.

Others who covered it with some success in the 1950s were Art Lund, and Lee Lawrence (in the UK). It proved to be what is known as an "evergreen hit" in the industry, making the pop, R&B, and country charts time and again. Everyone, it seems, cashed in on Artie Glenn's composition except the composer himself. He made very little off his work because he had signed a standard recording industry contract. "Crying in the Chapel" did not become his ticket to wealth and stardom. And though he went on to write another modest local hit ("Uranium," by Darrell Glenn and the Commodores—not to be confused with the later Motown group), Artie Glenn never had another national hit. He was what they call a one-hit wonder.

If the record industry was done with the Glenn family, God was not. Teenage Darrell enjoyed some fame from being associated with a hit record, but that was not why he was back in the news in May 1955. He was in a boat on Lake Worth with seven other people when the boat they were in exploded. Darrell suffered severe burns on his legs but still saved some kids who were thrown from the boat. He was treated at St. Joseph's Hospital and released. Unlike his father two years earlier, his brush with death did not inspire him to recommit his life to God or write a song. He would later say he performed for the next twenty years without giving much thought to his faith.[6]

Darrell Glenn eventually found his own fame in the music business, but not as a performer. Perhaps his brush with death had a delayed effect. He eventually came to believe God was indeed guiding his life. After enjoying modest success as a country singer, in the late seventies he went to work for evangelist Kenneth Copeland, writing gospel songs, one of which, "Only the Redeemed," went to the top of the gospel music charts. As he told it, "Crying in the Chapel" then gave him two things: it allowed him to "share God" with others and "give a witness" to his own spiritual journey. Ironically, for years he was confused with Darrell K. Glenn, also in the entertainment business as the president of Casa Mañana theater in the seventies. For years both men received phone calls from persons looking for "the other" Darrel Glenn.[7]

"Crying in the Chapel" has been recorded by more than six hundred artists over the years, including Johnny Burnette, Mahalia Jackson, Little Richard, The Platters, and Don McLean. The biggest hit was by Elvis Presley, who took it up the pop charts in 1965. It was his first chart-topping song since "Return to Sender" in 1962. It was a delayed hit, however, for the King had recorded it in 1960 because of his love of gospel music but was not pleased with how it came out. His label, RCA, was not displeased to shelve it because it did not fit Elvis's public image. Reluctantly, they included it as a cut on Elvis' first gospel album, *How Great Thou Art* five years later, and no one

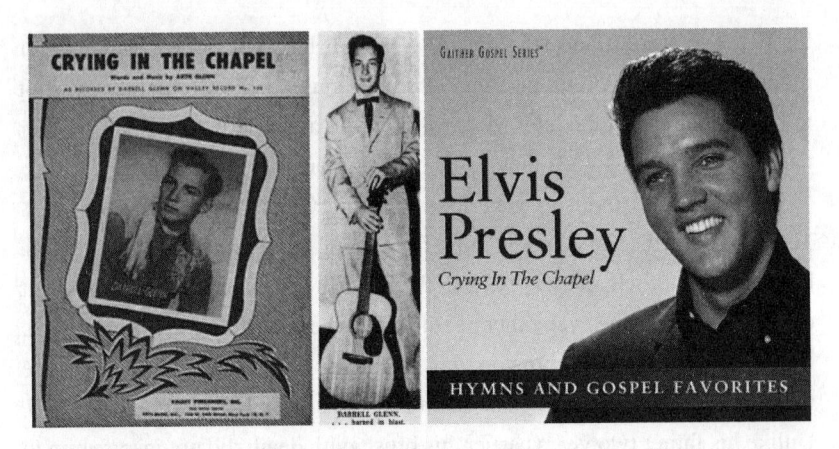

"Crying In the Chapel" has gone through several iterations:
Left: 1953 sheet music. Author's collection.

Center: Country singer Darrell Glenn with his guitar, 1955. Author's collection.

Right: Elvis Presley's 1965 version of "Crying in the Chapel." Author's collection.

was more surprised when the song broke out as a single and shot to the top
of the pop and easy listening charts both. In 1968 West Indian singer Bob
Marley released a reggae version. The song has never really gone away since.
It was part of the soundtrack of *American Graffiti* in 1973, and other movie
soundtracks have also made good use of it.

Artie Glenn died on July 25, 1994, of a heart attack. He was 79 years old.
Darrell Glenn had preceded him, passing in 1990 at the age of 54. Artie was
buried at Laurel Land Memorial Park in Dallas. He was survived by wife,
Foy, and son, Larry. His song will live forever.[8]

Chapter 14

Forget Colonel Tom Parker, Fort Worth Had Major Bill Smith

Colonel Tom Parker was the Svengali who made Elvis Presley the first star of rock 'n' roll. Several light years removed from the center of the music universe, Fort Worth had Bill Smith, promoter, producer, and empresario of the local music scene. Only Smith was a real major in the US Air Force before launching a career in music. Parker guided Elvis to three number one hits between 1961 and 1964. Smith took three different artists to the top of the charts in that same period, all of them homegrown talent: Bruce Channel, Paul and Paula, and J. Frank Wilson.

The Major was born William Arthur Smith on an Oklahoma farm on January 21, 1922, near Merle Haggard's hometown of Checotah. He grew up steeped in the country and gospel music of the southwest. Escaping the farm, he joined the Army Air Corps when World War II came and served in bomber command in the European theater until he was shot down and wounded over Germany. In 1946 the Air Force sent him to Carswell Air Force Base in Fort Worth, where he was public information officer, a job he proved a natural for because nobody had a gift for blarney like Bill Smith. He ended his Air Force career there and made the city home after leaving the service in 1958.[1]

His job as public information officer allowed him time to pursue other interests, which began and ended with music. He did not have the looks or the chops to be a musician, so he focused on the business side, writing, producing, and managing local talent. The first record he produced was "Lieben" with country artist Dan Alexander in 1953. He only pressed fifty records (78 rpms) and distributed them to local radio stations and record stores. This began Smith's longtime collaboration with Clifford Herring, who ran a sound equipment company and primitive recording studio ("Our Business Is Sound") at W. Lancaster at Burnet. Smith would record all his artists at Herring's studio for the next decade. The relationship continued after Herring moved his studio to 1705 W. Seventh "at the bridge." The building was bought by KXOL radio station in 1965, and Smith continued to use the basement as his recording studio.[2]

He slapped a variety of label names on his records based on whim and the deal he cut with the artist. Two of his labels, Le Cam Records and Le Bill Music, were named for wife Letitia and himself, and occasional songwriting partner George Campbell, respectively. Smith was no manager of artists; his focus was on discovering and promoting new talent. His business was the equivalent of a mom-and-pop operation that was more than a little shady. He signed naïve kids like Delbert McClinton to one-sided contracts and booked recording time by the hour, expecting his artists to cut a record in one or two takes. His first love was country music, which was reflected in the early artists he signed. He also continued writing music. In 1955 popular country artist Sonny James had a national hit with one of his compositions, "Twenty Feet of Muddy Water." He got his local artists on the radio, starting with hometown stations KCUL and KFJZ and, if they were lucky, KLIF in Dallas. He also booked his artists into local nightclubs like the Skyliner Ballroom on Jacksboro Highway. In 1959 one of his groups, the Team Mates, saw their record, "If Only I Had Known" reach number three on Fort Worth stations. At the time the music business was regional, and a promoter could make a nice living promoting local talent on local stations.[3]

The secret to success was owning the publishing rights, which Smith made sure he always did. The records were a byproduct. Publishers like Smith hoped one of their records would catch on and be picked up by a national label or recorded by a big-name artist. A record label like Le Cam would press maybe five hundred copies of a single, and if the song did well press another five hundred copies, always hoping a big company like Mercury or Capitol would come calling. His business practices were what one author calls "a racket."[4]

Smith broke into pop music (rock and roll) almost by accident. One of his proteges was a young Black Fort Worth artist named Ray Sharpe, who played the local "chitlin' circuit." In the summer of 1959 Sharpe had a national hit with "Linda Lu." By this time, however, he had moved away from Fort Worth, but Smith always claimed credit for discovering him, calling Sharpe "the greatest white-sounding black dude ever." Ray Sharpe was the first Black star to come out of Fort Worth in the rock and roll era.[5]

Bill Mack, legendary Fort Worth radio personality, would later say, "Major Bill signed everyone who had a song with potential to his label[s], and then took all the publishing and sometimes some of the writing credit, in the deal." Mack was one of many who admired Smith's chutzpah and ear for hit records, if not his business ethics. Singer-songwriter Delbert McClinton was the first act for whom Smith could claim rightful credit for guiding his career. Seventeen-year-old McClinton got his start in 1957 playing dives and honky-tonks on the Jacksboro Highway. He was knocking around as an in-demand session player when he hooked up with Major Bill. The local music fraternity was fairly small, with everybody connected to everybody else in a seven-degrees-of-Kevin-Bacon way. In September 1961 McClinton recorded a song at Clifford Herring's studio by an unknown Grapevine High School grad named Bruce Channel, at the time writing country-style songs with an Irving, Texas, songwriter, Margaret Cobb. Both Channel and McClinton were in Smith's stable of talent when they went into the studio to record some songs. The intended A side of a Bruce Channel single was supposed to be the Channel-Cobb composition "Come Back Jack." After getting that side down, they spent just thirteen minutes recording the Channel-Cobb composition "Hey Baby" for the B side. McClinton contributed the song's harmonica opening riff that caught the ear of the radio audience. It was the B side that took off, and by March 1962 it was number one nationally, replacing Gene Chandler's "Duke of Earl."[6]

Channel and McClinton got the star treatment with an appearance on Dick Clark's *American Bandstand* after-school TV show and a tour of the UK, where American rock and roll artists were still revered and the British Invasion was still two years away. When they played Liverpool, the pair met the resident band in the Cavern Club, the Beatles. It was Smith who created the oft-repeated legend that John Lennon learned to play the harmonica from McClinton then and there, inserting it into future Beatles records like "Love Me Do." The story was pure blarney, although Smith got a lot of mileage out of it in later years.[7]

A relentless promoter with enough chutzpah for an entire advertising agency, Smith would call up major record labels trying to cut deals for the national release of his local hits. As he told it, every single record was "another cotton-pickin' hit." By his grandiose count, he wrote and/or produced three thousand singles out of little Clifford Herring Studio. It was the golden age of the 45 rpm record, and he knew how to create three and a half minutes of pure pop delight. He bragged with false modesty that he didn't know a thing about musical composition, but he had "an ear" for hit songs. His claim to fame rests on discovering four North Texas talents and getting them on the national charts in a brief, two-year span, 1962–1964: Bruce Channel, Paul and Paula, and J. Frank Wilson. He didn't write the songs or play on the recordings, but he produced them and leased them to major labels that broke them nationally. Forty-fives were the name of the game in the sixties, so he didn't have to worry about recording full albums. That was up to the major labels after the singles broke. "Hey Baby," "Hey Paula," and "Last Kiss" went on to become classics of rock's golden age, subsequently covered by many other artists and even used in movies like *Dirty Dancing* (1987). Mint condition of the original 45s are collectors' items today.[8]

Smith struck gold in the fall of 1961 with Bruce Channel's "Hey Baby," cowritten with Margaret Cobb and recorded in Clifford Herring Studios, Fort Worth. Delbert McClinton, who was with Channel that day, provided the harmonica opening of the song. Smith did not have much hope for "Hey Baby," making it the B side of the 45, which means it was the A side, "Come Back Jack," that he pushed radio stations to play. Disc jockeys at KXOL broke the record, finding an audience for the B side. It also caught on with KFJZ and KLIF and in the nightclubs where young people danced the hully-gully to it. Smith placed it with Mercury Records subsidiary Smash Records for national distribution and by February 1962 it was number one on the charts, where it remained for three weeks. The lesson to be learned here was that Major Bill could break a record locally, but it took the big boys in the industry to make it a national hit.[9]

In the fall of 1962, two Howard Payne College (Brownwood, Texas) students, Ray Hildebrand and Jill Jackson, paired up to sing a song for a radio benefit that Hildebrand, a gangly basketball player, had written. The station engineer recorded the song, and it started getting local airplay. Ray and Jill were advised to take it to Fort Worth and see if they could get wider distribution with a 45 rpm record release. They showed up at Clifford Herring's studio on the same day that Smith had booked country singer Amos Milburn Jr. When Milburn failed to show, and the clock was ticking, Smith swore, "We're going to record something today if it's 'The Star-Spangled Banner.'" Ray and Jill took just thirteen minutes of precious recording time to cut "Hey Paula." The original version of Ray's song was longer, but Smith ordered them to cut it down to a more radio-friendly length. Hildebrand reworked the deleted verses into their follow-up record, "Young Lovers," which entered the charts and peaked at number six. "Hey Paula" broke on KXOL on November 6, 1962, then KFJZ and KLIF picked it up. A Mercury Records executive heard it because Gordon McClendon's KLIF station was a regional power in the music industry. Mercury leased it for their Philips label and credited the song to "Paul and Paula" to sell the pair as sweethearts. Truth be told, Ray had a steady girlfriend back in Brownwood. The record hit number one on the national charts in February 1963 and stayed there for three weeks, eventually selling two and a half million copies. Some consider it to be the greatest teen record of all time. It was not the dreaded one-hit wonder, but Jill and Ray's act was a one-trick pony. They appeared on Dick Clark's *American Bandstand*, toured with Dick Clark's Caravan of Stars, and were booked to tour the UK based on that one song.[10]

While record-buying teenyboppers loved the record, critics were less impressed. One reviewer a few years later termed it "a cute, teen-age, sugar pop song." The bigger problems were that Ray and Jill did not have a stock of songs in their pocket to perform in concert, and the constant touring got to them. Ray in particular missed his girlfriend back in Brownwood and felt his commitment to his Christian faith threatened by the rock lifestyle. Late that summer, while on tour with Dick Clark, he slipped a note under Clark's hotel door and headed for home. Clark finished out the tour singing as Jill's partner. Soon after, Ray called Major Bill and told him he was done touring. He tried to cut a couple of self-penned songs as a solo act, but he could not catch lighting in a bottle. In a short time, the music industry moved on from the wholesome goodness of Paul and Paula to the hippie pretensions of Sonny and Cher. Ray found his second act as a born-again Christian singing mostly gospel music, touring with the Billy Graham Crusade, and working with the Fellowship of Christian Athletes. Occasionally he came to Fort Worth to perform either with oldies shows or for church groups. There is no record that he and Major Bill ever got together for old time's sake on those visits. Jill also cut ties with Major Bill, touring for her record label with another "Paul."[11]

In 1964 Smith struck gold once again, this time with an ex–Air Force enlisted man named John Frank Wilson and his San Angelo band, the Cavaliers. Smith heard about them and about their cover of a Wayne Cochran song called "Last Kiss." The British Invasion was on, and tragic love songs like "Teen Angel" and "Tell Laura I Love Her" were passe, or so it seemed. "Last Kiss" was the last hurrah for the tear-jerker song, relating an actual fatal car accident in Georgia. Smith cut the record in the Clifford Herring studio, crediting it to "J. Frank Wilson" instead of John or Frank Wilson, for reasons only he knew, and leased it to Josie Records, a subsidiary of New York's Jubilee Records that specialized in novelty songs. It reached number two on the national charts in September 1964 and remained on the charts for twelve weeks, kept out of the top spot by The Animals' "House of the Rising Sun." The song had a macabre postscript when Wilson himself was badly injured in an auto accident shortly afterward. It was rereleased in 1974, then covered by Eddie Vedder and Pearl Jam in 1999, proving you can't keep a good song down.[12]

If Bruce Channel, Paul and Paula, and J. Frank Wilson were flashes in the pan, Delbert McClinton was a rare talent with staying power. He formed a country-rock group, the Rondels, and Major Bill released eighteen singles

Major Bill Smith's three biggest stars: Bruce Channel (*left*), J. Frank Wilson (*right, top*), and Paul & Paula (*right, bottom*). Author's collection.

by the group between 1963 and 1970. Their biggest hit was 1965's "If You Really Want Me To, I'll Go," written by McClinton, which shot up the local charts, convincing Smith it had potential as a national breakout hit. When he called up Huey Meaux in Houston and played it over the phone for him, Meaux offered him five hundred dollars for it, and Smith grabbed it. The record debuted at number ninety-seven on Smash Records but mysteriously dropped off the charts after a week because of legal complications typical of Major Bill productions. That did not keep Smith from continuing to release more than a dozen Rondels records in the next five years, hoping for at least one more golden egg from this goose.[13]

McClinton soldiered on through the good times and the bad, breaking with Major Bill long before he finally got a Top 10 hit in 1980, "Giving It Up for Your Love." That did not stop Smith from repackaging McClinton's old music in anthology albums years later sold on his Le Cam label. According to McClinton, Smith did not cut him in on the royalties.[14]

It is ironic that Smith had the least success with his most talented act. Music snobs could make fun of Major Bill's records, his unpolished musical acts, and his bush-league operation, but they could not argue with his Midas touch. His answer to the critics came after "Hey Paula" hit number one in February 1963: "They can talk about Nashville being the recording capital [of country music], but I wonder if our Chamber of Commerce realizes that this is the only time anyone has had the No. 1 song in the nation twice within the space of a year." Elvis Presley had accomplished that impressive feat several times over since 1956, but Major Bill could not be concerned with facts. Superlatives were his bread and butter. And Bobby Vinton would do it again later in 1963, though Smith had no way of knowing that.[15]

"Last Kiss" was Major Bill's last big hit, but scoring three huge hits in a row put him in the elite company of producers like Phil Spector and Quincy Jones. Disc jockeys on the area rock and roll stations KVIL, KXOL, and KLIF paid homage to him. Ron Chapman (KLIF) reportedly said, "When Major Bill says he has a cotton-pickin' smash, you'd better weigh him in." Unfortunately, his muse mostly deserted him after the British Invasion captured the American charts in the mid-1960s. His last hurrah was a song he cowrote called "I Wouldn't Trade You for the World," which was recorded by a minor British group, the Bachelors, and went to number four in the UK It is doubtful if anyone in Britain knew who Bill Smith was, but his name was right there on the label with two others right below the song title. Otherwise, Fort Worth's maestro found it nearly impossible to place his songs with major labels any longer, though he continued to push local talent like Larry & the Blue Notes. But nothing broke nationally.

For all his success, Major Bill was not a beloved figure. On the contrary, his relationship with even his most successful artists was toxic. Those who worked with him had nothing good to say after they were out from under his thumb. Delbert McClinton called him "a crooked old bastard," and Larry Roquemore of Larry & the BlueNotes remembered him as "loud, abrasive, and the joke was he didn't have to hit the control room intercom button to be heard in the recording studio." Producer Norman Petty, who discovered Buddy Holly and the Crickets, said upon hearing his name linked to Smith's, "I'd just as soon not have my name mentioned in the same breath with Major Bill, if it's all the same to you."[16]

More serious than the scorn were the lawsuits filed against him. November 1963, for instance, was not a good month. Jill Jackson (a.k.a. Paula) filed suit to stop him from using the name "Paul and Paula" to record other artists. She said the one-sided contract she signed with him was not binding because she was underage at the time and asked for $20,000 in damages. That case was barely settled when songwriter Margaret Cobb filed suit, claiming she had cowritten "Hey Baby" with Bruce Channel and received just a fraction of the royalties due her. She asked for $46,000 in actual and punitive damages. What both plaintiffs learned was that this was standard operating procedure in the business. Smith was not doing anything different from every other record company. The difference was that Major Bill did not have an army of lawyers on retainer. He settled both cases out of court.[17]

Bill Smith, "recording company executive," never quit chasing the next hit record. He made it back on the radio in 1978 with a novelty song, "Foat Woth, Ah Luv Yew!," which got a lot of local attention but did not enter the charts. His kind of music no longer had a radio audience, but his other problems were self-made. Smith's obituary in the *Dallas Morning News* in 1994 said he battled alcoholism, something not mentioned in the hometown newspapers, which still considered him a success story. In 1983 House Majority Leader Jim Wright of Fort Worth read a tribute to him into the *Congressional Record*: "He is a credit to his community as a civic-spirited citizen, and his contributions to the music industry, where he has earned nine gold records, are known far and wide."[18]

Major Bill did not go quietly into the good night. He seems to have preferred being laughed at occasionally to being ignored completely. He ran for both the school board and city council in different years. His platform in the school board race included introducing rock and roll into the formal curriculum taught in Fort Worth schools, while his platform in the 1981 city council race included expanding the city's water supply to handle future drought conditions and population growth. He lost every race for public office. He explored other paths to keep his name in front of the public, becoming a quotable gadfly on his favorite subjects: patriotism, Christianity, and Elvis Presley. He was particularly obsessed with Elvis. After Presley's death in 1977 he claimed the King had only faked his death, and that he was in regular contact with him. He even published a book in 1987,

Left: Major Bill in his office in 1979, still on the phone wheeling and dealing. Author's collection.

Right: Major Bill in 1982 showing off his gold records. Author's collection.

Memphis Mystery (*Requiem for Elvis*), detailing his fantastic conspiracy theories. His embrace of Elvis got him national press coverage, which he craved, but also got him labeled a kook in many circles. He seemed to have a direct line to Fort Worth newspapers while Dallas generally ignored him. He was in the news again in 1993 when he sued Graceland, claiming they had infringed on his free speech by halting an interview he was doing on the grounds with a Memphis radio station.[19]

The Elvis kook also had a kinder, gentler side not always recognized. He was a longtime member of the National Association for the Advancement of Colored People (NAACP), even serving on the board as the only white person. There is every reason to believe he was present in 1959 when Martin Luther King Jr. spoke at the Majestic Theater. More than a few white people were in the audience that night. He also worked tirelessly with the down-and-out in the city's population, first at God's Rescue

Mission, then later at the Union Gospel Mission where he was known as Brother Bill. Beneath the gruff, sometimes profane exterior was a big heart. He stepped up to the plate where his favored causes were concerned not by writing checks but by giving freely of his time and energy. For his musical and charitable contributions, Fort Worth Mayor Woodie Woods declared November 25, 1979, "Major Bill Smith Day."[20]

In the end we can say William Arthur Smith is the classic case of a man who outlived his time. He never lost his love of music and discovering new pop stars. His last release came in 1983 with "Dance, Baby, Dance" by Larry Moore, which had to wait another thirty years to become a hit (for Chris Cagle). The record went nowhere because music had moved on in both its style and format since the early sixties. Old pop dance tunes were out, as were 45 rpm singles and Top 40 radio. Disco and electronic music were in, and both were far beyond the capabilities of little Clifford Herring studios.[21]

By the time he died on September 12, 1994, he was known mostly to the current generation as a colorful character and a crank, not the World War II combat veteran and music impresario that their parents had known. His days as a producer with the magic touch were far behind him, much like his contemporary Phil Spector. But he could also say he was making rock and roll before the Beatles and outlasted them on the music scene. The difference was the Beatles went out on top. Bill Smith hung around. He was notorious around the *Star-Telegram* offices for his endless phone calls, most of which were to report his latest news about Elvis, whom he always said he had recently talked to. His calls drove *Star-Telegram* ombudsman Phil Record nuts, though Record was too polite to hang up abruptly.[22]

Some suspected that Smith's nutty behavior was a product of assorted physical and mental issues. A severely wounded war veteran with addictive tendencies, Smith himself admitted abusing drugs and alcohol for years. He claimed to have beaten both, but even if true, he couldn't beat the lingering effects of both. He was ill for years before death finally took him. In the end, however, he got a proper send-off with full military honors followed by interment in Greenwood Cemetery, a sacred burial ground in the city he put on the musical map in the golden age of rock and roll. He always said he would live and die "deep in the heart of Texas."[23]

Chapter 15

Kitty Barry
Fort Worth's First Female Reporter

Long before Dorothy Kilgallen, Barbara Walters, and other celebrated female journalists, Fort Worth's Kitty Barry was blazing trails as a female reporter. She did so by expanding women's role in journalism beyond the society page. She was the first female reporter with the *Star-Telegram*, landing a job on Louis J. Wortham's newspaper at a time when women could not vote in Texas, and even taking to the roads in one of the new-fangled automobiles was considered unlady-like. Nor was journalism a field that welcomed women. Isidore Miner Calloway was a trailblazer in the 1890s, writing a column for the *Dallas Morning News* under the nom de plume Pauline Periwinkle. Another nom de plume for women journalists was Beatrice Beeswax. Women did not use their own names because of an old maxim that a lady's name should only appear in public print three times: when she was born, when she married, and when she died. As late as the 1930s in Texas, reporter Louise Raggio was still battling professional resistance. For many years female journalists were referred to as "girl reporters."[1]

Katherine Barry was born in Sherman, Texas, in 1887 into a family that eventually gave her eleven brothers and sisters. She grew up fast, described as "one of the best known and most popular young ladies" in town. Barely out of her teens she went to work on the "reportorial staff" of the *Sherman Democrat*, setting her career path early.[2]

Her other great interest was horticulture, which was a lifetime love. Years later she found a way to combine her two great loves by writing gardening columns for the newspaper and running a "plant, tree and flower" business. She came to be a self-taught expert in the horticulture field.[3]

She graduated from North Texas Female College and Conservatory, an educational institution and notable school of music in Sherman, Texas, run by Mrs. Lucy Ann Kidd-Key for many years. Katherine focused her studies on English, with an emphasis on journalism and music. The latter served her well later when she became an arts and entertainment reporter. She enrolled in the University of Texas (Austin) in the fall of 1909 but did not graduate. She stayed long enough to be elected an associate editor of the campus newspaper, the *Daily Texan*. She supported her alma mater for years to come by recruiting new students for the struggling women's college and sponsoring exhibits of current students' artwork. During her brief tenure at UT she was a member of the Pierian Literary Society, but the life of a "University Girl" (coed) did not appeal to her. She was ready to launch a career. By 1910 she was working for the *San Antonio Express* writing "human interest" stories for the "society" section. They were good enough to be picked up on the wire by other newspapers, including one titled "A Talented Texas Girl," which could have been about herself but instead was about a "deaf and dumb" girl from Texas making a splash at the Chicago Art Institute.[4]

But Kitty's biggest journalistic coup was being the only woman covering the session of the Thirty-Second Legislature in Austin 1911. The *Express* gave her a full page with the headline, "Woman Sizes Up Texas Solons." Her erudite and snarky style stood out even at this early date. She wrote, "No use trying to figure out why gentlemen look at you. But anyway, no forbidding importance attaches itself to the swish of my skirts through the Capitol corridors, so the Legislature and I are very chummy."[5] She continued to report on state government, including Governor Oscar Colquitt, to the end of the session. She got an interview with the governor during which she tossed a few softball questions to him. She came away thinking he projected the calm assurance of a man who "had been Governor always." Her conclusion about the thirty-second session of the legislature was not nearly so complimentary. "If broad slouch hats, long frock coats and such other impressive garments as being a legislator demands constitute greatness, the Thirty-second Texas Legislature is the most illustrious body convened since the beginning of time." Still the gentlemen took appreciative notice of the feisty "girl reporter" and thanked her personally along with her male colleagues in the legislative *Journal* at the end of the session.[6]

Her columns attracted the attention of Editor Louis J. Wortham of the *Star-Telegram*, and he hired her in late 1911. She was just 23 years old, and though she was breaking the gender barrier at the newspaper, she was still lumped together with other female journalists known as "sob sisters" in the big-city eastern newspapers, assigned to the society desk covering births, engagements, marriages, graduations, club meetings, and other social events as opposed to "serious" stories. But at least Barry, unlike Isidor Miner, who wrote for the *Dallas Morning News* under the nom de plume Pauline Periwinkle, was able to write under her own name, a measure of the respect she had earned. Her columns even carried her picture, which placed her in very rare journalistic company. Hiring her made Wortham as rare a managing editor in Texas as Kitty was a female journalist, which is not to say the *Star-Telegram* was totally unfamiliar with female writers. The paper also employed a female writer of occasional doggerel under the byline Beatrice Beeswax. That same nom de plume was used a few years later by the writer of an "Advice to the Lovelorn" column in a Waco newspaper.[7]

Kitty was neither a Pauline Periwinkle nor a Beatrice Beeswax. She was a talented writer with the classic type A personality, and less sob sister than ace reporter in the vein of Hildegarde Johnson (Rosalind Russell) in the classic 1940 Howard Hawks film *His Girl Friday* (an update of *The Front Page*). "Hildy" saves a convicted man from hanging, which bears comparison to Kitty scooping her male colleagues in the Beal Sneed murder case in 1912.

She was initially assigned to write some human-interest fluff on the family of Captain A. G. Boyce, killed by Beal Sneed in a sensational love triangle. Beal Sneed's wife, Lena, was the lover of Al Boyce Jr. who had fled to Canada. Sneed couldn't get his clutches on Junior, so he took out his vengeance on the father. Lena Sneed was a key witness in the case, but the Sneed family had her under wraps at the Worth Hotel to prevent the prosecution from finding her. Kitty managed to track her down and knock on the door of her second-floor

Tragedy of Sneed-Boyce Families
to Be Reviewed at Trial Monday

John Beal Sneed and two children, Mrs. Sneed and Al Boyce.

Kitty Barry reports the sensational Sneed-Boyce murder trial, 1912. Author's collection.

room. When Lena opened the door her first question was, "How did you find me?" Kitty stuck her foot in the door and asked sweetly for an interview, to which Lena replied, "I can't talk to newspaper reporters." Kitty refused to take no for an answer, appealing to her not as a reporter but as woman to woman. What followed was not exactly an interview, but it was newsworthy enough to get in the newspaper the next day. Kitty had the scoop, but her roots as a society columnist shone through in the story. She called Lena "a distinctly feminine woman" and described in detail what she was wearing. The *Star-Telegram*'s readers ate it up.[8]

Her scoop on the Lena Sneed story and her regular columns attracted a readership far beyond Fort Worth society matrons and arts aficionados. She received fan mail from her readers that included the bunkhouse cowboys on the Diamond Ranch near Stanton, Texas.[9]

Kitty's bosses felt more respect for her smarts but remained stuck on the society desk for a while. She fought to distance herself from the sob sister label. Interviewed by a colleague, she insisted she was a "suffragist" not a "suffragette," refusing to describe herself with the feminine derivative for those crusading for women's right to vote. She allowed readers to see Kitty Barry the person in saying she hoped to "go up in an airplane someday" and admitting to being loud and hot-tempered.[10]

She cranked out routine pieces about the Harmony Club and a woman who ran her own farm "without the advice of any man," but occasionally she got to dig into meatier issues. In her self-styled crusading reporter persona, she latched on to the lack of safety regulations for milk sold in the city. With *Star-Telegram* sports reporter James R. Record she launched a campaign to provide certified milk to the city's poor children in the summer. She began writing about it in 1912, and a year later the newspaper embraced the campaign by starting an annual "milk and ice drive" to provide poor families with free milk and a chunk of ice to keep it cool in the hottest months of the year. She did not just report on the drive; she spearheaded it in her columns and in person. Even ignoring her gender, she was the kind of crusading reporter most Fort Worthers were unfamiliar with. She helped turn the *Star-Telegram* from a hometown newspaper into an activist journal of regional importance. She wrote about the plight of the city's poor children with erudition and compassion and along the way got her picture on the front page of the newspaper as one of the "directors" of the drive.[11]

She wrote another attention-grabbing story about how few of the city's high school graduates intended to go on to college. Her byline was in the newspaper regularly, though mostly on the back pages. The editor finally moved her closer to page 1 prestige for a story on a cooking-school event that attracted one thousand women. She was even given a photographer for the story.[12]

For a story about a fancy banquet, she became part of the story, attending the engagement dinner for Angie Ousley and John Rosser at the Westbrook

Hotel. Kitty got to sit at the head table, which probably had something to do with the fact that Angie Ousley was the daughter of the former owner of the *Fort Worth Record*, since absorbed by the *Star-Telegram* and now an editor with the latter.[13]

Putting her fondness for Mexico to work was what gave Kitty a second byline story. In the past she had visited Mexico on several occasions, spending some time there. It became a favorite destination for her and allowed her to get to know Mexican officials. It is presumed she spoke excellent Spanish. All that came together in September 1912 when she traveled to Mexico City on a vacation and tied it to her work by setting up an interview with Mexican President Francisco Madero. He had come to power the year before as a consequence of the Mexican Revolution. Two years before that he set up a government-in-exile in San Antonio, when he probably met Barry. By the time she was in Mexico City arranging an interview, the majority of the American press was savaging Madero, egged on by a hostile US government. Her own view was that he was a "scholar" devoted to constitutional democracy. Madero was a very formal gentleman, not particularly open to the press, but in this case he must have been glad to get some good press north of the border. So that is how Kitty Barry became the first American reporter to interview Mexico's president and the first female reporter to get a one-on-one interview with any head of state in the Americas. While she was a staff reporter for the *Star-Telegram*, other Texas newspapers picked up on the story. But rather than focus on the substance of the interview, they preferred to focus on the interviewer: "a young woman . . . very pretty, attractive and intellectual."[14]

She set the interview up through US Ambassador Henry Lane Wilson and did it at the historic Chapultepec castle. In her published account she reveals her admiration for Madero, describing him as a reformer, "a man of peace," and a "kindly man." She did not confine her questions to political issues but took a human-interest approach, asking him about his family, his favorite activities as a private citizen, and his dreams for the future. She got the famously reserved Madero to admit that he believed Americans were "too free." The interview lasted a while, and by the time it was finished, rain was pouring down. Rather than dismiss her with a polite sendoff, he took her by the hand and led her through his private quarters and back passageways until they arrived back at the reception area. By September 24 she was on her way home. Her interview was reported at length in the *Star-Telegram* then picked up on the wire by other newspapers across the country. This, her second reporting scoop, solidified her status as a serious news reporter, not just a Polly Periwinkle confined to the society desk.

The Madero story did not end there. On February 18, 1913, he was overthrown by General Victoriano Huerta and assassinated four days later. That led Barry's newspaper bosses to have her write a lengthy obituary of the man she had known personally if only briefly. She opined that his "undoing" had come about because of his "mild, kindly manner." As the leader of a turbulent country, he was not so strong as the man he had replaced (Porfirio Diaz) or the man who ousted him (Huerta). He was an aristocrat who also happened to be a "thorough democrat," whom his country was not ready for. He was a martyr as far as she was concerned, which was a much more sympathetic view of Francisco Madero than the majority of American newspapers took.[15]

It is impossible to say how much influence her Madero reporting had, but eight years later, Fort Worth in general and *Star-Telegram* president Louis J. Wortham in particular welcomed another Mexican president (elect), Alvaro Obregon, on a goodwill trip to the United States. Fort Worth was his second stop after San Antonio, and after visiting the state fair in Dallas, he returned to Fort Worth for a second round of kudos before setting off for El Paso. Wortham, who was at the *Star-Telegram* in 1912, might have reminded Obregon that the newspaper was a friend of Mexico.[16]

Sadly, Barry's journalistic fame was short-lived. The newspaper business was still a boys' club that did not know what to do with a reporter like Kitty Barry. Despite the two scoops she had scored, first the Lena Sneed interview then the Francisco Madero interview, she found herself banished to the back pages of the newspaper again.

The biggest change in her life was giving up the life of the career woman on October 31, 1913, to marry Jasper Garfield Crawford, a fellow *Star-Telegram* columnist. He was already a veteran newspaperman when he came to the *Star-Telegram*, starting as a printer's apprentice at the age of 12 and working his way up to publisher of his own newspaper before

Left: Kitty Barry as cub reporter for the *Fort Worth Star-Telegram*, ca. 1911. Author's collection.

Right: Kitty Barry as nationally known columnist, 1912. Author's collection.

coming to Fort Worth in 1909. His forte was political writing, and he even campaigned for office a few times over the years. Kitty and Garfield knew each other for two years, though working in different parts of the building, before they decided to tie the knot in a secret ceremony. Why they did not announce their engagement ahead of time is a mystery, but the Halloween wedding may have been Kitty's idea. She was known to have a wry sense of humor. The ceremony may have been secret, but the marriage itself drew the attention of the *Austin American-Statesman*, which declared that "newspaper men always have the most charming wives." The *Star-Telegram* was more blunt, calling theirs a "newspaper office romance" that began the first day she came to work.[17]

What may have begun as an office romance proved enduring. Kitty and Garfield remained married until his death in 1970 and were professional colleagues as well as soulmates. Their collaborations included having a family and starting their own publication. A daughter, Jane Anderson Crawford, was born in December 1914, and exactly one year later they launched a weekly magazine, *The Critic*, devoted to "art, music, politics, amusements, business, education, and humor." Subscribers paid only a dollar a year for fifty-two issues. (The majority of the revenue was obviously to come from advertising.) Garfield handled the political beat while Kitty handled the cultural stuff. Calling itself "militant and independent," *The Critic* promised to "champion the causes and protect the elements that make Fort Worth the best town in which to live and do business in the Southwest." While pitching in with the editing, Kitty juggled motherhood and writing two columns every week, "The Week at the Theater," and "This Week at the Hippodrome" (Fort Worth's premier vaudeville theater).[18]

Growing their family had to be put on hold, and *The Critic* never got off the ground because in the winter of 1916 Kitty contracted tuberculosis (TB), the "great white plague" of history. Glamorized as consumption, the "disease of sophisticates," it was incurable and almost always fatal in a slow and painful way, causing its victims to waste away. Even those lucky enough to survive found they could never return to "top speed" again. Kitty refused to accept the fate of being a permanent invalid. She had too much she wanted to accomplish, so she and Garfield set out to find the best medical treatment available, which brought them to Carlsbad Sanitarium just outside of San Angelo, Texas. (She calls it simply a "Midwest" sanitarium in her writings.) The dry climate coupled with a rigorous diet-and-treatment program was supposed to be beneficial for patients. Kitty spent most of the next four years battling TB. Back home, Garfield tried to relaunch their publication, changing its name and focus to the *Texas Oil Critic* that offered advice to investors in the booming oil business.[19]

Kitty herself could not be content as just another patient. She kept busy bucking up her fellow patients. Others might come to such places to die, but not Kitty Barry. She intended to get well and resume a professional career. One of her fellow patients was a woman she called "Hulia" in her writings.

Kitty Barry's good friend and fellow tuberculosis survivor, Katherine Anne
Porter, ca. 1921. Author's collection.

Not until September 1921 did she reveal Hulia as author Katherine Anne
Porter. They had bonded over their shared illness and love of writing, becoming lifelong friends.[20]

Kitty returned to Fort Worth with her tuberculosis not cured but in remis-
sion. As she had done in her professional life, Kitty Barry Crawford beat
the odds for survival. Contemplating what she wanted to do with the rest of

her life, she approached her former employer, the *Star-Telegram*, about writing a series of articles on her medical journey. The former society columnist wanted to do a mixture of investigative journalism and human-interest reporting. Managing Editor James M. North accepted her offer, and at the end of June 1921, she began a series of articles that she cryptically titled "Counterpane Land." In them she talked candidly about "all the beautiful, tragical, ironical things I have seen and experienced." She described her own treatment—both the highs and the lows—at a place she alternately called "the San" and "the Home." She also told poignant stories about her fellow patients, hoping that by telling their stories she could help others grapple with the debilitating disease.[21]

The series began on June 28 and continued through the end of August 1921. She wrote not just as an observer but also as a patient battling the disease herself. She tried to put a positive spin on life as a victim of tuberculosis. Among the things she claimed to "love" about her condition was "fatness, pure, old avoirdupois." She went on, "Another is short hair. Just enough of a mane to tuck up in the back is sufficient for me. And I am fond of low-heeled shoes, loose clothing, being called 'Kitty Crawford' with the 'Barry' left out . . . and a chance to help a human being toward an equal opportunity at life."[22]

She described how the disease had first taken hold of her, a detail her family were not happy about her sharing. Yet after apologizing for going into such detail, she explained how she and Garfield had been walking to work one cold day in January when she coughed up blood. It was the first clue that she was seriously ill. She kept coughing up blood as her husband hustled her to the nearest doctor's office, where she passed out. That was the beginning of a journey she later described as "four lost years."[23]

In subsequent columns she described the exhaustive and terrifying admission process to get into one of the few TB hospitals, the doctors' exams and spartan living conditions, the loneliness so far from home, and finally her determination to get a TB clinic for Fort Worth so that others like herself wouldn't have to go so far to be diagnosed and treated. "So many times, tuberculars struggle to get well, but there is lack of a definite [treatment] program, or lack of money and misdirection all along the line. So they have only their tears for their trouble."[24]

The columns made Kitty a national celebrity when they were picked up by other newspapers. In making lemonade out of lemons, she achieved far more professional recognition than she would ever have received as a society columnist. The columns brought her bags of fan mail from readers. There were so many letters she could not answer each one personally but expressed her gratitude in her columns. One letter came from US Representative Fritz G. Lanham, who wrote from Washington that he had been following her columns and wanted to commend her on "all the good" she was doing. Other TB sufferers did not write; they came to see her in person as some kind of pilgrimage seeking wisdom to cope with their disease.[25]

Kitty did not resume full-time work but kept doing freelance writing and being active in her church (St. Alban's Episcopal) and the Fort Worth Garden Club. Her freelance writing included the occasional column for the *Star-Telegram* and the introduction for Howard Peak's memoir *A Ranger of Commerce*. She was also a big supporter of Fort Worth's Diamond Jubilee in 1923.[26]

But the cause nearest to her heart was opening a TB clinic in Fort Worth. She spoke and wrote tirelessly to drum up support. In September 1921 the idea was endorsed by the Tarrant County Medical Association at a meeting where she and Katherine Anne Porter both spoke on behalf of the clinic. The Tuberculosis Society went to work selling Christmas seals to help raise money to open a clinic as part of the City-County Hospital. It was a remarkable campaign largely driven by two women.[27]

She and Garfield got to see daughter Jane graduate from Paschal High School (Fort Worth) in 1932 and begin performing on the stage as a dancer while studying ballet. She was part of the Pan American Exposition in Dallas in 1937. They also got to see her when she performed at the Majestic Theater as "one of the two prettiest girls in the chorus," and saw her marry and settle down in Arlington.[28]

Kitty and Garfield settled on a two-acre tract of land in Arlington in 1941. On November 1, 1963, they celebrated their golden (fiftieth) wedding anniversary. They were living in Arlington when he died in 1970. He was a civic activist and public relations man to the end, helping to put on Fort Worth's Diamond Jubilee in November 1923 and the Texas Centennial Celebration in Dallas in 1936. He is given credit on the earlier occasion for giving away ten-gallon Stetson cowboy hats as a Cowtown promotion, an idea that Amon G. Carter embraced enthusiastically thereafter. He and Kitty shared a mutual interest in planting and growing things. He leaned toward fruits and vegetables; she leaned toward flowers. He was buried in Fort Worth's Greenwood Cemetery.[29]

Kitty Barry Crawford died at home on August 25, 1982, of cardiac arrest complicated by chronic lung disease (COPD). Though she had fended off TB, her body eventually just gave out. She was 93 years old, a remarkable age for a survivor of tuberculosis. The service was conducted in Arlington's St. Albans Episcopal Church, and she was buried beside her beloved Garfield in Greenwood Memorial Park.[30]

Seventy years after breaking the glass ceiling at the *Star-Telegram*, she might have found it ironic that Garfield got much the bigger obituary in the newspaper. It listed all his professional accomplishments, while hers simply noted her passing and survivors. From sob sister columnist to pioneering journalist to bare mention in her obituary, Kitty Barry's life had come full circle.

Chapter 16

Stansell T. Brogdon
Gadfly or Just a Kook?

Mixing religion with our politics is a long-standing Texas tradition, and if a little assault is involved, how much more Texan! Stansell Brogdon was a fundamentalist Christian who, unlike his hero, William Jennings Bryan, was highly educated. Like Bryan he had big political ambitions, and also like Bryan he was a passionate crusader for the causes he believed in. It's just that his causes were seldom other people's causes. He traveled to the beat of a different drummer than most folks.

Though not born in Fort Worth, Stansell Tennyson Brogdon lived here longer than anywhere else, so we can claim him as an adopted son. He was born in Robertson County, Texas, on January 27, 1877, to William Joseph Brogdon, a "pioneer schoolteacher," and Laura Hix Cook Brogdon. With a name like Stansell he found it easier to go through life by his initials, S. T. He was the firstborn of six children. If his father ever called Robertson County home, it was not for long. Many years later he was fondly remembered as a "Brazos County pioneer," and he died there in 1921. Laura continued to live there until her death in 1946. His parents were Primitive Baptists, and he held similar fundamentalist beliefs his entire life, though not as a member of the Baptist church. He was intelligent and motivated to seek higher education. Not for him the life of the farmer or the stockman. He attended public school in Bryan, then went to Texas A&M, where he graduated in 1898 with a BS degree in mechanical engineering and architecture. He counted himself a loyal Aggie the rest of his life. In the years to come he would put both degrees to work, but his spiritual faith and love of learning always came first.[1]

Reportedly, he enlisted as a volunteer in the Spanish American War (1898), but if so, he did not see combat. He next turns up in Beaumont, Texas, in 1903, where he opened an architect's office and was hired as assistant city manager and then city engineer in his first foray into politics. A career in architecture, engineering, or even politics did not really excite him. In 1908 he resigned as city engineer, closed his architecture office, and enrolled in Chicago's Moody Bible Institute, a private, evangelical Christian school founded by Dwight L. Moody in 1886. The school's mission was training students to be full-time ministers. Brogdon would later say he graduated from Moody in 1910, but the list of graduating seniors in April 1910 does not include him.[2]

According to the proceedings of the Methodist Episcopal church, in 1910 he was enrolled as a third-year student at Vanderbilt University (in Nashville) It is unclear when exactly he joined the Methodist Episcopal Church, but he remained a member for the rest of his life. He said he did "graduate work" in Greek and Hebrew at both Vanderbilt and Yale, and he certainly became proficient in Greek somewhere. In December 1910 he attended the seventy-first annual Texas conference of the Methodist Episcopal Church South at Galveston. It was there that Bishop William B. Murrah appointed him a minister to the Beaumont District, which gave him the right thereafter to use the title "Reverend." In the years to come he would often refer to himself as a "Methodist minister" and seldom missed a Texas conference of the church.[3]

After completing his education, he knocked about for a bit, spending a year as US postmaster at Amelia, Texas, and doing a little preaching in Texas and Oklahoma. When World War I came along, he registered for the draft but did not have to worry about being called up because he was missing two fingers off his left hand.[4]

He moved to Fort Worth after completing his education and settled in the Polytechnic area, until 1922 an unincorporated suburb of Fort Worth. He bought a home on Court Street and took a job teaching at Polytechnic

High School. Never shy about putting himself out front in everything he did, he ran for the school board, unsuccessfully as it turned out, which characterized many of his endeavors. But defeat never discouraged him. He also started a newspaper, the *Texas School News*, which he published weekly from his home on Court Street. The newspaper covered far more than just school news. Brogdon considered himself an investigative journalist and took on the Ku Klux Klan, which was particularly strong in Fort Worth at the time. The Klan was a serious enemy for a smalltime crusading journalist, but that did not keep him from publishing a series of articles denouncing them. And he joined the Citizens League of Liberty, an anti-Klan organization. Unfortunately, the Klan was especially strong in local law enforcement, in both the sheriff's office and the police department.[5]

In between teaching and publishing a newspaper, he found time to be a spokesman for his deeply held religious beliefs. In 1920 he set up a debate with Reverend Tice Elkins of the South Side Christian Church on the necessity of "water baptism" for salvation, taking the negative side of the proposition. It was the great age of debates in Protestant churches, with eager audiences treating those debates as both entertainment and religious instruction. The baptism issue is one Brogdon would come back to repeatedly over the years. In 1929 he tried to set up another debate, this time with Reverend J. D. Tant of Memphis, Tennessee. He asked permission to use the Sixty-Seventh District courtroom for the three-day event, promising "there will be no wrangle and the debate will be educational." He also promised to quote from his 1,500-year-old Bible written in Greek and Latin to win the debate. County commissioners weren't persuaded. They turned him down, forcing him to call off the debate. He did not give up though. Nine months later he put out a press release over the wire challenging all comers to debate him on the question, "Resolved, that the apostolic church did not practice water baptism in any form." He invited anyone interested to contact him either by mail or telephone. No debate followed, so it may be assumed he got no takers, a surprising development since Fort Worth was deep in the heart of the Bible Belt and baptism was a cornerstone of mainline Protestant theology.[6]

The year 1922 was a headline-making one for Brogdon. He was approached by author W. C. Witcher to print his book manuscript, *The Unveiling of the Ku*

Klux Klan. Brogdon was an enemy of the Klan, but he was also a businessman. He set the book in type but refused to print it or return the manuscript until he was paid $56.65. Witcher sued him for $1,000 in Seventeenth District Court, and Brogdon countersued for the money he was owed. Six months later Judge R. E. L. Roy handed down a judgment in favor of Brogdon.[7]

This same year Brogdon set up the Protestant Bible Society as a "benevolent and charitable institution" chartered by the state of Texas. As director he planned to put his printing press to work publishing "Biblical literature." He also hoped to use the society to hit the lecture circuit with parent-teacher organizations around the state and to lead archaeological trips to the Holy Land. Education and faith were his guiding lights.[8]

But Brogdon scored his biggest headlines in 1922 for a physical altercation of epic proportions: the crusading editor against the police chief. On Friday morning, July 14, he went to the office of Fort Worth Police Chief Harry Hamilton to quiz the chief about the connection between "special officer" commissions and Klan membership. The commissions gave their holders the right to be armed and exercise police powers. Hamilton was a proud member of the Klan whom Brogdon believed was creating an auxiliary force of armed Klansmen, giving them official cover to abuse individuals and groups they disliked.

Brogdon demanded a list of all the men holding special commissions with the FWPD, which set off Hamilton, who regarded the names as protected police records. (Membership lists for the Klan were secret.) He accused Brogdon of publishing anti-Klan screeds, then came around his desk to strike the pesky editor several times with his revolver. Brogdon was seated at the time and unable to defend himself. Then Hamilton ordered him out of his office. Brogdon left only to go straight down the hall to District Attorney Jesse Brown's office, where he filed a complaint charging Hamilton with assault and battery. As proof he showed a bruise on his forehead, a swollen cheek, and "lacerations" around his right eye. He did not get in to see Brown, but an assistant DA informed him the proper place to file such a complaint was with Fire and Police Commissioner John Alderman.[9]

In the meantime, Chief Hamilton was also busy. He went downstairs to his desk sergeant and placed himself under arrest. Then he posted the twenty-dollar minimal bond and went back upstairs to summon reporters. He told them Brogdon had threatened to "write him up" and admitted he might have struck the editor but only once and then only after removing his pistol out of fear that Brogdon "might attempt to use it." He insisted he was the aggrieved party, not Brogdon. Jesse Brown also talked to reporters that day, telling them Brogdon's complaint would be handled just like any other complaint and would "probably" be turned over to the grand jury, which was not the way such complaints were usually handled. Since no grand jury was in session at the time and there was no date on the calendar for swearing one in, that was an empty promise.[10]

In the end the little dustup was resolved quietly. The chief and the editor appeared in city court (a.k.a. police court) a few days later. Judge H. O. Gossett required Hamilton to enter a plea of "guilty" to the assault charge and fined him ten dollars. For his part, Brogdon apologized and admitted he might have "provoked" the chief. He even magnanimously insisted that the fine be remitted to his attacker. Gossett instructed the two to shake hands, which they did, and the book was closed on the affair. Or almost. Mayor E. R. Cockrell waded in with his own statement to the press. He said an officer of the law, "like an army officer," cannot be so thin-skinned as to allow himself to be insulted. He "censured" Hamilton and said the city commission and grand jury would both investigate. No further action was taken, and the affair passed quietly from the news.[11]

Brogdon liked being in the news, and when he was not the story, he made up for it by writing fiery "Letters to the Editor." He used that forum to express his support for Jim and Miriam Ferguson, better known as Pa and Ma Ferguson when they served as governors of Texas, 1915–1917 and 1925–1927, respectively. Endless controversy surrounded the pair. Pa was impeached at the beginning of a second term and forbidden from ever holding public office in Texas again, something Brogdon considered a miscarriage of justice. Pa got around the prohibition against holding office again by engineering Ma's election as governor, which everyone knew put the reins of government back in his own hands. None of that kept Brogdon from coming out four-square for the pair. After Ma was elected, he praised her in a letter to the editor for loyally supporting her husband "through [his] years of suffering and trouble"

Left: Stansell T. Brogdon, newspaperman, educator, and public figure. Author's collection.

Right: Brogdon antagonist Fort Worth Police Chief Harry Hamilton, 1922. Courtesy of retired FWPD Sergeant Kevin Foster.

and for being a role model for all the "young women of Texas." Brogdon never lost his faith in the Fergusons.[12]

Brogdon was a restless soul always working on some new project. He opened his architect's office in Fort Worth and in 1925 served as the "supervising architect" on some buildings on the Texas Tech (Lubbock) campus. Four years later he put up a five-story addition to the Hotel Lubbock. In between he bought the defunct Meridian Junior College from the Sons of Hermann for $36,600 and reopened it as Meridian College, with himself as president and a focus on vocational training and teacher education. The sale was completed in the summer of 1927, and he announced resumption of classes that fall. He imposed his own unconventional standards on the school, which included banning athletics, requiring all students, male and female, to wear uniforms, and inviting the ROTC to put a unit on campus. He explained that "the Almighty frowns on collegiate athletics," citing as evidence the tragedy of the Baylor basketball team that died when the team bus was hit by a train. He took out ads in newspapers across the state touting Meridian as "the only college in Texas where girls are treated as the equal of boys." For a junior college it was a pricey education. A year's tuition was "about $500."[13]

It would seem the Almighty did not smile on Meridian College either. The school never got off the ground in the fall of 1927. Brogdon announced its closure on October 1 citing "lack of support." He returned to his other love, which was Bible study, not architecture. With the Protestant Bible Society, he was able to do the Lord's work and make money at the same time. The society had financed his purchase of Meridian College and presumably taken the hit when he closed it. In 1930 he finally got his chance to lead a tour of Palestine under the aegis of the society. This was not just a sightseeing excursion. He issued an invitation to all Fort Worth and Dallas "theologists" interested in "delving into the ancient lore of the Holy Land." There is no record of how many signed up to go. They went in May and spent the next several months exploring "Palestine's old ruins." Brogdon made a geological "survey" of the River Jordan and the Sea of Galilee and brought back a trove of ancient manuscripts that the locals were willing to sell. On his return he wrote a report of the trip for the *Star-Telegram* and a scientific paper on his findings. He also made a public appeal to "every Fort Worth friend" to contribute to his "exploration fund" so he could go back to the Holy Land.[14]

He went back in February 1931 to conduct further research on behalf of the Protestant Bible Society. Beside his archaeological diggings and "charting the Sea of Galilee," he searched monasteries and bazaars for ancient Bible manuscripts. His prized find was a "1,000-year-old" manuscript that he said was "given to him by an old monk." On his return he also announced that John the Baptist ate barley cake, not locusts, which he said was a mistranslation in the Bible by those who did not understand ancient Greek. He also made a third "research and exploration" trip in 1932 to seek the "lost cities" of Bethesda and Capernaum and visit more "old monasteries" in hopes of finding more "ancient manuscripts."[15]

These trips established his bona fides as a biblical scholar of the first rank and added to his growing collection of relics and manuscripts.

He claimed to have a "1,500-year-old Bible," hand-written in Greek. In the summer of 1933, he displayed a few of his treasures, including a Codex Sinaiticus and a Codex Alexandrinus, at Leonard's Department Store in the book department. The newspaper reports of his travels made him an even bigger public figure, which would come in quite handy when he turned his attentions toward state office.[16]

Brogdon loved to write letters to the editor, lambasting whoever he disagreed with, which was a lot of people. Often his rants were pointless rather than constructive. For instance, when the trustees of Texas Woman's College (formerly Polytechnic College) planned to close it in 1933 for lack of both money and students, he attacked that decision as well as any thought of keeping it a women-only institution, which he said violated the vision of the man who had donated the land in the beginning. In a letter to the editor, he called both actions a "reproach" to the Methodist Church, which had chartered the school, and a "breach of trust" with its benefactor, George Tandy. Instead, he offered a counterproposal: If the Methodist Episcopal Conference was determined to abrogate the original charter, then the school should be "transferred" to his own Protestant Bible Institute (an offshoot of the Protestant Bible Society), loosely "patterned on the more famous Moody Bible Institute." He vowed to keep the school open and reinstitute its original coed admissions policy. He ended with a ringing appeal: Fort Worth "more than any other city in Texas" was the perfect place for an institution "that would draw the support and patronage" of Christians across the state. And, of course, he would be at its head.[17]

After calling Fort Worth home for some fifteen years, Brogdon moved to Stephenville in 1936 to take on a construction job—he still considered himself a working architect—but then he stayed on as "music instructor" at John Tarleton Agricultural College (part of the Texas A&M system). Composing music was another of Brogdon's talents. It is unclear when or where he acquired such a talent, but he was not shy about touting it. Always looking for a bigger audience, he refused to be tied down to a mere teaching job. While still at Tarleton, he launched a quixotic run for governor's office two years later. Entering the race was not hard. He was a Democrat and only had to pay a one-hundred-dollar filing fee to the Democratic Executive Committee to enter the race. He kicked off his campaign with a rambling speech on the Stephenville courthouse lawn on January 7, 1938.[18]

As one of nine candidates in the race for the party's nomination, he was given zero chance by the Kerrville newspaper because "nobody knows him." Before he could even face the electorate he would have to get through the Democratic primary in July. Whoever won that would by all odds be the next governor. He took out ads in newspapers and stumped the state tirelessly. He described himself as "an architect," and his ads said he was a man "Who Is Convinced That the Great State of Texas Should Be the Leader in These Great United States." It wasn't exactly an appeal that jumped off the page. Still, as he was an adopted son of Fort Worth, the *Star-Telegram* followed his campaign, which he had to finance out of his own pocket, to the tune of about $750 in the beginning.[19]

If nothing else, his campaign platform drew attention, and he needed all the free publicity he could get. It had just three planks, but they were doozies. He borrowed from the New Deal to advocate a state pension of thirty-six dollars a month for "everyone 65 years or older." Secondly, he favored prohibition in general (repealed by the Nineteenth Amendment in 1933) with an exception being made for seventeen cities that had the police to control drunken driving. But it was the third plank that caused jaws to drop. He favored "the annexation of Mexico by the United States." He also displayed a xeno-phobic fear of Japan in his argument for annexing Mexico. "The Japanese will soon invade Mexico [in force]," he warned in 1938, and the United States would be next. He was right in his prediction of war between Imperial Japan and the United States, but that was hardly far-fetched in 1938. He was no Nostradamus, but he was all over the map when it came to taking a stand on the issues. He also spoke out in favor of restoring "political rights" (meaning the right to run for office) to impeached Governor James "Pa" Ferguson and of opening the Confederate Home in Austin to "all aged Texans," whether Civil War veteran or not. Staking out radical stands on peripheral issues was his bread and butter as a marginal candidate for public office. He did not so much campaign for votes as use his platform to spout wacky beliefs.[20]

He was an energetic campaigner. Crowds came out just to hear what he had to say, probably with no intention of voting for him. He

BROGDON
for Governor

Born and reared in Brazos County, and graduated in 1898 from Texas A. and M. College, I am seeking support on the basis of a three-plank platform.

I favor pensions for all, of 65 years or older, of $30 per month.

I favor annexation of Mexico by the United States.

I favor prohibition of liquor sales at highway stands, believing it should be confined to cities with an adequate police force, in order to reduce drunken driving.

A vote for me will be a vote for good government for all the people of Texas.

S. T. BROGDON

Help Me Fight Your Fight

1938 campaign ad for Brogdon during unsuccessful run for governor. Author's collection.

crisscrossed the state in the summer of 1938, hitting thirty-two towns in June alone. The Democratic state primary was scheduled for July 23, and his goal was to hit every good-sized town in the state. Sometimes he made three stops in a single day, like he did when he spoke at Denton, Sherman, and Gainesville on June 20. He was the butt of more jokes in the state's newspapers than serious consideration. The *Brownsville Herald* called his campaign a lot of "Hot Air," describing him as "a rather misguided, 61-year-old, gray-haired gentleman." A tireless campaigner and a happy warrior, he racked up the miles on both his automobile and his voice. On Friday, July 1, he stopped in Fort Worth long enough to speak at the Englewood Heights Methodist Church. The small turnout knew him mostly as a former schoolteacher and Methodist minister. They must have been shocked at his campaign platform. He ended his campaign in Austin on Saturday night July 16 before returning home to Stephenville for the last week before the primary. He must have drawn some heat for his annexation proposal because he assured his Austin audience that annexation would in the long run "assure permanent friendly relations with Mexico."[21]

Resting at home in Stephenville did not keep him quiet. If anything, his rhetoric became more inflammatory. In a message that would resonate with later Lone Star politicians he said, "The hour has come for Texas to dictate to Washington . . . to prevent the injury and ruin of the economic life" of the state. He was particularly concerned with Mexican influence extending across the Texas border. He spoke of annexing Mexico "by force if necessary" to "protect" the nation. His rhetoric did not win him any friends in the Rio Grande Valley district of Texas.[22]

Brogdon did not win the Democratic nomination or the governorship. Both honors went to W. Lee "Pass the Biscuits, Pappy" O'Daniel, another uniquely Texas character with a flair for showmanship whose claim to fame was selling flour and fronting a hillbilly band (the Light Crust Doughboys). O'Daniel vanquished twenty-six Democratic and Republican challengers on his way to winning the governorship. Surprisingly, however, Brogdon came in third in the Democratic primary with 892 votes to O'Daniel's 573,166 votes. The respectable showing encouraged his future political ambitions.[23]

However, Texas had not heard the last of Stansell Brogdon. He returned to Bryan, Texas, and remained active in the Methodist Episcopal Church. He did not give up on politics either. In 1946 he ran for the House seat of incumbent Bert Horne. World War II was over. Japan was a devastated nation. His campaign platform called for the annexation of Japan, with Congress taking the lead in setting policy (over the president). He was at his least consistent in advocating for the annexation of Japan. In 1938 he had called for the United States to annex Mexico "to keep the Japs out." The original "Make America Great Again (MAGA)" candidate, he now believed annexing Japan would "make the United States greater" while at the same time opening a new missionary field for Christianity. It was a nutty idea, out of left field. No surprise, he lost this race, too. He was always more of a curiosity than a serious candidate. He went back to something he was good at: leading archaeological trips to the Holy Land, where he could acquire more "souvenirs" for his relics and manuscripts collection. He loved showing his treasures off and pontificating about the Greek text that only he could read. The collection was highly regarded enough that several institutions offered to give them a home. In 1959 he gifted to Texas A&M University a manuscript of the Jewish Torah estimated to be three hundred to five hundred years old. Unfortunately, he did not properly document his intentions, which caused a legal battle later.[24]

Stansell Brogdon died on May 2, 1960, in an Austin hospital. He was 83 years old and had been sick for some time with pancreatitis, so no one was surprised by his passing. He had some family members around him at the end, just not a wife or children. He never married or started a family. Whether that was because he did not have time or he just was not bent that way is unknown. The body was brought back to Bryan for the funeral, which took place the next day. Two Methodist ministers tag-teamed on the funeral sermon, and he was interred in Bryan's Alexander Church cemetery alongside his parents.[25]

The surprise came after his death when the family sued Texas A&M to get the supposedly donated manuscript back. The case brought out some of the big guns in the legal community, including the assistant attorney general of Texas. A district court ruled in favor of the family and ordered A&M to return the manuscript. The school appealed to the Court of Civil Appeals, which upheld the original verdict, ruling that although Brogdon had intended to give the document to the college, he only "gave" it to his sister who only "loaned" it to Texas A&M.[26]

Stansell Brogdon was a pistol his entire life; many would have described him as a kook or a crank. A more charitable observer might have said he was a nonconformist or gadfly. Whatever term is used, it is undeniable that controversy followed everywhere he went. He was also a Renaissance man: architect, engineer, publisher, crusading journalist, teacher, music composer, Hebrew scholar, preacher, and politician. In his mixture of evangelism, architecture, and archaeology, he was a combination of Billy Sunday, Wyatt C. Hedrick, and Indiana Jones, with a little P. T. Barnum thrown in for good measure. Fort Worth has not seen his like since his passing and probably never will again.

Chapter 17

The Gridiron Stars of North Side High School

One of the most remarkable football teams of all time in this area—after the Dallas Cowboys of 1993–1995 and the TCU Horned Frogs of 2022–2023—was the North Side High School team of 1915–1916. In those years they were the "red and white," not the "maroon and white" of today, and they were not yet known as the Steers. (Their choice of a mascot came nine years later.) The school had only been playing football since 1909, and in 1916 they only graduated thirty-four, at the time the largest class in its history.[1]

The stars of those 1915 and 1916 teams and their coach went on to put Kentucky's Centre College on the national map. The stars of those teams were Alvin Nugent "Bo" McMillin and his brother Reuben, Madison "Matty" Bell, Jim "Red" Weaver, Bob Mathias, James Ralph "Sully" Montgomery, Bill Boswell, Bill James, and Roscoe Minton. Their coach, Robert L. Myers, came to North Side in 1912 to teach English. Coaching football was an additional duty, and a new one, but one at which he excelled. When he came to town the *Star-Telegram* had him playing big-time college football at the University of Kentucky, probably because the writer had never heard of tiny Presbyterian College in Danville, Kentucky. Myers was a personal friend of the legendary Glenn "Pop" Warner, who put Carlisle Indian School on the map. He got coaching tips from Warner and taught his North Side boys to play disciplined, hard-nosed "Carlisle style football," producing winning teams for the next four years. North Side was also riding high after moving into a new building on Twenty-First Street in 1914. Myers left North Side after the 1916 school year to take the coaching job at his alma mater.[2]

Three North Side players left school after the 1915 season without graduating: Bo McMillin, Red Weaver, and Thaddeus McDonald. They would need additional high school credits before entering college. It was no accident that they chose to continue their education in Kentucky. Until 1916 the little Kentucky school was called Central College, an all-male institution that would remain that way until going coed in 1962. It had fewer than 270 students when the first Fort Worth boys arrived in 1916, so most of the football players had to play both offense and defense because the football team was so small. Coach Myers was a graduate of Central College, class of 1907, who took over the football team from Orville B. "Bo" Littick before the 1917 season. Myers had been enticed away from North Side by the opportunity to coach on the college level, not by the pay, which is what caused Coach Littick to resign. Myers took over a rebuilding program at a school that had fielded a football team since 1880, but most years they were a punching bag for larger schools.[3]

The school's teams were the Colonels, an appropriate name for a Kentucky team. In the 1917 season before taking the field to play Kentucky, Coach Myers suggested they pray. After winning the game 3–0, they made a prayer part of their routine before every game, which is why amused rivals began referring to them as the "Praying Colonels," a name they embraced. Legend has it they were the first team ever to pray together before taking the field, which got them as much press coverage as their victories on the field. Myers's successor, Charles B. "Charley" Moran made it clear the boys did not pray for victory, only that they come through the game uninjured and play their hardest. History repeated itself in 1924 when the West Point football team adopted the same practice. Today, many teams do that.[4]

The 1916 team coached by Bo Littick did not have all its stars in place yet, but it was no slouch led by three former North Siders: Madison Bell at quarterback, Reuben McMillin at tackle, and Bob Mathias at fullback. They only

North Side High Makes Bid for State Honors

COACH MYERS   CAPTAIN McMILLIN

The stars of North Side High School's 1914 championship football team, Coach Robert L. Myers (*left*) and Captain Bo McMillin (*right*). Author's collection.

lost one game, to Kentucky State. The other three North Siders who came to Kentucky spent the school year enrolled at Somerset High School to pull up their grades. The 1916 Somerset team with Bo McMillin, Red Weaver, and Thad McDonald did not lose a game and all three graduated in the spring.[5]

Robert Myers reaped the reward of the North Side exodus to Kentucky. As a former Centre (Central) College player-turned-coach, he was the reason they came. Centre did not give athletic scholarships; it was the personal connection that built a championship football team. One Danville newspaper commented admiringly on the Fort Worth connection on that 1916 team with Bo McMillin, Bob Mathias, Bill Boswell, and Red Weaver. Added the writer, "It's easy to see that the Texas boys have brought their fighting spirit with them to Centre [College]."[6]

One more piece remained to be put in place; that was an assistant coach. Myers brought in 39-year-old Charley Moran, whose hiring was either a stroke of genius or a case of pure luck. Hiring successful coaches can be attributed to either or sometimes both. Moran's son Thomas was on the team at the time, and papa came to see him play in November 1917. He stayed and accompanied the team to Chattanooga to play Sewanee. That decided Myers to recruit him as an assistant coach. "Uncle Charley," as they called him, had an impressive football resume of his own, having coached winning programs at Vanderbilt University and Carlisle Indian School. He also had roots in Texas football as head coach at Texas A&M, 1909–1915. Coaching is a precarious profession, and Moran was fired by the Aggies, not because he was unsuccessful but to smooth over relations with the University of Texas. He was the only coach who had ever beaten Texas twice in the same season. He landed at Carlisle, where he worked under the legendary Coach Glenn Scobey "Pop" Warner. Moran would move up to be head coach after Myers moved up to be athletic director and led the Colonels to the greatest glory before moving on to Bucknell College (Lewisburg, Pennsylvania) in 1924. His opening speech everywhere he coached was the same: "I didn't come here to lose." Football was his job only in the fall. In the summers he was a National League baseball umpire. Like Myers, he was also well-known to Fort Worthers from spending his summers umpiring for the Texas League— along with another beloved North Sider, Charley McCafferty.[7]

It was Myers and Moran who built a championship team. They knew they had something special with the 1917 team, defeating the Kentucky Wildcats 3–0 on a McMillin drop kick and finishing 7–1. The Colonels capped the season as Kentucky state football champions. In February 1918 every member of that team received a little souvenir gold football as a memento. Myers's and Moran's gold "pigskins" had to be mailed to them at their homes in Fort Worth and Horse Cave, Kentucky, respectively.[8]

In 1918 World War I interrupted their march to fame and glory. Star quarterback Bo McMillin left school to enlist in the US Navy, returning for the 1919 season to join Red Weaver and James Madison "Red" Roberts as the heart of the team. The players dubbed McMillin "the Colonel," overlooking the fact that the navy does not have colonels. The three of them played both ways, as was customary at Centre, and Charley Moran carried on what Robert Myers had started with the same meager number of players. The traveling team carried only seventeen boys plus the Black trainer Joe McDonald. That was all they needed to beat West Virginia in Charleston, 14–6, and Indiana, Kentucky, and DePauw on the way to nine wins in 1919.[9]

By the end of the season, Centre's prowess had spread beyond the borders of Kentucky. The *Boston Globe*, which usually only followed Harvard, sent a reporter to Danville. After interviewing the locals, he sent in the following report on the reasons for their success: "Danville folks will tell you that it is, first, the material, second the coach, and third, the spirit. But I believe to solve the secret you have got to dig deeper than that. First—There is faith in themselves not born of over-confidence. Second—Coach Charles Moran. Third—The material. Fourth—The firm belief of the material in, and its almost filial affection for, that coach."[10]

McMillin and Red Weaver made Walter Camp's first All-American team, announced after the 1919 season. Weaver at 5' 10" and 185 pounds played center for the team, the smallest center ever to be named All-American. McMillin was another mighty mite at 5' 9½" and 175 pounds. The competition was about the same size, but McMillin was a superb athlete who could pass, run, punt the ball, and call plays. He was the complete football player. His physical skills and mental acumen were matched by a personality that inspired teammates to play their hearts out. Wise beyond his years, he told adoring fans, "Football is the greatest game of all, but a boy has to love it to play well. It's just too rough and tough for anyone to play, or anyone to coach, unless he loves it more than anything else. It's not right to have to urge a boy or pay him to play football." Bo's nickname (the Colonel) and the success of the team inspired a new tradition first announced by Kentucky Governor Edwin P. Morrow—making the team's captain an honorary colonel on his staff every year.[11]

In 1920 the Praying Colonels continued to be giant killers. They knocked off Indiana and West Virginia, losing only to powerhouse Harvard, 31–14, in the second of three meetings, and to Georgia Tech, 24–0, on the way to an 8–2 season. The postseason saw them inflict a humiliating defeat on Texas Christian University on January 21, 1921, in a bowl game dubbed the Fort Worth Classic. TCU came into the game riding high as the champion of the Texas Intercollegiate Athletic Association. Centre came into the game as the first football team from east of the Mississippi "to invade Texas." The Praying Colonels did to TCU what King David did to the Philistines, handing them a 63–7 defeat. It was the first and the last Fort Worth Classic.[12]

The Praying Colonels were 10 and 1 in 1921. McMillin saved his best for the game against their biggest opponent, the Crimson of Harvard. At the time the Crimson were one of the country's powerhouse teams, undefeated in five seasons, a twenty-five-game winning streak. In the fourth quarter he broke through the line and raced thirty yards to the endzone for the only score of the game. Newspapers of the day called it "the biggest surprise in football history." Eighty-four years later the *New York Times* called it "the upset of the century in college football."[13]

In the 1921 postseason the unbeaten Colonels come to Dallas to play Texas A&M in the Dixie Classic, forerunner of the Cotton Bowl. The Colonels lost 22–14, but they were not done on their march through major college programs. The next season they won eight of ten. That 1922 season also saw them play the rubber match against Harvard, with the Crimson winning as they had done in 1920. The team bounced back for the 1923 season when they went 7–1–1. After 1923 the Praying Colonels started a long slide into irrelevance.[14]

Bo McMillin played one more season after 1921, his fifth as a Praying Colonel. The extra year of eligibility was allowed because of his time in the service. He was not the only veteran serviceman on the Centre College team. H. Y. "Shanks" Lipscomb also played on those remarkable teams. Some losing opponents groused that the Praying Colonels were winning with ineligible "professionals."

During five years as coach at Centre College, Charley Moran compiled an .868 winning record. The team played in three bowl games, winning two, the East-West Christmas Classic and the Fort Worth Classic, both played in 1921. They went from playing before crowds of a few hundred to playing before thirty-five thousand and more. They went from fielding a team of sixteen players when Moran arrived to fielding teams of twenty-two or more players. For most of that time he had just one assistant, meaning he coached offense and defense and did the laundry. He was a walking endorsement for Texas football, telling reporters he "favored Texans on my teams believing the best of gridiron talent hails from the state." What his later teams lacked was the stars of those early years, starting with the North Side boys.[15]

The stars of those glory teams went on to achieve great things of their own after college. After graduating in the spring of 1922, Bo McMillin went to work that fall as football coach for Centenary College (Shreveport, Louisiana). Other coaching stops followed in a notoriously peripatetic profession before he landed at Indiana University. He took the Hoosiers to an undefeated Big Ten championship season in 1945. He left Indiana in 1948 for the professional ranks, coaching the Detroit Lions and Philadelphia Eagles. As a coach in the pros, he never enjoyed the success he had with his college teams. He ended his coaching career with a 146–77–13 record. Among his contributions to football were the Crazy T formation and the five-man backfield. His greatest accomplishment was that at every school where he coached, he inherited teams that were average to poor on paper and turned them into winners. Before every season he bemoaned the state of his team, calling them "mah pore little boys," but this was a rope-a-dope tactic made famous by Bear Bryant with his Texas A&M and Alabama teams.[16]

Bo's teammates also had distinguished careers. After Madison Bell left Centre College in 1919, he coached at TCU (1923–1928) and SMU, taking the Mustangs to the Rose Bowl and a national title in 1935. Bill James became coach at Texas A&M. James Ralph "Sully" Montgomery married his North Side High School sweetheart while he was in college. After graduating in 1922 he played professional football with the Chicago Cardinals and Philadelphia Eagles, became a heavyweight boxer who was seventh in line for a title match, and served as Tarrant County Sheriff from 1946 to 1953. And it was not just in sports that those North Side boys made their mark. The Greines brothers, David, Sol, and Abe, who anchored the line on those 1911–1912 teams, and S. D. "Dave" Shannon, who was a backup, all went on to great success in their chosen fields in medicine, business, and law. The North Side boys were overachievers, every single one of them, although they would have a hard time making the junior varsity today. Sol Greines weighed only 145 pounds, David Greines weighed 150, and Abe Greines weighed 175.[17]

The Centre College coach did not do too badly either. Besides coaching winning football teams, Charley Moran enjoyed a long career as a National League umpire, noted for his famous quip to players who questioned his calls, "It ain't nothing until I call it."[18]

There was one other member of those Centre College football teams whose name does not appear on any team roster. He was their African American trainer, Joe McDonald, remembered only as "Black Joe," whose job description included a little bit of everything. He was beloved by a generation of players who called him their "faithful valet" and "team mascot" for thirty years. He was part of the traveling squad every year except 1920. He had to miss that history-making season because he was in the Danville, Kentucky, jail for some unspecified offense. The players lamented his absence. There is a certain irony to this because some of those same players were the former North Side High boys who put on a minstrel show every year (its purpose was to raise money for the North Side High School Athletic Association.) They saw no contradiction in their warm regard for Joe McDonald and their blackface performances in high school.[19]

The Praying Colonels should have been a headline story all over the country: "the Little Team That Could!" "David vs. Goliath on the Football Field!" And North Side High School should have been known as a football

Top: Centre College football team, 1919 champions. Author's collection.

Bottom: North Side High School football team, looking for football success one hundred years later. Author's collection.

factory for all the talent it produced. Unfortunately, both Centre College and North Side High had their run before "ballyhoo" took over the national news, turning sports into the stuff of legends. They needed a Grantland Rice or a Damon Runyon to tell their story, to move them from the sports page to the front page.[20]

Fort Worth residents need to remember that before Paschal and Arlington Heights dominated Fort Worth high school athletics, North Side was a powerhouse, producing such future professional stars as Rogers Hornsby (baseball) and Yale Lary (football). North Side played their biggest rival, Paschal, in an annual series of football games that began in 1912. The 1946 game was a classic played on Thanksgiving Day before the biggest crowd ever to see a game at Farrington Field (25,000). North Side won 14–13, thanks largely to running back Yale Lary. Years later, who remembers North Side High School's glory days?[21]

Chapter 18

Jesse Williams
Forgotten Hero of the Spring Palace Fire

If you grew up in Fort Worth or have lived here long enough, you have heard of Al Hayne, the hero of the 1890 Texas Spring Palace Fire. If not, you can drive down Lancaster and see his memorial standing near the intersection of Lancaster and Commerce. Poor Al is a little weather-beaten after so many years exposed to the elements, but he is still recognizable.[1]

Hayne is remembered for his heroic actions on the night of May 30, 1890. It was the last night of the Texas Spring Palace's second season when the building erupted into flames. At the time the building was crammed with visitors—estimates say as many as seven thousand—enjoying the last night of the grand exhibition. It was about 10:00 p.m., and the Elgin Watch Factory Band had just concluded their concert. The Cotillion Ball was about to begin on the second floor, so many people were making their way there. Elsewhere in the building people milled around taking a final look at the exhibits under the electric lights. The next thing anyone knew, the place was on fire. Exactly how it started was in dispute afterward, but all agreed it started on the east end of the second floor. The jangling of the fire alarm in the northeast corner got everyone's attention, causing a "great rush" for the exits. However, the building had not been built with swift evacuation in mind. The designers had other things in mind besides a disastrous fire. While the structure had ten

The Burning of the Texas Spring Palace.
COPYRIGHTED BY O. A. McCORMICK.   On the Night of May 30th, 1890.   J. E. DANIEL, PHOTOGRAPHER

Artistic rendering of 1890 Texas Spring Palace Fire. It happened too fast for photographers to set up and get a picture. Linda Jo & Scott Barker Collection.

"large" exits on the first floor, there were only two narrow staircases to the second floor, one at either end of the building.[2]

Al Hayne, the English-born civil engineer who had called Fort Worth home for ten years, was there that night. He sprang into action, finding a rope somewhere that he used to lower women and children to safety from the west tower. He also helped reunite frantic mothers and crying children and point them toward the stairs. With the building beginning to collapse in upon itself, he raced back into the inferno one last time to see if anyone was left. Instead of the rescuer he risked becoming another victim. Too weak to save himself, he was leaning against a wall with flames all around him, moments away from a fiery death, when another hero came charging through the flames.[3]

That second hero was Jesse Williams, who had been standing on the grounds watching the festivities when the fire erupted. He could not join in those festivities because he was Black and racial segregation was a fact of life, but he was not the kind of man to stand aside when disaster loomed. In 1890 he was 36 years old, born into slavery in Virginia. Sometime after 1870 he found his way to Fort Worth, a part of the Black Exodus that fled the South after the Civil War to build new lives. In 1880 he was working as the porter (janitor) in an uptown boarding house on Houston. One of the residents of the house was Fort Worth Mayor John J. Brown. Williams's circumstances had not notably improved ten years later. In the summer of 1890, Jesse, who described himself as a hostler (stableman), was looking for work. He had what he described as "good recommendations," which may have included former Mayor Brown, and felt he was qualified to be a "general utility man," which meant glorified porter. He had no known family in town.[4]

Jesse could have hung back at a safe distance and watched the Spring Palace go up in flames as thousands did that night. But something drove him to jump in and help save people he did not know and who would not have given him the time of day under ordinary circumstances. He sprang into action without being asked, catching one lady being lowered to the ground by a rope from the second floor. He looked up and saw Al Hayne in a doorway about to collapse. Jesse rushed into the building, putting his own life at risk to save a man he could not have known.[5]

By the time Jesse got to the Englishman, Al was lying on the floor, a scorched form with second and third-degree burns. Jesse picked him up and carried him back down the stairs out of the building. He carefully laid the grievously injured Hayne on the ground where others ministered to him. Jesse's own coat was on fire, and his hair was singed. He shucked his coat then disappeared into the crowd. Hardly anyone noticed the Black man leaving. They were focused on getting Hayne to the city's only hospital, St. Joseph's Infirmary. It was too late for Al Hayne. He died in St. Joseph's Hospital within the hour, reportedly in an agony of pain.[6]

From the first cries of "Fire" it had taken just four minutes for the entire building to catch fire and another eleven minutes after that for it to be reduced to a pile of smoldering embers. It is amazing only one person died. In the days that followed, the newspapers gave credit to getting everyone safely out of the building to a number of folks: E. F. Fudge, T. P. Keater, Russell Harrison, E. F. Segerson, and B. B. Paddock, among others. All of them coincidentally were white. But Al Hayne was mentioned most notably because he alone lost his life. The *Fort Worth Gazette* dubbed him "the Hero of the

Spring Palace Fire" and said, "No truer hero ever died on American soil or for the American people."[7]

The newspapers finally got around to mentioning the "brave colored man" who "did his best to save poor Al Hayne's life." In that telling of the story, Hayne was "the hero" while Williams had merely "performed a heroic act." It was an important distinction. The only other African American connected to the Spring Palace fire was an unnamed "Negro boy" whom some sources blamed for the fire, saying his energetic dancing had ignited it when his shoe struck a phosphorus match. That theory, for that is all it was, is akin to the legend that Mrs. O'Leary's cow starting the great Chicago Fire of 1871.[8]

Six days after the fire, an anonymous person wrote a "note" to the *Gazette* pointing out there were two heroes that night: "The white hero, Al Hayne, who gave his life to save others," and "a black hero, Jesse Williams, who risked his life to drag the white man from the burning Palace." After that, for all practical purposes, Jesse Williams dropped off the face of the earth. The only notice his hometown took of him was a few ads he placed in the "Help Wanted" columns as a "young colored man" looking for work. At the time he was living over Bill Love's saloon on Twelfth. Love was a leader in the Black community and may have been one of the "excellent recommendations" Jesse referenced in his "help wanted" ad. There is no way of knowing if he found a job, though it is hard to imagine why someone would not hire the man who risked his life to save Al Hayne.[9]

Fort Worth would never forget Al Hayne. Three years after the fire the Woman's Humane Society erected a monument in his honor in front of the T&P passenger station. The Al Hayne memorial was the first thing people saw when they emerged from the train station. And in Fort Worth Fire Department history he was transformed into a full-fledged fireman. (A full-time fire department was created the same years the memorial was put up.)

As for Jesse Williams, he was almost erased from the pages of history. Al Hayne fared little better. It took only fifteen years for the *Fort Worth Telegram* to lament the "obscure hero's memorial" that people knew almost nothing about beyond what happened that fateful night. The irony of that story is that if people knew so little about Al Hayne, they knew even less about Jesse Williams. *Star-Telegram* columnist Amos Melton tried to keep

Left: Bronze bust of Spring Palace Hero Al Hayne atop the Al Hayne Memorial. Author's collection.

Right: Jesse Williams, Mystery Man. No photograph of the fire's other hero is known to exist.

Williams's memory alive in 1930 when he wrote a recap of the fire, crediting Jesse with "rushing into the building to pull Hayne from the structure." Sixty-plus years removed from the events of 1890, a couple of old-timers still remembered Jesse when interviewed by newspaper reporters. D. E. Claypool told a *Star-Telegram* reporter in 1950 that he had helped an unnamed "Negro" pull Hayne from the fire that night, and seven years later Clay Sandidge told a *Press* reporter that he remembered "the Negro who braved the wreckage to pull Hayne out." Unfortunately, memories are not the same as monuments, so Jesse Williams remains a forgotten hero.[10]

Even tracking Jesse Williams the man through the historical record is a lost cause. From the 1880 Census record we learn that he was born in Virginia about 1854. As a Black man growing up under slavery and Reconstruction, he was fated to remain practically invisible for the rest of his life.

Barring some descendant coming to light now, we do not even know where or when he died. By 1900 he is no longer traceable through Census records. He could have still been living in Fort Worth and just been overlooked, or he could have moved somewhere else and still been missed in the census. He virtually drops off the face of the earth after his fifteen minutes of fame on the night of May 30, 1890, a mysterious Black man who stepped from the crowd to perform a heroic deed, then returned to obscurity.

Chapter 19

John Birch
The Man, the Society,
and the Preacher

John Birch was a Baptist missionary murdered in China in 1945. The John Birch Society was an ultraconservative political organization founded in 1958 and named for him. It was J. Frank Norris, founder of modern Christian fundamentalism in America, who inspired Birch to become a missionary. Birch, Norris, and Christian fundamentalism all came together in Fort Worth in 1940. That was the year Birch graduated from Norris's Baptist Bible Institute in Fort Worth and went to China for his first mission post.

Birch was Norris's golden boy, seemingly destined to be a missionary. He was born in Landour, India, in 1918 to missionary parents, growing up deeply immersed in scripture, especially what believers call "the Great Commission." After their Indian mission, his parents made their home in Macon, Georgia, where he enrolled in Mercer University in 1935. He graduated magna cum laude four years later. Even as an undergraduate he was already a lightning rod for controversy as the spokesman for a group that charged the Mercer faculty with teaching "religious modernism." He was also already pastoring a local Baptist congregation even before graduating. Not content to follow a conventional career path, he set his sights on carrying the gospel to China. In October of that same year, he came to Fort Worth to join the inaugural class of what was then called the Fundamental Bible Baptist Institute. The flamboyant pastor of

First Baptist Church who headed the institute viewed its purpose as training missionaries, preachers, and evangelists to carry the gospel all over the world, saving souls while fighting godless communism. Birch completed his studies in June 1940 and immediately applied to the World Fundamental Baptist Missionary Fellowship to go to China, a risky posting because China had been at war with Japan since 1937.[1]

While other foreigners fled China as fast as they could, some two hundred Baptist missionaries stayed on in the war-torn country. Birch asked to be posted to the Shanghai and Hangchow districts. On June 25, 1940, he left Fort Worth for Shanghai. One hundred and fifty members of First Baptist Church, including Norris, saw him off at the T&P passenger station, which echoed with their prayers and singing as Birch boarded the train. On July 1 he set sail from Seattle, Washington, for Shanghai on a Japanese freighter, reporting to the Sweet Memorial Baptist Bible School as soon as he arrived. A committed fundamentalist and eternal optimist, Birch embraced the challenge of trying to convert five hundred million Chinese to Christianity. The boys' school where he taught was deep in the war zone. His upbeat reports to the missionary society back home told of performing exorcisms (!) and achieving miraculous things through fervent prayer.[2]

When war followed between Japan and the United States on December 7, 1941, Birch chose to stay on in China even after the State Department ordered all missionaries to leave. Instead, he volunteered for the American Military Mission to China. He happened to be in the right place at the right time to rescue Lieutenant Colonel Jimmy Doolittle and his crew when they crash-landed after the Tokyo raid. He led them to safety, then stayed in country to join General Claire Chenault's China Air Task Force (a.k.a. the Fourteenth Air Force). He was commissioned a second lieutenant and worked as an intelligence officer. He got his commission on the recommendation of Doolittle and impressed Chenault, who called him "the pioneer of our field-intelligence network." He used his fluency in Mandarin and familiarity with Chinese culture to operate deep behind enemy lines and gather information. As the Fourteenth's chaplain and an intelligence officer both, Birch saw himself quite literally as a "soldier for Christ." His intelligence gathering was of such high quality, he was transferred to the Office of Strategic Services (OSS),

The
John
Birch
Society

A
REPORT

CAPTAIN JOHN BIRCH
U.S. ARMY

"John Birch Society: A Report," Sunday supplement to the *Chicago Tribune*, November 15, 1964, showing Birch in the US Army captain's uniform that he wore for only a short time before his death. Author's collection.

forerunner of the Central Intelligence Agency. His brashness was not only useful in gathering intelligence but also made fellow officers worry that sooner or later he was going to "run into trouble" of his own making. But his luck held, and before the end of the war the army awarded him the Legion of Merit (created in 1942) for "exceptionally meritorious [wartime] service"— in his capacity as an intelligence operative, not chaplain.[3]

By 1945 Birch had become what was soon dubbed an "Asia Firster," believing that America's peace and security in a postwar world would be decided in the Far East, not Europe. This was a historic policy shift in American thinking. Asia Firsters believed faith and foreign policy should go hand in hand, with Americanism and fundamentalism "winning" over Asia the same way European colonialism and Christianity had "won" Africa in the nineteenth century.[4]

When World War II ended in August 1945, John Birch was a US Army captain. After being demobilized he stayed on in China, resuming the missionary duties he had left in 1941. But first he had one last mission to carry out for the OSS—an information-gathering mission into communist-controlled Jiangsu province. It was to be his last mission. Intercepted by Red Chinese soldiers, he informed them he was an American and refused to obey their orders. Unimpressed, they shot the arrogant American dead. It was August 25, ten days after VJ Day. There was a certain irony that John Birch died on a mission, though it was not the sort of mission he had envisioned as his life's work.[5]

Word of his death was slow in getting back to America. He was just one of thousands of American soldiers who had died in foreign lands during the war, neither more nor less important than any other GI. His death was not reported in any major newspaper, not even in Fort Worth surprisingly. Only the *Macon Telegraph* carried an obituary. The pride of the Baptist Bible Institute remained largely forgotten until J. Frank Norris and Robert Welch elevated him to sainthood, Norris by naming the institute's classroom building "Captain John Birch Memorial Hall" in October 1945, and Welch by publishing a worshipful biography, *The Life of John Birch*, nine years later. Robert H. W. Welch was the retired president of the namesake candy company whose second career was promoting archconservative causes. Both Welch and Norris took liberties in the telling of Birch's story to support their respective causes. Welch blamed his death on communist sympathizers inside the US government who "sold out" China and made Birch "the first casualty of the Cold War." Norris used his star graduate to put a face on the Bible Baptist Institute. Thanks to the two of them, John Birch was elevated to a martyr to the cause of liberty and the gospel. His death was no tragic accident; it was

Top: Newly opened John Birch Memorial Hall in late 1945, part of First Baptist Church of Fort Worth. Author's collection.

Bottom: Robert Welch, founder of the John Birch Society, at his desk with a picture of John Birch behind him. Author's collection.

the work of the Prince of Darkness, putting Birch the missionary in the same conversation with John the Baptist. While Norris and Welch were alive, the memory of John Birch, American saint, could not die.[6]

Years later, after Norris died in 1952 but while Welch was still alive, the truth finally came out thanks to Lieutenant Colonel Gus Krause, an officer with the OSS during the war. It was Krause who sent Birch out on his final mission. He told a newspaper reporter how Captain Birch really died: "He was a real fine gentleman . . . but he was pretty forward and spoke harshly with the Chinese." He went on to explain that Birch brought about his own death. "He didn't die the hero he was supposed to have died," explained Krause, choosing his words carefully. Another soldier on the same mission who lived to tell the story concurred. "There was no lesson in Birch's death and certainly no glory," he stated.[7]

However, by this time there was no knocking the legend off its pedestal. John Birch was larger than life, a Christian martyr to everyone who entered the Bible Baptist Seminary and the namesake of the conspiracy-loving John Birch Society. To question his story was to question God and American patriotism.[8]

Eventually, the John Birch Society faded from the news but not before enlisting some very prominent Americans. One of the most prominent was Phyllis Schlafly, a conservative social activist who was against not only communism but also the cause of women's rights as represented by the proposed Equal Rights Amendment to the Constitution. But long before the society faded as a political action group, its namesake suffered one more posthumous insult. In 1956, when the Bible Baptist Seminary moved from its downtown Fort Worth location to become Arlington Baptist College, John Birch Hall was razed along with the rest of the old building. Five years later, *Time* magazine inquired rhetorically, "Who Was John Birch?" The article concluded that he was "a loner with a somewhat overbearing manner." It was the latter that got him killed more than being an American field agent or a Christian. Today the name John Birch barely stirs a flicker of recognition when mentioned to anyone not a member of the Baby Boomer generation.[9]

Chapter 20

Mayor William S. Pendleton's "Fatal Infatuation"

The biggest scandal ever to hit Fort Worth politics and the only mayor ever to be driven from office both involved the same man, William Smartt Pendleton, brought down by a sex scandal in 1890. Pendleton may not have been the first mayor to cat around, but he was the first to have his dirty laundry aired in the newspapers, not just in Fort Worth but all over the country. The city had not gotten this kind of bad press coverage since Luke Short shot Jim Courtright in 1887. Unfortunately, the story made headlines across the country at the same time as the Texas Spring Palace, which was supposed to mark Fort Worth's arrival on the national stage. The Pendleton scandal completely upstaged the Spring Palace.

Pendleton was born in Tennessee in 1850. His large family eventually included five brothers and sisters. After graduating from Manchester College (Indiana) in 1869 he came to Texas. He passed the bar exam and settled in Fort Worth in 1873, beginning a long, successful career climb. His siblings did well, too. One sister, Octavia, married Confederate hero and Fort Worth banker Khleber Van Zandt; brother George became speaker of the Texas House of Representatives; and brother Edmund became a successful cattleman.[1]

HON. THOMAS J. POWELL.

The Honorable Thomas J. Powell, 1908, former mayor of Fort Worth (1900–1906), candidate for Congress, and erstwhile law partner of W. S. Pendleton. Author's collection.

Pendleton was what they used to call "a man on the make." It did not take him long to make a name for himself in the politics and civic life of Fort Worth. He got himself appointed secretary of the celebration that followed the coming of the Texas & Pacific railroad to town in July 1876. About that same time, he opened his law office in the Huffman building on the square. In the next decade he went through a succession of law partners that included the brothers N. B. and C. R. Bowlin, Thomas J. Powell, and Henry M. Chapman. The only one that stuck with him through the scandal was Chapman, who became his law partner in 1886. Powell went on to be city attorney of Fort Worth, then mayor (1900–1906), leaving their partnership off his resume. Among Pendleton's clients over the years was ex-Marshal Jim Courtright, whom he defended in several scrapes in the 1880s.[2]

Pendleton had his fingers in many pies. He was a self-styled "land agent," buying up properties in town and in the country. He was also what we might call a venture capitalist today, joining every new business venture that came down the pike. Those included the Fort Worth Electric Light Company, Fort Worth Natural Gas and Water Supply Company, the Town and Improvement Company, the Democrat Publishing Company, the Fort Worth and Tarrant County Immigration Association, Western Manufacturing Company, and Fort Worth Refrigerating and Export Meat Company. He joined the western railroad-building boom by investing in a proposed line from Fort Worth to "central New Mexico," along with such other distinguished gentlemen as Khleber M. Van Zandt and Max Elser. He was a charter member of the board of trade (forerunner of the chamber of commerce) when it was organized in 1889 and was a backer of the Texas Spring Palace (1889–1890). He was a member of the exclusive Commercial Club (forerunner of the Fort Worth Club). No surprise for someone with the middle name Smartt, Pendleton was also something of an inventor. He secured a US patent in 1882 for "improvements in [railroad] car axles and wheels" and held a financial stake in the Suren hotel annunciator and time alarm.[3]

Pendleton liked to quote German poet Johann Wolfgang von Goethe who said, "What you can do or dream, you can begin it. Boldness hath genius, power, and magic in it." Pendleton was certainly not lacking in boldness. All his business ventures did not prove profitable, but he did parlay his real estate

William S. Pendleton, member of the Nineteenth Texas Legislature representing Tarrant County in 1885. State Preservation Board, Austin, TX.

holdings into a portfolio worth at least $50,000 by 1890. Unknown to most of his fellow Cowtown capitalists, however, he was "land poor." He never had much money in the bank. Still, he managed to keep up appearances. He built a nice home two miles east of the courthouse, then a few years later a "fine residence" in town (corner of Cherry and W. Seventh).[4]

As a business and civic leader, he was a younger version of K. M. Van Zandt, albeit without the war record. He also had political ambitions. He went into politics the same way he went into everything else, full-bore. He joined the Democratic Party because no other political party mattered in Texas. In 1878 he ran for office for the first time—county attorney. The *Fort Worth Democrat* endorsed him, and he won—then was reelected two more times (1880 and 1882). His success got him a seat on the city's Democratic Executive Committee, which chose the (usually winning) candidates for all city offices. He was elected to the Nineteenth Texas Legislature in 1885 representing Tarrant County and became a power in state politics. He was on the winning side of the prohibition fight in 1887, and in 1888 he was a delegate to the state Democratic convention, which met in Fort Worth that year.[5]

Pendleton had a dark side. He was ingratiating but also tended to be hot-headed and impulsive. As county attorney Pendleton got into brawls with opposing lawyers on several occasions. In 1882 he was cited for mixing it up in court—twice. He received a reprimand and paid the five-dollar fine but apparently learned nothing. A year later he was at it again, this time in fisticuffs with Henry Marshall Furman. They were separated and each fined fifty dollars. Four years later, now in private practice, he exchanged blows with another member of the bar and fellow Democrat Frank W. Ball over submitting a deposition in court. Pendleton accused Ball of drunkenness, Ball took strong exception, and as the *Galveston Daily News* described it, "a lively rough-and-tumble fight took place." A deputy sheriff finally separated the two, and the judge fined each fifty dollars for contempt of court. His scrappy ways were notorious all over the state. Pendleton was also a speculator in real estate, the problem being that he bought much more than he sold. He financed his dealings by borrowing money from family and friends and taking out liens that his brother-in-law cosigned on. He was frequently "hard up" for cash, asking his creditors to carry him, which they did because of who he was.[6]

Like everything else he did, Pendleton married well—three times. Being successful and nice-looking, he was a good catch for any woman— "a man of medium height and slender build with a brown [imperial style] mustache scarcely hiding the mouth upon which determination is plainly written, and an intelligent and pleasant face." This description is important because in a time before mass newspaper photography, all newspapers across the country had was a sketch in the July 20 *Dallas Morning News*. His first wife, Elizabeth Isabelle Shelton, apparently liked what she saw. Lizzie Belle, or Lizzie as she was usually called, was the daughter of John F. Shelton, a respected Fort Worth doctor and drugstore owner. She was born in Kentucky in 1855 and came to Fort Worth with her parents as a 3-year-old. That made her seven years younger than Pendleton. They married about 1876, though no marriage record exists, probably because the Tarrant County Courthouse burned on March 29, 1876, taking most of the records with it. Though Pendleton would later lament they were not "well matched" from the start, he did his duty as a husband. In eleven years Lizzie bore five children, sons Herbert, Walter, and George Maurice, and daughters Anna Belle and Edna. Little George Maurice died in infancy. Pendleton had no trouble fathering children, but he left their rearing up to her. To all appearances they were a proper Victorian family.[7]

When not bearing children, Lizzie enjoyed a very comfortable existence. They had an active social life that included a trip to Dallas to see famous stage actor Edwin Booth in 1887 and vacationing at the beach in Galveston. He was frequently absent, but she did not sit at home alone while he was away. In April 1885 she went with her sister and brother-in-law George Pendleton and his family to the World Cotton Centennial in New Orleans. While she enjoyed a life of genteel domesticity, her siblings went on to distinguished careers. Brother John M. Shelton became a wealthy cattleman. Sister Anna went to college and became a successful businesswoman, civic leader, and founder of the Fort Worth Woman's Club. Anna never married, reputedly because of the shame of her sister's marital scandal. As one biographer puts it, she chose to "eschew traditional women's roles" in favor of being what would later be called a "liberated woman."[8]

Pendleton's name and political track record were good enough to get his party's nomination for mayor of Fort Worth in 1890. It did not hurt that brother George was being talked up as the next lieutenant governor of Texas. Pendleton steamrolled his opponents rather easily. He was a dynamic orator, able to speak in a "fair, manly and forcible way" on the issues. He had no trouble beating out William J. Bailey, a pioneering developer, as the nominee of the city's Democratic Executive Committee, which gave him the right to face incumbent Dr. Hiram S. Broiles, who as an independent lacked strong party backing. He shrewdly cast himself as a "liberal progressive" with one foot in the business camp and one foot in the workingman's camp. On the stump he said it was "not his own desires but circumstances that impelled him to make the race." The crowds loved a reluctant candidate who only entered the race to throw the (incumbent) rascals out. And he certainly benefited from what happened in the middle of the race. On the night of March 29 his 22-month-old son, George Maurice, died after a long illness. The next day, as he was preparing to give a campaign speech on the corner of Main and Twelfth, someone interrupted the event to deliver the breathless news that his son was dead. The whole thing seems staged, and if so it had the desired effect. The personal tragedy got him the sympathy vote, which helps explain why he won by 705 votes, a margin of victory that "even his most sanguine friends did not anticipate." Otherwise, it was the quietest city election anyone could remember. Taking office on April 8, he admitted he did not know much about "the affairs of the city" but said he had studied the subject since his election and come to the conclusion that "they are really complicated." At his first press conference he spoke in vague generalities about fixing the waterworks and the sewer system and building a new city hall "as good as any of our neighbors." His term of office was off to a good start. The Democrats had recaptured city government, the city was in good financial shape, and the mayor was seemingly a man of the people.[9]

But Pendleton had a dirty little secret that not even his wife or law partners knew about. The 41-year-old husband and father had been carrying on an affair for nearly two years with a girl young enough to be his daughter. As a New York newspaper later commented, "How two persons in such widely different walks of life and positions in the social scale became acquainted is interesting." His wandering eye, sense of entitlement, and the stars aligning brought the affair on. Pendleton's law office was on the second floor of the First National Bank (corner of Houston and Second), which also happened to be the home of the Erie Telephone Exchange on the third floor.

Nineteen-year-old Adelaide G. Cullen was a "telephone exchange girl" whose job was connecting callers to the phone numbers they wanted to reach. She caught his attention as she passed up and down the stairs. He was immediately smitten with the "Telephone Venus" as one Dallas newspaper cheekily described her. Addie, as friends and family knew her, was a simple country girl blessed with the kind of face and body that make men forget themselves. Born in Natchez, Mississippi, in 1871, she was the youngest of five sisters in a large Catholic family. While her sisters went to work in the cotton mills, the beautiful Addie did not have to do such physical labor. After her father died, her mother, Anna, and three of the girls, including Addie, moved to Fort Worth, perhaps following sister Elizabeth, who had married Fort Worth grocer W. F. Fanning. Addie, Stella, and Katie all got jobs as telephone operators, which was good employment at the time for young, unmarried girls. But Addie was the golden child. Her "beautiful features and magnificently developed form" were her ticket to a better life. She was said to be "the handsomest girl in Fort Worth." Pendleton seems to have been her first beau; until she met him, she was "above reproach." He came into her life in 1888. Love blossomed, turning into obsession on his side. He began writing her letters—almost one a day—and then dropping by the house at 1507 Main where she lived with her mother and three sisters. Though Mrs. Cullen and Katie did not approve, Addie was flattered by the attentions of the older, distinguished gentleman. Her family acted as chaperones during his visits.[10]

According to Elizabeth (Mrs. Fanning), who of all the family members was closest to Addie, the couple were never left alone together. After the affair went public later, she insisted, "Addie was as pure and innocent as any girl that ever lived, and if she was ever alone one hour with Pendleton before her marriage, I do not know it." For his part, he pledged undying love to the girl, promising to give up everything for her. He told her family that his relations with his wife were "not happy," though he admired her "character and virtue." They had "slept apart" for months, he said, and agreed on a separation. All the while Pendleton continued playing the role of the dutiful husband at home. Lizzie gave birth to their fifth child in 1887.[11]

After more than a year of secret courting, Pendleton was nearly crazy with unrequited desire. He spent more and more time away from Lizzie and the children. In July 1889 he left town, telling her that he was going on a business trip to "form a company for promoting some new patent." He stayed gone for months, not returning until just before Christmas. While in New York City he secured the services of W. D. Hughes & P. H. Campbell, divorce lawyers. They told him they could get him a quick divorce in Illinois for $265 paid upfront. He believed a trip to Chicago and a short stay there would get it done. When he got back to Fort Worth, he told Addie he had gotten the divorce on the grounds of "incompatibility of temper" and showed her the paperwork to prove it ("Court Doc. No. 123,624, William S. Pendleton vs. Lizzie B. Pendleton"). He then tried to get her to marry him immediately. He approached St. Patrick's Father Guyot about doing a Catholic ceremony but was turned down flatly. Pendleton told Lizzie nothing, and they continued to live as husband and wife for the next seven months. In the meantime, little George Maurice took sick. That spring he busied himself with his mayoral campaign, stealing time whenever he could to be with Addie.[12]

Things finally came to a head that summer in what would become known all over the country as the "Pendleton Scandal," "the Pendleton Affair," and "Fort Worth Sensation." The instigator of all this uproar moved into city hall and commenced his duties as mayor of Fort Worth in April. But his mind was not on civic matters. Dear sweet Addie was all he could think about. He gave her expensive gifts, including a gold watch and a diamond pin, the sort of things a poor working-class girl from Mississippi could never have dreamed of owning. In the beginning of July Mrs. Cullen packed Addie off to Natchez, Mississippi, hoping the time away would bring the girl to her senses. But sister Elizabeth, Addie, and Pendleton had something else in mind: a secret rendezvous in New Orleans to tie the knot. Then, he assured her, they would come back to Fort Worth, and she would "assume her position at the head of his house." Pendleton sent Lizzie and the children off to visit relatives in Kentucky for her "health." She had never fully recovered her health from the distress of losing their youngest in March, and Pendleton was not providing much comfort. He lovingly kissed them good-bye at the station. As soon as they were gone, he got a leave of absence from the city council, ostensibly to go to Corpus Christi to "recuperate his energies" at the seashore. Instead, he met up with Addie and sister Elizabeth in New Orleans, where the two lovers were married before a justice of the peace with Elizabeth as witness. Addie had brought along her trousseau for the expected honeymoon. The next day, July 5, he wrote a letter to Mrs. Cullen addressing her as "Dear Mother" and informing her that he and Addie were married. He hoped she would understand. Anna Cullen wasted no time sharing the news around Fort Worth. This was the first most people knew of the affair.[13]

When word got out, everyone from city fathers to bartenders and boot-blacks was talking about it. Most professed to be outraged. Many knew the Pendletons personally. Fort Worth was still small enough that people were used to seeing "Hizzoner" on the street. He was not some remote politician in the capital. Fortunately for Lizzie Pendleton, she was not around to be harassed by reporters, but they soon learned of her whereabouts and fired off a tele-gram which caught up with her in Jonesboro, Tennessee, where she had gone to visit a longtime friend. The local news hounds skipped the niceties and got right to the point: "Do you know your husband has secured a divorce from you and is remarried to Addie Cullen?" She told them she was totally ignorant of everything, a response they wired back to Fort Worth, where it was printed in the papers. They described her variously as a "sweet-faced little woman" and a "delicate little woman dressed in black and heavily veiled." She responded to their hectoring questions by bursting into tears.[14]

Newspapers in Dallas and Fort Worth had jumped on the story as soon as the word got out, the Dallas newspapers with more enthusiasm. Almost as quickly it went out over the Associated Press and United Press wire services. Fort Worth was still recovering from the disastrous Spring Palace fire of May 30, but this pushed that out of the news. Newspapers from New York to California and everywhere in between related the story of the "Fort Worth Sensation." Other newspapers took a Fort Worth or Dallas story and rewrote it to a greater or lesser extent to fit the space allotted and the priority assigned to it. Newspaper editors even then knew that sex sells. At home the consen-sus seemed to be that Fort Worth's mayor had "sacrificed everything for love," in the process committing "political suicide." He was finished in Fort Worth. Friends wondered how he could "throw his honor to the wind." The *Dallas Morning News* opined gleefully that the man who had been untouched by "defeat" before had fallen victim to a "fatal infatuation." For his part,

Pendleton asserted to a New Orleans reporter that he did not believe he was "guilty of any wrong in assuming his new marital relations."[15]

The perspective of the various newspapers was wholly male because their editors and reporters were male, as were the members of city government and Pendleton's law firm that were interviewed. The *Dallas Times-Herald* focused on "Pendleton's Plight" over Lizzie's or even Addie's. His friend and law partner, Henry Chapman, would only admit that Pendleton "may have been indiscreet in paying attentions [*sic*] to the young lady." Their misogynist focus also explains the grudging admiration that was felt at all the "obstacles" he had overcome to achieve his heart's desire. Even after the full story broke, his friends continued to "sympathize" with him as much as they did Lizzie. Such sentiments were not going to save his political career, however. Thirty-one of the Fort Worth's most prominent citizens went on record calling for a public meeting at the courthouse to discuss "impeachment." Those who crowded into the courtroom that night got an update on the situation as it then stood. Pendleton had secured an illegal divorce eleven months prior, then came home and resided with his wife while making plans to marry his lover. Before the evening was over, a series of resolutions were adopted condemning Pendleton in the strongest terms and demanding that he resign or face formal charges. The thought was expressed in Fort Worth and elsewhere that the mayor had lost his mind, delicately termed "an aberration of intellect."[16]

Rumors had the newlyweds headed off to Niagara Falls on their honeymoon. It was widely believed Pendleton would not dare show his face in Fort Worth again. Some newspapers also suggested that they were in upstate New York not for the scenic falls but because of the nearness of the Canadian border, just in case the law came after the runaway mayor. In Fort Worth a few voiced doubts about the validity of his Chicago divorce, but their voices were drowned out by the expressions of outrage and sympathy for Lizzie Pendleton.[17]

Meanwhile, Pendleton's story was already falling apart. Reporters who reached out to Chicago found out there was no divorce decree for Pendleton vs. Pendleton. Perhaps he had filed for divorce under an alias? "Colonel" Robert McCart, distinguished lawyer and public figure, set off to Chicago on

July 12 to look into it. Three days later he wired the results of his investigation back to his law partners in Fort Worth. It would have been impossible for Pendleton to secure a divorce in Chicago when he said he did because Illinois law required a year's residence before one could file for divorce. That simple fact made Pendleton not only a liar and a scoundrel but also a bigamist if indeed he had married Addie Cullen. Early on, public opinion was divided between those who believed the worst and those who thought it was all just ugly gossip spread by the mayor's enemies. Newspapers addressed columns of newsprint to "unraveling the plot." Within a week, however, public opinion had turned totally against him. The *Dallas Times-Herald* printed a scathing editorial calling him "a forger and a bigamist" and Addie "a miserable dupe." Even his brother, George C. Pendleton, denounced him. The talk was not just of kicking him out of office but of prosecuting him.[18]

The Pendletons cut their honeymoon short after they got word of the outrage back home. They returned to New Orleans on July 16, registering at the Denechaud Hotel as "W. Pendleton and wife, Mississippi." Reporters dogged their every step, fascinated not just by the juicy scandal but also by the lady in question. They described her as "a strikingly beautiful woman with bright blue eyes and a wealth of rich brown hair . . . tall and stately, of fine figure and very ladylike in appearance." Pendleton announced he would leave for Fort Worth immediately to clear his name. New Orleans detectives also kept an eye on him and notified the Fort Worth authorities that he was in town. They were prepared to arrest him if they received a warrant. Pendleton wanted to send Addie to Natchez, Mississippi, but she insisted on going back to Fort Worth with him to face the music. Instead, on the eighteenth he put her on a train to Fort Worth, kissing her goodbye and pressing four hundred dollars into her hand. He assured her he would join her there as soon as it was safe. In the meantime, he would be staying with friends "somewhere on the Gulf coast." But that was not what he did. On the nineteenth he took a night train for Chicago to get to the bottom of his fraudulent divorce. A few days later he wired his New Orleans hotel to forward his mail to No. 319 Michigan Avenue, Chicago. While the newshounds continued to follow his movements, there is no indication Addie had any idea where her paramour was.[19]

What Pendleton did not tell reporters in New Orleans and maybe not Addie was that he had already submitted a letter of resignation. While the couple was honeymooning, he sent a telegram from Buffalo, New York on July 14 to "the Honorable City Council of the City of Fort Worth." He got right to the point.

> Gentlemen:
> I herewith tender my resignation as Mayor, to take effect immediately.

The news of his decision did not break until July 19, by which time it was out of his hands. He also wrote a letter to longtime friend and political ally M. B. Loyd asking him to close out all his financial affairs, including paying off his debts and making arrangements for "Belle and the children."[20]

It was about the same time that Lizzie for the first time revealed that she had known long before July that her husband was having an affair. As she related it, "one Sunday afternoon" in March she had "accidentally" come across some damning papers in her husband's coat pocket. They included a new will with Addie named as the beneficiary and some saccharine notes between them. She kept only the will and one note, but Pendleton found out she had them and forced her to give them back, at the point of a gun she said. Then he broke down crying and said he no longer loved her, adding he "did not love any woman." She begged him to break off the affair, and he begged her for a separation. Neither got what they wanted. When she subsequently announced her trip to Kentucky, he tried to persuade her to stay there, but she refused, setting up the donnybrook when they were all back in Fort Worth.[21]

The principals were all coming together for the first time. Lizzie Pendleton and her children arrived in Fort Worth by train on the night of July 17. She was met at the station by her brother-in-law (George Pendleton) and her brother (John M. Shelton), who escorted her and the children home. There she and the children remained in seclusion, a "broken-hearted woman." In the weeks following she was seen on the street only once, when called to testify before the grand jury investigating her husband. Addie arrived from New Orleans on July 19 to be met by her sister and driven to their mother's home. She did not leave "the yard" thereafter except to put in an appearance before the grand jury, not on the same day as Lizzie. Reporters would not leave her alone. To them she expressed shock that her marriage was a fraud, but beyond that she would not say what she intended to do. Elizabeth Fanning went further, threatening to instigate legal action against all the newspapers that had been printing scurrilous lies about her sister. On July 20 Lizzie commenced divorce proceedings, charging adultery and naming Addie Cullen as the co-respondent. Her petition asked for alimony and "proper" division of all assets. The bad news for Pendleton was coming fast and furious now. Mrs. Cullen and Elizabeth Fanning stood squarely between him and Addie, and since the council had removed him from office on July 9, his return to Fort Worth would only be for damage control and a possible divorce court appearance. Through friends Pendleton attributed his divorce debacle to being flimflammed by one of New York's notorious "divorce mills." He was a victim as much as Addie, he claimed.[22]

As of July 9, Fort Worth was short one mayor. Councilman J. P. Nicks served as mayor pro tem until a special election could be held on August 4. John Peter Smith's name was entered in the race, and no one knew of any scandals on his record. Other newspapers in the state lauded him as "the Moses who will lead Fort Worth out of the wilderness" and save it from the "flesh pots" of sin. His opponent was the same man Pendleton had defeated in April, Hiram S. Broiles. The *Fort Worth Gazette* editorialized before the vote that Smith was "as sure to be the next mayor as that the sun will set on the day of the election." No surprise, Smith won.[23]

The last loose end to be tied up was Lizzie's divorce. It was finalized in October in Judge R. E. Beckham's court, but only after deeds transferring property had been recorded in county court. By the terms of the divorce decree, she received all property "in and near Fort Worth," including their home on W. Seventh. He kept all accounts for his law practice and his stock and patent holdings. Describing the final settlement, the *Dallas Morning News* referred to her as "Mrs. W. S. Pendleton proper" and Addie as "Addie Cullen-Pendleton." All financial arrangements agreed to beforehand were entered, and Lizzie got custody of the children. The newspaper added that now the odd couple were free to get married.[24]

Neither principal was at court. They left matters to their attorneys, J. Y. Hogsett for Lizzie and Henry Chapman for Pendleton. Elizabeth Fanning was also present, still claiming to be looking out for little sister's interests. She testified to being a witness to their marriage in New Orleans, which was another strike against Pendleton, making him a certified bigamist since his Chicago divorce did not count. On the street it was rumored that Pendleton had been "dodging in and out of Fort Worth in disguise" and had asked Addie to meet him at a Dallas hotel. Elizabeth vehemently denied those rumors while admitting that Addie heard from him "daily."[25]

Once the divorce was finalized, the people of Fort Worth were "inclined to let the whole matter drop." There were so many other things to focus on: the new electrified street railway, the new packing plant, planning for a new city hall, and talk of a second Spring Palace season. The Pendleton affair may have been settled, but it would not soon be forgotten. The *Laredo Times* summed up the impact of the scandal with this: "Never before has any affair so taken hold of the people of this city."[26]

On Sunday, October 19, Addie Cullen left Fort Worth for good, taking a train for St. Louis, where she was reportedly to meet up with Pendleton. After that they headed to New York, where he had his law practice she said. A crowd of citizens gathered at the station to see her off, including reporters. The lady was still a big news story. They fired questions at her hoping to get enough for one more column and even made note of what she was wearing.[27]

As it turned out, Pendleton had no intention of settling in New York. The principal reason he was there was to file charges of fraud, forgery, and a few other crimes against lawyers W. D. Hughes and P. H. Campbell. He also wanted back the $265 he had paid them. He vowed he would see them go to prison. While he and Addie were there, they tied the knot again, going to Jersey City, New Jersey, on October 22. This time their marriage took.[28]

It is unclear how long they stayed in the east, but William and Addie settled in Shawnee, Oklahoma Territory, where he reinvented himself as an upstanding lawyer and jurist. They never had children but remained married until her death on June 25, 1906, following a long illness. She was just 35 years old. One local newspaper praised her as "a lady of splendid attainments and great personal beauty" whom her husband "worshipped." Another called her "a pure, high-minded and highly accomplished Southern lady" and said, "None was more highly esteemed nor more deserving of the universal affection with which she was regarded." Pendleton was with her right to the end. She received a proper Catholic funeral and interment in sacred ground. Nobody remembered the Addie Cullen of Fort Worth.[29]

Pendleton was not the kind of man to live alone for long. On October 20, 1907, he married for the third time, not counting the bogus first marriage to Addie. This time the lucky woman was Miss Rosa Prather of Shawnee, Oklahoma Territory. Curiously, her middle name was Addie. She was also the same age, 19, as the first Addie when he legally married her. The 45-year-old judge needed the permission of her father, Samuel Prather, to wed the girl. Rosa moved into his house in Shawnee. The marriage did not take; they were divorced sometime before 1920. He spent the last thirteen plus years of his life living alone.[30]

Putting the past behind him, Pendleton became a "political power" during Oklahoma's territorial days. He was there when Oklahoma became a state in 1907 and wielded power for many years thereafter. He died on March 22, 1933, at home. His Oklahoma obituaries barely mentioned his public service in Fort Worth so many years earlier. Oklahomans remembered him as a "pioneer Shawnee lawyer" and the Pottawatomie County judge who served longer than any other in the county's history. (He was defeated in his last race in 1929.) It is doubtful if anyone knew of the forty-year-old scandal that drove him from Fort Worth. No one had been more upright than Judge Pendleton since coming to Oklahoma. His past was so nebulous the newspapers were not even sure of his age; they guessed 86 or 88. He was 85. One obituary mentioned that he was survived by a sister and a son, both living in Fort Worth. Another spoke of a daughter, "Mrs. K[hleber] M. Van Zandt, Jr. of Fort Worth." It seems no Fort Worth relatives were interested in being identified with him. His passing was barely noted in the city's news-papers, probably out of respect for their feelings. It only rated perfunctory mention near the bottom of page 10 in the *Star-Telegram*, right above an ad for BC headache powders. A black sheep in Fort Worth and headache to city fathers, a model citizen in Oklahoma! The *Dallas Morning News* may have seen the irony, reporting his death on page 1. His third wife, Rosa, remarried and died in Muskogee, Oklahoma, on January 31, 1966.[31]

Lizzie kept her married name after the divorce. She also continued to live in Fort Worth because her family was there, and that was the only home she had known for most of her life. She occupied their house at W. Seventh and Cherry for years until moving into a boarding house at 618 W. Seventh. She was known to the people of Fort Worth only as Mrs. Pendleton or Belle to her friends. The details of her solitary status were not discussed in polite company, and in the 1910 Census she described herself as "widowed."[32]

Lizzie Belle Pendleton died on August 15, 1911. She was 56 years old, and her death, like her marriage, was a tragedy. She had gone to visit her son Herbert in Shamrock, Texas. At Sunday supper they ate some bad canned goods, and she died of ptomaine poisoning two days later. The body was shipped back to Fort Worth for interment, and her funeral was held on Thursday, August 17. Her obituary said nothing about her marriage to William Pendleton, only that she was "a member of one of Fort Worth's pioneer families." She lies in Oakwood Cemetery today.[33]

Chapter 21

Sammie Howard
Undercover Policewoman, Pioneering Feminist

Sammie Howard was a pioneering feminist before feminism was a cause. She did not march for the right to vote or carry a picket sign, and she did not burn her bra. Her vehicle of choice for making her statement was law enforcement. She went to work for the Fort Worth Police Department at a time when "policewoman" meant the "matron" in charge of women and juvenile in the jail. Jail matrons seldom if ever ventured onto the mean streets of the city. Sammie Howard was different. She was described in the press as a "detective" working undercover for the FWPD. She was only on the job a couple of years before moving on. No longer a curiosity, she dropped out of the public consciousness. In our modern era that cries out for nontraditional heroes, it is time to rescue Sammie Howard from undeserved obscurity.

She was born Sammie Ezell Howard on August 7, 1889, to Robert H. and Willie C. Howard in Logan, Arkansas. She was the second of five children. Clyde preceded her in 1885; Roena, Jeanette, and John followed between 1893 and 1899. Sammie does not seem to have been short for Samantha—no surprise, perhaps, since her mother was named Willie (known to friends and family as "Pinkie"). Her father was a teacher-turned-evangelist who heard "the call" in 1874 and joined the Church of Christ. The next several years were spent moving from one small rural church to another, taking him from

Callahan County, Texas, to Logan, Arkansas. In 1889 he came back to Texas and entered business to support his growing family. Then about 1899 he became pulpit minister at a small Church of Christ in Snyder, Scurry County, Texas, 229 miles west of Fort Worth. In the next few years, he would uproot his family again to take the pulpit in a church in Stephenville, Erath County, sixty-three miles south of Fort Worth.[1]

Daughter Sammie had bigger ambitions than being a wife and mother. She may have been inspired growing up by stories of New York journalist Nellie Bly, who achieved fame for her undercover reporting and being the first woman to go around the world in shorter time than Jules Verne's fictional Phileas Fogg. Her father saw to it that she had a good education in both academics and practical things. She went to nursing school, where she earned a diploma and also learned stenography and bookkeeping. And she was athletic enough to do high kicks. She was a Renaissance woman for her day. Yet when it came time to picking a career, she chose teaching, living like a proper maiden schoolmarm with her parents in Stephenville, employed in the local school. In 1913, when Robert Howard took the pulpit of a Church of Christ in Mannsville, Oklahoma, Sammie stayed behind. She was 24 years old when she took a teaching job in Lipan, Texas, sixty miles southwest of Fort Worth. Next, she took a teaching job in Huckabay, seventy-four miles southwest of Fort Worth. No longer living under her father's roof, she began to think about the world beyond small-town schoolrooms. Fort Worth was the nearest big city, and to Fort Worth she moved, but not to teach.[2]

She moved into a proper boarding house (614 Taylor Street) and went looking for work. In November 1914 the law firm of Mays & Mays hired her. Brothers Charles and William Mays had founded the firm in 1911, and by 1914 they were among the most respected criminal defense lawyers in Fort Worth. Women working undercover was nothing new. Department stores had used them for years to catch shoplifters, though it was always left to male officers to make the actual arrest. The only woman with the FWPD was Mrs. Ollie Hargrave, the police matron at the city lockup.[3]

Sammie's first assignment was to infiltrate the city's vice operations. It was one of the senior partners who "suggested" she don male clothing to pose as a 16-year-old boy so that she could "mix with a certain crowd in town" on a

Friday night. Exactly what "crowd" they had in mind was not specified, but it was clear she was going undercover. We are left to wonder what vital information a teenage boy might have gathered, but she accepted the challenge. This was a far different world than anything she had experienced as a member of Reverend Howard's family. It is nearly impossible to believe he would have approved of his daughter's chosen field She pulled on trousers and a man's shirt and donned a wig bought at a five-and-dime store. Then she sallied forth. Her undercover disguise must not have been too convincing because on the way out of the house, the housekeeper cast a disapproving eye at her and said, "You'd better be careful, little girl." She did not go alone. She had taken the precaution of asking fellow boarder W. L. Thayer to accompany her. On their way down Seventh Street, she attracted stares from passersby. A pair of girls spied her, and one blurted out, "What a small, delicate little man that is!" Replied the other, "That's not a man; that's a girl!" Others turned and simply stared as she passed. She felt completely crushed but kept on, thinking the ugly wig was the giveaway. She asked Thayer if he knew of a quiet, out-of-the way barber shop where she could get her hair chopped off. He took her to one on Main near Second, and she told the barber to make her look like a boy. He was just finishing up when Fort Worth detectives came in. They took her and Thayer into custody and hustled them off to headquarters. Thayer was quickly released after explaining that he was only a friend to the girl. She had to wait until Mays & Mays posted her two-hundred-dollar bond.[4]

She did not know it at the time—although Mays & Mays should have known—but it was against the law for a person to dress "in drag" as we say today. In Sammie's case that meant wearing men's clothes, specifically trousers and a shirt as opposed to a dress or skirt and shirtwaist. On her way down the street, someone had called the police to report her, and detectives tracked her to the barber shop. The law she was breaking was not a mere Fort Worth city ordinance but the law all over the country. Two years later, when sisters Augusta and Adeline Van Buren traveled cross country on motorcycles, they were repeatedly arrested along the way for wearing khaki leggings and leather riding breeches, which were considered men's clothing. The newspapers criticized them mercilessly for supposedly trying to escape their lives as housewives to become bohemians.[5]

Miss Sammie Howard's 1914 *Star-Telegram* photo that made her a public figure. Author's collection.

After October 10 everybody knew who Sammie Howard was. With her cover blown, it was doubtful she could be an effective undercover agent in the future, but that did not prevent her from giving interviews and posing for pictures. The former small-town schoolteacher was not shy about offering her professional opinions to anyone who would listen, and since she was news, there were plenty of reporters willing to listen. She predicted the "female city detective" would be the next innovation in law enforcement. She acknowledged male resistance to the idea but said it was bound to happen "sooner or later." She went so far as to say "the woman is superior to the man" for undercover work, explaining that the woman was less likely to be made as a police officer. She added women also brought "finesse" to the job and were therefore more likely to win the confidence of the criminal subject. "Imagine," she said, "sending a big policeman out to investigate a society robbery." Her audience of male reporters nodded in rapt agreement, scribbling in their notebooks as she concluded, "These are delicate jobs which must be handled by women." She did offer one caveat: any girl wanting to enter the law enforcement profession must be able to handle any situation she might find herself in.[6]

Sammie was also a quick study. Somewhere between the classroom and Fort Worth, she learned what it takes to be a detective. She knew the proper way to tail a man on the street: follow him from the other side of the street. Tailing a woman was even easier. Whereas a woman would quickly catch a strange man eying her even from across the street, she would never suspect a girl was tailing her. Even if a woman suspect noticed her, all she would see were clothes, complexion, and hairstyle.[7]

Mays & Mays were impressed enough to keep her on as their only female operative. They gave her non-dangerous cases "to work up," befitting her gender and tender age. Those included a divorce case and a personal injury lawsuit. She was especially proud of her work on the divorce case. The husband filed for divorce after the couple had been separated for a time. He wanted custody of the two children but knew courts almost invariably awarded custody to the mother. Enter detective Sammie. She wormed her way into the woman's confidence and learned she was a "drug fiend" and intimately involved with another man. She revealed the information to the surprised husband and bragged that surely the court would give custody of the children to him. Yet another case sent her to Oklahoma "in search of a lost daughter." She found the girl performing in a stock stage company and ingratiated herself into the chorus. She finally revealed herself to the girl and brought her back home.[8]

None of these cases involved risky undercover work, which she would have accepted without hesitation. But the Victorian code of male honor kept her bosses from putting the lady in any kind of danger or dubious situations. She was able to keep her feminine appearance on the job and use her feminine wiles to make cases beyond the confines of the office.

Sammie's biggest case came in November 1914, when Mays & Mays had her infiltrate a white slavery ring (human trafficking) operating in Fort Worth run by a couple calling themselves Professor Robert Lustress and Madame Zella Warsaw. They were recruiting girls to work the Panama-Pacific International Exposition (a.k.a. World's Fair) in San Francisco, opening in 1915. They advertised in the newspaper for girls who believed in spiritualism and wanted to travel. The advertisement promised the girls fifty dollars a week. The authorities got a tip when they detained a 16-year-old Fort Worth girl who had answered the ad. Sammie may still have been working for Mays & Mays, but on this case she worked with county and city officers, posing as a young girl named Mabel Hammond looking for adventure and spiritual awakening. Likely the only reason she used a cover name was because most of Fort Worth by this time knew the name Sammie Howard. She had certainly been in the papers often enough. City probation officer Sam Calloway asked her to go to the professor and Madame Warsaw's "studio" posing as the girl answering the ad. Over the course of four visits, she won their confidence and gathered information on their operation. On her fourth visit she took along six officers as backup, and they placed the professor under arrest. He was subsequently convicted of pandering and sentenced to forty-five years in prison.[9]

Sammie was back in action a couple of weeks later, again working with county and city officers. Her job this time was to get close to a suspect and get him to incriminate himself. How she did that was up to her. As with Professor Lustress, her target was a Black man running a vice operation. Apparently, the authorities believed such perps were more likely to open up to a white girl than

Sammie helped bust a sex-trafficking ring connected to the 1915 Panama-Pacific Exposition (postcard). Author's collection.

anyone else, a line of thought based on the racial stereotype that Black men were especially lustful for white girls. Neither the authorities nor Mays & Mays would have put her in a dangerous situation with violent criminals, but apparently sex fiends were okay. She was sent to the shoe shop of 50-year-old W. R. Pearson at 1211 St. Louis Avenue, said to be a front for a "disorderly house" (bordello). She went disguised as a schoolgirl from the nearby high school, complete with "curls, dimples, wind-bitten cheeks, and an innocent smile." For her costume she donned a little-girl frock that stopped three inches above her ankles, carried her shoes under her arm, and held a schoolbook dangling from a strap over her shoulder. Sammie must have been quite an actress because the 25-year-old did not arouse the proprietor's suspicions. She left her shoes to be repaired and promised to come back to pick them up in two days. The newspaper does not report what they said to each other, but when she returned later she brought four officers who arrested Pearson and charged him with running a disorderly house.[10]

The authorities were delighted to have her assistance, but nothing was said about hiring her full-time. Truth be told, most male officers of her day would not have accepted working with a woman any more than with a Black or Hispanic officer. In their minds there were just two kinds of women— ladies and all the rest—and no lady would be caught dead in the environments Sammie was asked to investigate.

Sammie was so sold on the life of the independent, career woman that she tried to dissuade her sister Jeanette from walking down the aisle. Sister had come down from Oklahoma for a visit and caught the eye of Alexander George, whose only negative to observers was that he was Greek. She went so far as to call up the county clerk's office to try to prevent the issuance of a marriage license. She failed, and the girls' parents in Mannsville, Oklahoma, were notified after the fact. It was the only significant failure on Sammie's record so far.[11]

Despite her talents for detective work and her independent spirit, Sammie did not see undercover work as a longtime career. She had been raised in a conservative, God-fearing household where a girl's highest calling was marriage and a family. As the *Star-Telegram* quaintly put such things, "Cupid finally caught her." She married fireman Dudley M. Culley of El Paso sometime before 1920 but kept her hand in teaching. In 1920 she obtained a US passport to go to Mexico to teach. When Dudley passed away in 1926, she resumed her unattached life, working as a practical nurse and an elementary school teacher in Texas and New Mexico. She eventually moved to Oregon, where she met and married Claude T. Springs on April 24, 1937. He was a barber by trade and ten years her junior. They moved to California in 1939, where she operated the Springs Resort Home in Sonora. Sammie Springs died in the hospital at Sonora on January 25, 1971, following a long illness. She was 81 years old. She was buried in Mt. Shadow Cemetery. Claude outlived her by another ten years. She never had any children by either husband. Of her other family members, the only ones still alive were sisters, Roena and Jeanette, both in Oklahoma.[12]

Sammie Ezell Howard was a remarkable woman for several reasons. We might see her as a preacher's kid who went out into the world and found a calling that allowed her to break away from her strict upbringing. But she was far more. She found her niche as an undercover detective and worked the streets of Fort Worth without ever going over to the dark side. She remained a lady in a tough profession.

From 1930 on Nancy Drew was a literary phenomenon that thrilled millions of girl readers. She could have been Sammie Howard only with a car and better clothes! Author's collection.

She was the first woman to operate on the street in Fort Worth law enforcement. She was also ahead of her time in using the media of her day—newspapers—to her advantage. After her first arrest for breaking the law against wearing men's clothes, she called a press conference, describing herself as "a detective who usually gets what I go after." That was sheer blarney since this was her first undercover job, and she was arrested after barely getting out of the house. She did not stop there either: "I didn't mean this as a wrong, although I know it isn't good looking for a woman to go about in man's attire. You see, it was a matter of business with me. I meant no offense. I have a father and mother, and I love them so dearly that I would not wander so far into the paths of wrong. . . . There are lots of worse things that I could have done." Mentioning her parents while explaining she had no desire to offend was brilliant, as was referring to unspecified worse crimes she might have committed. She instantly won the hearts of the news reporters covering her story, who all happened to be male.[13]

Sammie's success as an unaccredited policewoman almost certainly influenced the FWPD to hire its first female police officer, Mrs. Emma Richardson, in April 1915. The department had used occasional female "volunteers" before and employed a woman as a jail matron, but Emma was the first to be commissioned a police officer.[14]

It is not too far-fetched to say Sammie could have been the prototype for famous fictional girl detective Nancy Drew, the creation of author Edward Stratemeyer in 1930. In the hugely popular series of juvenile books, Nancy was a teenager living at home with her father while solving crimes, but otherwise, she was a slightly younger version of Sammie Howard, with the same self-confidence, quick wits, and pluck. There is no indication that Stratemeyer or any of his numerous ghostwriters (under the name Carolyn Keene) had Sammie in mind when they wrote Nancy Drew, but Sammie's story made it into the newspapers and could have found its way to Stratemeyer and crew. If nothing else, Sammie's stated desire to see more girls grow up to be detectives was realized in the fictional Nancy Drew.

Chapter 22

Joseph Z. Wheat
The Man and His Building

I t is not very often that a building is more famous than the man it is named for. But that is the case with the Wheat Building. Also unusual is when the namesake owner insists that his name remain on the building forever, writing it into his will. That also describes the Wheat Building. Joseph Z. Wheat's namesake property was part of downtown Fort Worth history for more than half a century until it fell to the wrecking ball.

Joseph Zaharia Wheat was born in Columbia, Kentucky, on December 21, 1855, to Joseph Zaharia Sr. and Myra Ellen Smith Wheat. His father died when he was a child, and he and his mother had to move in with her family. He was too young to fight in the Civil War and lacked the education to go into the professions. He became just another restless postwar youth who had to go west to make his fortune. He left Kentucky sometime before 1880 to come to Texas, bringing with him a young wife, Virginia Sampson Wheat. He had married 19-year-old "Virgie" in Louisville, Kentucky, on March 31, 1882. They got off to an inauspicious start in the Lone Star state. His first job on record was working as a farmhand in Tarrant County. Later reports had him and Virgie living "briefly" in Cleburne before relocating to Fort Worth where the opportunities and social life were far greater in 1885.[1]

In Fort Worth the Wheats found a permanent home, though he strug-gled at first. He was unable to pay the rent on their first place, and they were evicted by court order. Things improved after that, and he brought his widowed mother to live with them in 1892. She died in Fort Worth seven years later and was buried in Oakwood Cemetery. Wheat quickly made friends among what one account calls "the most prominent businessmen of the city." One of those who was not a friend was saloon man Charles Scheuber, who took him to court over some division of "personal property," which suggests some kind of joint investment. He began life in the big city on a small scale as proprietor of the Lindell Hotel on the courthouse square. He did his socializing in the town's saloons. Virgie took up with a different group of folks, becoming an active member of First Baptist Church.[2]

Wheat did not spend long behind the desk of a hotel. In the next decade he became a "sporting man," or what the 1900 census described more bluntly as a "gambler." "Sporting man" was how gentlemen gamblers described themselves. He did well enough that he was able to move his family into a nice house, where they threw a big fifth birthday party for their daughter, Rose Nell ("Nellie"), that was attended by children from some of the city's most respectable families. At the same time he retained friendships with other members of the gambling fraternity like Jake Johnson, Luke Short, and Frank Fossett. In 1900 Fossett was an escaped fugitive wanted for murder in Fort Worth. The two gamblers were close enough that Wheat went to El Paso on the train to help his fugitive friend, which got him crossways with Tarrant County Sheriff Sterling P. Clark.[3]

Wheat's efforts to recast himself as a respectable businessman were in conflict with his sporting persona. He owned the Stag Saloon (702 Main) and was a regular at the tables above the White Elephant Saloon. County Attorney O. S. Lattimore hauled him into court on a gambling charge, and he swore on the witness stand that he had "parted with his interest in the Stag Saloon." Subsequent events would show that Joe Wheat was still very much a sporting man. Still, he cultivated a respectable image. Many years later Virgie would describe her dearly departed husband as a "builder and real estate man." To the extent that was true, it was a sideline to his gambling interests. There is no known record of any real estate dealings before 1901. That was the year he acquired the empty building on the northwest corner of Eighth and Main for a song. That particular corner and the building on it have an interesting history all their own.[4]

The property began as the homestead of Thomas B. James, an early sheriff of Tarrant County (1869–1876) who came to town from Birdville when Fort Worth was still a clutch of rough buildings on the bluff and purchased it from E. M. Daggett. The wholesale dry goods firm of Sidney Martin and Joseph H. Brown purchased it from James and hired Fort Worth Loan and Construction Company in 1890 to build them a six-story building, which by Fort Worth standards was practically a skyscraper. Fort Worth was booming at the time thanks to the Texas Spring Palace (1889–1890) and new railroads coming to town. Martin-Brown was riding high, advertising regularly in the *Fort Worth Gazette*. They wanted a magnificent home for their booming dry goods company, which had been around a few years. They hired an architect and instructed him to spare no expense creating an "elegance of design and proportions." What they got was an old-fashioned Richardsonian Neo-Romanesque structure, a style named for American architect Henry Hobson Richardson. Its height, granite stonework, deeply recessed windows, rounded archways, and high stone steps made it a landmark on Main Street. The interior was not so impressive though it did have a birdcage safety elevator connecting all six floors. The contractor, Fort Worth Loan & Construction, had a track record of building grand structures, which included the Texas Spring Palace and Hurley office building. They spent between $90,000 and $100,000 on the work, extending easy-pay loans to the owners. Unfortunately, Joseph Brown died in October, and Martin could not pay construction costs, which meant Fort Worth Loan & Construction could not pay off their subcontractors, who were disagreeable enough to drag them into court. In the meantime, wholesale grocer Chas. A. Sandergard occupied the building, but he could not make a go of it when the financial panic of 1893 hit. Reportedly, he lost the building in a poker game to an unnamed cattleman who had no use for it and could not move it. Sometime in the late 1890s this white elephant was sold on the courthouse steps to Merchants' National Bank, which leased the ground floor to a grain exchange while they tried to unload it.[5]

The iconic Wheat Building (corner of Eighth and Main) with the Victoria Building next door, ca. 1925. The Wheat Building was a favorite subject of postcard makers, photographed from a variety of angles and distances. Gregory Dow Collection, Fort Worth, TX.

That is how Joe Wheat came to acquire the building in March 1901 for $40,000. One story has it that he won the purchase money "in a poker game at a cattleman's convention," which conflates the story of another transaction from an earlier time with Joe Wheat's involvement with the building. However he came by the purchase money, instead of trying to "flip" the building, he decided to turn it into prime real estate by remodeling the interior into an office space of seventy-five rooms. He spent upward of $50,000 transforming what had basically been a warehouse. Everything "save the walls and interior columns" was torn out and a steel frame added to the interior to support the soaring stone walls. This upgrade alone transformed it from a traditional stone building to skyscraper status. In addition, all the plumbing and wiring were redone, and fireplugs installed on every floor connecting to a five-thousand-gallon tank on the roof. He also added an artesian well in the basement for the pure water one could not get from the public water system. When he was finished, the Wheat Building was "the finest appointed building of the kind in the state of Texas."[6]

One of the first tenants was the "district headquarters" of the New York Life Insurance Company, which leased a "suite" of five rooms. To keep his building in the news, Wheat teased the public with hints that he was "figuring" to add two additional stories in the future. Those plans were purportedly driven by reports that Fort Worth National Bank was planning to erect a six-story building at Main and Fifth. "Skyscraper envy" was a real thing. Another blue-ribbon tenant was the St. Louis–San Francisco Railroad (a.k.a. the Frisco). They rented most of the fifth floor for their Fort Worth headquarters.[7]

The biggest makeover to the building was what he did with the roof. With other buildings the roof was a dead space, the location of the elevator machinery and a haven for birds. As the owner of the tallest building in Fort Worth, Wheat had something else in mind: a "roof garden" with restaurant and stage. It would be the first such venue west of the Mississippi. Such places were popular among the smart set in eastern cities where tall buildings were common. This was before air conditioning, so performance venues in the summer had a hard time attracting a crowd, no matter the entertainment. Cowtown's idea of a fancy night spot was the White Elephant Saloon or Greenwall's Opera House. A posh roof garden promised an elevated, breeze-cooled spot for Fort Worth society to gather on summer evenings. The elevator would whisk patrons up to the roof, where they would be greeted with potted palms and planter boxes. He installed a canopied stage, a full-service bar (requiring a liquor license), a soda fountain, and a first-class kitchen. By the time he was done, he had invested a small fortune.[8]

In the next couple of years, Wheat added another touch to attract nighttime fun seekers: a basement saloon that he named the Stag Annex, in effect franchising the name of a well-known watering hole that he may or may not have still had an interest in. In doing so he revealed his true colors; he was still a sporting man first and foremost. He was shrewd enough to use the Stag Saloon name, hoping to attract the same clientele. Businessman Wheat had an innate talent for marketing his properties. He advertised the Stag Annex as "not the cheapest, but the best" saloon in town with "fine wines, liquors and cigars." It was a "resort for gentlemen" like himself, which meant sporting gents. This latter was an important marketing ploy, because the Wheat building was right on the edge of Hell's Half-Acre, hardly known for classy venues. To get people to come to the south end of town, he had to draw a clear line between his establishment and the dives in the Acre. The basement saloon did not have even a single window to ventilate the place, but that did not keep him from advertising it as "the coolest place in the City"—more evidence of his marketing smarts. By adding another attraction (a saloon) to the Wheat Building, he hoped to draw the after-hours crowd that no other office building catered to. It was a novel business model by a born entrepreneur.[9]

The transformation of the Wheat Building inspired the owner of the Victoria building next door to add two more stories to its original two stories. Otho Houston, banker and cattleman, had recently purchased the building and did not want it to look like a low-rent wing of its towering neighbor. This would not be the last addition to the Victoria building. Two more stories were eventually added, bringing the structure up to six stories, with a magnificent capital topping it off. The Victoria building shared a common wall with the Wheat building that left them conjoined like Siamese twins.[10]

With its skyscraper height and fancy roof garden, the Wheat Building was the new showplace of Fort Worth. It got another distinction in 1904 when one of the first wireless telegraph transmission towers was erected on the roof. It was part of the American DeForest Wireless Telegraph system being installed around the country, first demonstrated at the Louisiana Purchase Exposition in St. Louis in April 1904. In Texas the first two sending-receiving stations went up that summer in Dallas and Fort Worth. The system was supposed to connect Fort Worth to St. Louis, New Orleans, and Memphis in the next two years. In the meantime, the installation of the tower atop the Wheat Building called for an open house attended by the bigwigs of both Fort Worth and Dallas.[11]

Fort Worth's first "rooftop terrace" had its opening season in the summer of 1902. When initially announcing it, Wheat had said he would offer "comic opera almost exclusively," an Italian import favored by sophisticates. What he actually put on was variety theater, a combination of musical and comedy acts that did not require fancy sets or high-class actors. Customers could enjoy their entertainment under the stars while imbibing the newly fashionable cocktails or a soft drink called Strawberry Betsy. Fort Worth society enjoyed being high above the hoi polloi on the hot, dusty streets below. The challenge was putting something on the stage night after night. It wasn't just the cost of booking acts; the show had to be good enough to please a discriminating clientele. To fill the bill, he put together his own stock company. Thus, Joseph Wheat found himself theater owner and manager both.[12]

Rooftop summer evenings in Fort Worth lasted just two seasons. Finicky Texas weather was not congenial to year-round rooftop gatherings. Gusty wind blew off hats and knocked over potted palms. On summer evenings the heat could be almost unbearable, and when a freak rainstorm blew in, everything stopped as customers ran for the stairs and the elevator. Another problem: rooftop terraces with their planter boxes and gravel paths were still an architectural novelty. Planter boxes were not properly sealed off from the offices below. Instead of water being channeled off the building as it was with traditional roofing, it accumulated beneath the planter boxes and walkways, ultimately soaking through to the ceilings below. The novelty of the terrace idea quickly wore off, and it staggered to the end of the season. That winter Wheat announced that he was putting an iron roof over his roof garden. He had lost several nights of revenue the first season because of rainy weather. He did not intend to have the same problem the next season.[13]

The cost of putting a roof over it and booking expenses finally doomed the roof garden. The 1903 season opened on May 4 without a roof and with most nights filled by his stock company. Admission was twenty or thirty cents, with a few seats down front for fifty cents, except customers could see variety acts in almost any saloon for free any night. The roof garden was a losing proposition. At the end of the 1903 season, he closed it down and tried to figure out a way to get some return on his investment. He decided his biggest asset was a "fully rehearsed and costumed" stock company with its own scenery. He would take them on the road. His tenure as manager of an acting troupe proved even shorter than as a theater empresario. The company closed in Smithfield, Texas, on Saturday night, October 24, and were back home the next day. He told a *Fort Worth Telegram* reporter, "I am out of the theatrical business," although whether he meant managing or owning or both is unclear. He added, "There may be money in the business, but I don't want any of it." He sold all the "scenery, seats, etc." of his roof garden-theater to the Sour Lake, Texas, group. His elegant rooftop terrace had turned out to be a white elephant, not a cash cow.[14]

He announced he was pulling the plug on it and planning to put a seventh floor on the building for office space. He did it up very nicely, matching the design and stonework of the original floors while also putting his imprint on the building by having his name carved into the space between the sixth and seventh floors: WHEAT BUILDING. He spent more than $15,000, including adding a restaurant to the basement with tile floor and marble wainscotting. Fortunately, he found a high-end tenant, the Santa Fe Railroad, to move in and filled up the other floors with a variety of attorneys, merchants, insurance companies, and a bank.[15]

Joe Wheat, sporting man, had arrived as a member of Fort Worth society. He was the respected businessman Virgie described years later as a "builder and real estate man." He was elected to the board of trade and was one of the first men in town to own an automobile when they were still a luxury toy for rich men to tool around in, joining fellow owners like Mayor Thomas Powell, councilman Bill Ward, and banker M. B. Loyd. He turned management of the Stag Annex over to Tom Dougherty. Still, the old gambler's instincts did not die easily. He continued to meet with his card-playing buddies for regular afternoon games of "jackpot poker" either over the Stag Saloon or at the Metropolitan Hotel just across the street from the Wheat Building. In March 1906 the friendly game was raided by sheriff's deputies. Ordinarily, such high-class games would have been immune from raids, but perhaps Sheriff John T. Honea, running for reelection, was trying to make points with the church set. Wheat and friends were arrested but did not spend any time in jail. Their arrest was a bigger blow to their reputations than to their pocketbooks. It would have been a bigger embarrassment to Virgie among her Baptist friends.[16]

Fortunately, she did not have to face them immediately. Joseph, Virgie, and their two daughters had moved to San Antonio in the fall of 1905 for "business reasons," though he retained extensive property holdings in Fort Worth. What was not generally known was that his health was failing. Besides suffering from diabetes, breathing had become difficult, and he had a hard time swallowing. He may have felt San Antonio had better medical facilities. He and Virgie spent the summer of 1906 in the east (seeing doctors?) and even visited Canada. They traveled in luxury because he could easily afford it. Perhaps seeing the end coming, he took out a life insurance policy for $100,000 and drew up his will. They passed through Fort Worth on the way back to San Antonio. Less than two weeks later he was rushed to the hospital in San Antonio suffering from pulmonary edema complicated by diabetes. He needed emergency surgery, and doctors operated on him the next day, Saturday, November 17. He died on November 20, 1905, just 51 years old. Fort Worth and Dallas newspapers both covered his passing. The news shocked his many friends, who had not known how sick he was. Virgie had the body shipped back to Fort Worth for the funeral service and interment. They had lived in Texas for more than twenty years, all but a few months of that in Fort Worth.[17]

Since they had sold their house with the intent to move permanently to San Antonio, the funeral service was held in the home of Robert B. Smith, husband of Joseph's Aunt Annie, a librettist of note. The tenants of the Wheat Building sent a magnificent floral arrangement. Interment was in Oakwood Cemetery in the same plot as his mother. Pallbearers included Fort Worth notables William Bryce and W. G. Garvey.

Virgie did not remain in Fort Worth after the funeral but returned to her home in San Antonio. She would come back to Fort Worth regularly in the years to come. Friends and real estate interests drew her back. The Wheat name continued to be newsworthy in Cowtown. When daughter Rose Nell married a San Antonio man in 1908, it was reported in Fort Worth.[18]

In Joe Wheat's will, dated July 31, 1905, he disposed of property holdings worth an estimated $150,000, entirely separate from his enormous life insurance policy. Though Virgie was named executrix, his property holdings, with one significant exception, were placed in the hands of three named trustees to be conducted "as they see fit," which presumably meant without any input from Virgie The big exception was the namesake Wheat Building, his pride and joy, now worth three times what he paid for it in 1901 and considered by many to be the finest building on Main Street. On it he placed a deed restriction that barred Virgie or her daughters from selling it "so long as they shall live," or from mortgaging it or "pledging it in any way." He directed it be maintained "as at present" with whatever income it earned divided, half to Virgie and one-quarter each to daughters Rose Nell and Virginia. The restrictions also extended to their husbands, present and future, and their children. Should either daughter die while the other was still alive, her portion would pass to her sister, and after their deaths to their children, and if they had no children to their mother. If Virgie died first, her portion would pass to her daughter(s). The children/grandchildren could do anything with it while any one of the three was still alive. Only after all three had died could the building be disposed of. These were the ironclad terms of Wheat's will, a man determined to control his building even from beyond the grave.[19]

Everything rocked along smoothly until 1935. Virgie, who proved to be no slouch in the real estate world, had acquired her own portfolio over the years, which brought her back to Fort Worth frequently. For their part, daughters Virginia Wheat Finley and Rose Nell Wheat Rowland were anxious to get out from under the "antiquated" building and put the property to more lucrative use. They brought suit in Forty-Eighth District Court to break the will, putting them at odds with their mother, who still counted the building in her portfolio. Their petition said the forty-year-old building was bringing in "diminishing revenues," and as a result they wanted to demolish it and put "a more modern office structure" on the site. Both sides hired lawyers, and the petition languished in court proceedings for the next four years. Finally, in 1939, Judge Robert Young granted their petition to break the will. He gave as legal reason to "protect the investment."[20]

In May 1940 the daughters returned to Judge Young's court for a permit to raze the old building, which stood defying both time and the owners' wishes. Two things complicated getting permission. For one, the building shared a wall with the Hickman building next door, which required securing

Top: Razing the Wheat Building in the name of progress, 1940. Author's collection.

Bottom: The John L. Ashe building went up on the former site of the Wheat Building. Author's collection.

the permission of its owner, Dr. C. A. Hickman. They got that by agreeing to pay for the demolition work on his building. The second complication was the family had not paid taxes on the building for eight years. The tax debt added up to more than $7,600. The petitioners had to borrow against any new construction to settle the tax lien, the largest tax settlement ever paid in Tarrant County up to that date. The Wheat Building finally came down that summer. One of its longest resident tenants, John L. Ashe men's store (tenant since 1927) built a new store on the empty lot that opened in October 1940.[21]

Virgie and her daughters felt no guilt over the fate of papa's building. They had never been emotionally connected to it the way Joe Wheat was. In 1942 she moved in with Rose Nell (Mrs. R. A. Rowland) at Weslaco, Texas, though still visiting Fort Worth and San Antonio regularly. She took to her bed in early 1958 and on July 12 passed away quietly in her sleep. She was 85 years old and had been faithful to Joseph's memory for more than forty years. The family brought her back to Fort Worth to be buried beside her husband in the town they had called home for twenty years.[22]

Joseph Wheat lived an enviable if too-short life, but he left Virgie comfortably fixed so she never had to worry about money. Wheat himself is still something of a mystery. For a man who was so prominent for more than twenty years, no photo of him is known to exist. Apparently, he managed to avoid the camera. The building is better remembered than the man! His idea of a roof garden also outlived him. Both the Westbrook Hotel and Hotel Texas created garden spots atop their buildings, to be enjoyed by Fort Worth society, not the hoi polloi.

If one believes in such things, the Wheat Building could be described as jinxed, not haunted but certainly with more than its share of bad luck. One of the partners who built it, Joseph Brown, died before it was completed. Several of the owners who followed could not make a go of it, letting it sink into bankruptcy to be sold on the courthouse steps. The new owner's fancy roof garden failed miserably, and while Joseph Wheat always considered it the jewel of his real estate portfolio, his tenants suffered from a string of tragic misfortunes, which included a rash of break-ins in 1908 when juvenile delinquents pried open desks and stole money. Seven years later a tenant fell to his death in the elevator shaft. The building's cranky 1890 elevator machinery frequently broke down, and owners refused to invest the money to replace it. On another occasion four years earlier, the cage dropped abruptly, injuring a woman inside who filed suit for her injuries. Finally, after the building's new owners took it off the family's hands, they unceremoniously kicked out all the tenants preparatory to razing it in 1940. By that time, Joseph Wheat's former pride and joy had become an eyesore, still standing tall on Main Street out of sheer orneriness.[23]

Chapter 23

Townes Van Zandt
Fort Worth's Troubled Troubadour

The list of musical celebrities who once called Fort Worth home, as we have already seen, includes such diverse talents as Willie Nelson, Van Cliburn, Delbert McClinton, John Nitzinger, and T Bone Burnett. Those are just the names the public recognizes. We should add to that list Townes Van Zandt, a singer-songwriter beloved as a country music legend but barely known by the nonmusical public.

John Townes Van Zandt was born in Fort Worth on March 7, 1944, to Harris W. and Dorothy Townes Van Zandt, which explains where he got his middle name. He came from a most distinguished Fort Worth bloodline. His great-uncle was Khleber Van Zandt (1836–1930), Civil War veteran, pioneer banker, and city builder. The Van Zandts were a large family with many children and grandchildren, amounting to a Fort Worth dynasty. But great-uncle Khleber, great-grandfather Isaac Van Zandt, and father Harris Van Zandt never played a lick of music.[1]

Fort Worth was home for only his first nine years. A revealing photograph shows Dorothy Van Zandt at a Colonial Country Club event with little Townes clutching one hand and big sister Donna clutching the other. He attended Arlington Heights Elementary through the third grade. Though he seemingly

Khleber Van Zandt (*seated, middle*) was married three times, fathering fourteen children, most of whom lived to adulthood. Three generations of the vast Van Zandt clan are pictured here. Author's collection.

had every social advantage, his was not a happy childhood. He later said, perhaps ironically, that all he remembered about Fort Worth was, "I ran away from home a lot." Such a troubled beginning as a boy did not bode well for life as a grown man. His parents got him counseling and sent him to exclusive private schools where he had the best teachers and the most helpful administrators. After high school they sent him to the University of Colorado, hoping he would take his place in the family oil business. He had other ideas, however.[2]

Like Woody Guthrie he was drawn to the life of the vagabond trouba-dour, only it was country music that drew him, not folk music. His songs were more about his own pain and despair than those of society at large. His family worried about his mental state, particularly after such tricks as going off a fourth-story balcony "just to see what it felt like to fall" that distance. Doctors diagnosed him as a "schizophrenic-reactionary manic-depressive," which was psychobabble for a young man with a boatload of mental problems. He was institutionalized and subjected to insulin shock therapy which did not "cure" him; rather, it probably contributed to serious memory loss later in life.[3]

He broke free of family and academic convention to follow his muse in 1966. That did not make him a black sheep, just an odd duck traveling to the beat of a different drummer. He spent the rest of his too-short life passing through the world most of us inhabit, but he lived inside his head, composing brilliant music while battling frightful demons. He dropped his first name because it was a connection to an unhappy past. Besides, not counting James Taylor's example, Townes Van Zandt was more artistic sounding than the kind of conventional names the Silent Generation bestowed on their kids.

As a musician he was a self-taught guitar player who used the traditional fingerpicking method rather than a plectrum (guitar pick). He sat virtually motionless while performing, his voice gruff and almost monotone. His vocal shortcomings perhaps reminded listeners of another reclusive troubadour, Bob Dylan. While reflecting the darkness in his own soul, his songs touched the emotions of countless fans. During his lifetime he was better known for others' covers of his music, among them Willie Nelson, Merle Haggard, Don Williams, and Emmylou Harris. He never achieved breakout commercial success but was cited as a major influence by Lyle Lovett and Steve Earle, among others.[4]

He settled in Houston, where he married his first wife, Fran Peterson, in 1965. It was there while playing in small clubs about town, performing both covers and original music, that he recorded his first album in 1968 (*For the Sake of a Song*). In the next nineteen years he recorded nine more albums, none of which made the Top 40 charts but raised him to "near-legend status" on both sides of the Atlantic. The despairing tone of his music reflected his belief that he would die young. Yet he never lost faith in his music. Prophetically he told his third wife, Jeanene, more than once to hang on to his songs because once he passed away, "you'll be a busy girl."[5]

Van Zandt never figured marriage out, though it was not for lack of trying. He and Frances divorced in 1970. His second marriage was to Cindy Morgan in 1978. They divorced in 1983. His third marriage was to Jeanene Munsell in 1983. That one lasted until 1994. He fathered three children along the way. He was reportedly an absentee father to all three. He remained on good terms with Jeanene. He always found it easier to court the women than to be a good husband and father. More bluntly put, he was impossible to live with.[6]

Still chasing his muse, he relocated first to Austin then to Smyrna, Tennessee, the latter because he wanted to record in Nashville, the country music capital of the world. He continued writing but performed only rarely. He and his wife lived one step away from homelessness in shacks without a single modern convenience. Being a vagabond was part of his eccentric image. *Sing Out!* magazine labeled him a "self-destructive hobo saint," which did not hurt his reputation for eccentric genius. He returned to Fort Worth to perform a few times, the last in 1992 at the Scott Theater. His very last performance came four years later on December 3, 1996, in London. By then he had a devoted following on both sides of the Atlantic. His eccentricity and reclusiveness only added to his appeal among the musical cognoscenti. He was the tortured artist, one of the most enduring tropes in literary and musical history.[7]

Drugs, alcohol, and mental illness made his life a living hell, which affected both him and those around him alike. Like other musical giants before him whose lives were cut short by the same problems (Janis Joplin, Jimi Hendrix, Jim Morrison), his death was mourned as a great loss by the music world. Some of the leading artists of his day paid tribute to him. A documentary about his life and music, *Be Here to Love Me*, came out in 2004. The Americana Musical Association, an advocate for "the authentic voice of American musical roots," bestowed their President's Award on him posthumously in 2007. He was the subject of a tribute album by Steve Earle and inducted into the Austin Music Memorial in 2010 for his contributions to that city's music tradition.[8]

Like Woody Guthrie and Pete Seeger before him, he felt a special affinity for "the disadvantaged and downtrodden." His personal life was much closer to Guthrie's than Seeger's. Like Guthrie he battled debilitating mental and physical issues his entire life that made it difficult for him to interact with others socially. In his last year alone, he suffered a broken hip and a heart attack. And like Hank Williams, another legendary singer-songwriter, he fell

Left: Townes Van Zandt was by inclination a country artist, 1970s. Author's collection.

Right: Van Zandt could also play "Joe Cool." Author's collection.

victim to substance abuse, both alcohol and drugs. He considered Williams a hero, and his life paralleled his hero's life in many ways. Besides being a country singer, he adopted Williams's stage persona with the cowboy hat and a cigarette dangling from his lips, strumming an acoustic guitar. Mental demons can produce both genius and tragedy. Van Zandt wrestled publicly with his demons. His institutionalization was the subject of the last thing he wrote, "Sanitarium Blues," a spoken poem released after his death.[9]

Van Zandt died of cardiac arrythmia, as fate would have it, on the same date as his hero Hank Williams, January 1—Williams in 1953, Van Zandt in 1997. He was just 52 in human years but two or three times that old in experience years. The *London Telegraph* called him "one of the most colorful and original songwriters of his generation." He was cremated according to his wishes. His remains were buried in the tiny Dido Cemetery. About twenty miles from Fort Worth near Saginaw (12341 Moris Dido Newark Road). The inscription on the granite marker is an abbreviation of one of his most famous songs, "To Live's to Fly," which is the way he sang it. At the time of his death, he was working on a new studio album, *A Far Cry from Dead*, which was not released until June 1999.[10]

Townes Van Zandt has been a cult figure since his death, another artist whose genius was snuffed out early. One of his admirers, a fellow musician, says "he should have a statue like Stevie Ray Vaughn has in Austin." He does have a hotel named for him in Austin with a music club named for his dog, Geraldine. Fort Worth has hosted "HomeTOWNESfest" every year since 2014 at the Southside Preservation Hall and Rose Chapel (1519 Lipscomb). Though it is well attended, there is no telling how long it will continue going forward as Van Zandt's contemporaries pass away and musical tastes change.[11]

It is a curiosity of the arts that the more eccentric and self-destructive an artist is, the more adored he is by his fans. Van Zandt could be exhibit A for that phenomenon. His devoted fans in the music community swear he was not the dour, troubled soul he has often been depicted as. They prefer to focus instead on his "musical genius," his rare humility in a profession known for large egos, and his "wicked sense of humor" that the public did not see.[12]

However, unhappiness has dogged even his legacy. His former managers, labels, and wives battled over control of his estate—like vultures, according to those who loved him. And like the artists Prince or Jimi Hendrix, his catalog was seen as a potential gold mine that could keep producing for years. It only encouraged the legal wrangling that he made contractual commitments over the years that were legally vague, to put the best face on his business decisions. As a result, more than a few people have tried to cash in on his music and his personal possessions both. His music lives on in documentaries and biopics, plus various artists have come together to record tribute albums to him, and his songs have been used in films (e.g., *The Big Lebowski*, 1998). In addition, three biographies to date have been published to mixed reviews. As labors of love, they are more hagiography and reminiscence than biography. There is to date not a Townes Van Zandt Museum, but Fort Worth, Houston, and Austin can all claim a piece of him. Who winds up ultimately in possession of his legacy remains to be seen.[13]

Chapter 24

The Lady in the Lake
Alias Patricia Ann Harmon

She was a leap-year baby, born February 29, 1928, which superstition says brings a long, happy life. Superstition also says being a leap-year girl comes with the privilege of popping the big question to her beau rather than waiting to be asked to marry. But not in the case of Alta Marie Hancock, who changed names like others might change hair styles. She went through a telephone book's worth of names in just twenty-five years. She is remembered in Fort Worth history mostly as Patricia Ann Harmon, a "beautiful" girl with big dreams who fell victim to bad habits and ended up a corpse in Benbrook Lake in 1953.[1]

Her story begins with her birth in Fort Worth to Lawrence B. and Edna Gatlin Hancock. The couple had married on September 17, 1921, in Dublin, Texas, and came to Fort Worth two years later. Their older child, Ruby Jean, was born in Fort Worth in 1924. Alta Marie was born four years later in Dublin. The name confusion begins immediately. Her birth certificate gives her name as Estalene, but thereafter she is known as Alta Marie. A clue to that name comes from the fact that Lawrence Hancock was a truck driver for Alta Vista Creamery in Fort Worth.[2]

We will call her Patty here because that is how she was known at the time of her death. We will introduce her other names as they come up during her lifetime but always return to her last known name. Using her birth name would be pointless pedantry.

Lawrence and Edna ("Eddie") Hancock's marriage was not a happy one. He could not keep a job and was abusive and unfaithful. They separated in April 1927 and two months later she filed for divorce, accusing him of calling her vile names, striking her, and having sexual relations with other women. The suit was dismissed at their request the next day, but they separated for good in 1930. Lawrence Hancock remarried and died in Comanche County, Texas, on February 27, 1942.[3]

Neither parent wanted the two girls, so they were shipped off to Comanche County to live with their maternal grandparents, Thomas and Ada Gatlin. Ruby Jean grew up to be a normal, happily married woman. She lost track of her little sister for more than ten years. The girl whom Thomas and Ada Gatlin called Alta Marie grew up on their farm, later creating her own backstory. As she told it, she was looked after by a Black servant named Hattie and was taught by private tutors. Patty's difficulty with the truth casts suspicion on everything she ever said and makes it very difficult to track her life. The fact that she lived her final years in the criminal underworld makes it even more difficult.[4]

She became a "foster child" in fact if not in name, passed from family to family. Sometime before turning 12, she returned to Fort Worth to live with Mr. and Mrs. C. L. Woodward. Since her grandparents were still living, it is not known why they gave her up. Nor can it be explained why she wound up with the Woodwards. There was no family connection and no court documents to explain it. He was a retail grocer. The Woodwards enrolled her in school. She attended Jennings Ave. Junior High, then R. L. Paschal High School. By the time she got to Paschal, she was living with the family of a girlfriend and going by the name Patty Jenkins, which is how her classmates remembered her later. Her last foster parents were William E. and Edna Joe Jenkins. He was a restaurant cook, and she was a waitress, hardly glamorous enough for Patty's self-image. She would later claim her father was noted orchestra leader-composer Gordon Jenkins, though it was William Jenkins who provided the information for her death certificate. Gordon Jenkins as father was a creation of her imagination.[5]

Her family connection also confused her classmates. Years later, one of them told a researcher, "None of them [her family] seemed kin to each other. There was a woman, a couple of girls and a boy. Don't ask me who they all were. I could never figure it out. I don't know what she used for money. But she dressed pretty well for a high school girl."[6]

As a Paschal student her grades were poor in academic courses. She only excelled in home economics. It was her looks and her social life that stood out when classmates remembered her years later. One anonymous classmate remarked admiringly that her looks "took the school by storm." The same classmate said, "Patty liked to sing and had a passable voice," but it was her looks not her voice that got her an invitation to "front" a local band. The classmate summarized Patty as a "happy, popular girl," which is at odds with her life after high school. It is hard to believe this is the same girl who sank into a life of crime and debauchery in the next seven or eight years.[7]

No surprise, her popularity was highest with the boys. She had a date "nearly every night," recalled another one of those anonymous friends, and only went out with the "nicest" and most popular boys. Some of those boys went on to become prominent Fort Worth businessmen who had conveniently forgotten they ever knew her by the time she was a headline story. Being mature beyond her years and not reined in at home, she also dated college boys from nearby TCU. She never got serious with any of them. Patty's ambitions did not include marriage and a family. She dreamed of being a big-band singer and movie star during hours spent listening to records.[8]

The school newspaper, the *Pantherette*, found her a ripe subject for gossip and was not shy about naming names. Snide editorial comments there prove that "Mean Girls" was a real thing long before it was a movie. One item asked rhetorically, "Can it be possible the ones who have been criticizing PATTY JENKINS are just jealous? Probably so . . ." Another was phrased in Q&A form:

Who: Patty Jenkins.
Identification: Pretty Girl.
Talent? Making the girls jealous.
See the other night—PATTY JENKINS and GUY PROCTOR.

Left: Patty Harmon's high school montage, published in the *Fort Worth Star-Telegram* in 1944. Author's collection.

Right: Patty Harmon's faked graduation picture, inscribed, "Loving you always, Patty." Author's collection.

The student editors of the newspaper were very interested in who Patty was dating, especially toward the end of the school year: "PATTI JENKINS and DONALD SCOTT made a cute couple at DeMolay's Show." The last item in 1944, which should have been her graduating year, was another date report coupled with a dig at her peroxide-blond hair: "Lots of Paschal girls would like to choke PATTY JENKINS for ruining SONY HAMILTON'S beautiful hair—some wonder how she could spare the peroxide."[9]

Former classmate George Grammer still had vivid memories of her some sixty years later. "I remember Patty Jenkins as a bright flicker in a long-ago, forgotten time. Although my friends and I were innocent bystanders, just seeing Patty I the hallways at old Paschal was a rare thrill. [She] was a standout in a large student body. We were not in the same classes. She was our Bridget Bardot, and her smile set the hormones twirling. All eyes were on Patty wherever she went. She was a star-quality blonde."[10]

It was not just for the *Pantherette* that Patty made good copy; she was also good copy for the *Star-Telegram*. On February 24, 1944, the newspaper profiled "Patty Jenkins" (looking very blond and much older than her 15 years) for a page-one story about leap-year babies. By then she would have been in her senior year and thinking about life after high school.[11]

Despite the size of her Paschal legend, Patty did not stick around long enough to graduate. School officials would later tell reporters that that she spent "less than a year" enrolled, but her sense of the theatrical led her to pull a joke on the graduating class by posing in full graduate regalia in the spring of 1944. Her faux graduation picture shows a girl with blond hair beneath her mortarboard, and the inscription "Loving you always" signed by someone who must have been in on the joke.

One big reason she did not stick around to walk across the stage was that her next stop was before a judge or justice of the peace to marry Billy Jack Harmon of Weatherford, Texas on July 29, 1944. She was just 16—which does not jibe with being a senior—while he was 20 and a pilot in the Army Air Force. We can only speculate on why she traded in her dreams of being a professional singer or movie star to become Mrs. Harmon. Perhaps she was swept off her feet by this older man in uniform, or perhaps the fact that he also moonlighted as a trumpet player in local nightclubs convinced her he was her ticket out of Fort Worth. When Lieutenant Harmon was discharged from the army on January 9, 1946, the couple moved to Los Angeles. They were living in LA when a child was born on February 24, 1946. They named her Bunny after famed jazz trumpet player and bandleader Roland Bernard "Bunny" Berigan (1908–1942), whom Patty later claimed was her father in another flight of imagination.[12]

Less than two years later, on December 29, 1947, Patty and Billy signed divorce papers. He returned to Fort Worth while she stayed in Los Angeles. She got custody of their daughter. Three months after getting divorced she went to work for Charles Cull, a venetian-blinds and drapery installer. Her job was going door to door selling drapes on commission, and apparently she was quite good at it. She moved in with the Culls, putting Bunny in foster care with the Dyer family. The Culls thought Patty did not "much care for the child" and that she was determined never to have another one.[13]

Patty enjoyed the party-hearty single life while living with the Culls. She went out almost every night, frequently to the "colored" Zombie nightclub, bringing home men she met at the clubs. Some of them were Mexicans of whom the Culls did not approve. One of her pick-ups was Armando Joseph "Pat" Contreras, a musician at one of the clubs who still lived with his parents. It was while living with the Culls that she also began to use heroin, a common drug among musicians. Though the Culls did not mention it later, that may have been one of the reasons they asked her to move out and find a boardinghouse. She moved out, but instead of finding a boardinghouse, she moved in with Pat Contreras's family, telling the Culls they had gotten married, which they had not.[14]

Mrs. Cull said later that she liked Patty personally but did not trust her. She explained: "Patty apparently is a pathological liar. You can find probably that you can't believe a word she says. She told us innumerable stories of her past life, all apparently untrue—for instance that her father was Bunny Berigan the trumpeter."[15]

Life got more complicated for Patty at this point. The Dyers were moving to San Diego and were no longer willing to keep Bunny. Mrs. Cull agreed to take the little girl in until Patty could make other arrangements, but she also contacted Billy Harmon in Fort Worth to tell him of the situation. He came to LA and offered to take back mother and child both, but Patty was not interested. She insisted she was in love with Pat Contreras and believed he would help raise the child. There is no indication he ever agreed to any such thing, and besides, Billy Harmon would not agree, so with Patty's blessing he took custody of Bunny and the two of them returned to Fort Worth.[16]

Patty, now going by the name Patricia Ann Contreras, entered the criminal justice system for the first time on March 27, 1948. She was arrested in Long Beach, California, and charged with possessing unspecified narcotics. She got off because there was insufficient evidence to prosecute her, but she was already well-known to the Long Beach police as a prostitute and addict. She did not stay out of trouble long. She was arrested again on September 30, 1948, by US Customs agents and charged with smuggling narcotics into the country from Tijuana, Mexico. She was caught at San Ysidro, California, traveling in a car driven by Lorenzo Umel Cacayan. A customs inspector recognized her from a photo posted at the station. A female agent and doctor conducted a full body search, finding fifty-seven grains of heroin hidden in her vagina. She claimed that she had acquired the heroin in Tijuana for her own personal use, and her companion did not know she was carrying the illegal drug. A search of the car and the driver found nothing, but that did not get her off the hook.[17]

She was charged with importing and concealing illegal narcotics and tried in federal district court in San Diego. She pleaded guilty and Judge Jacob Weinberger sentenced her to eighteen months in prison. He added the recommendation that she serve her time in a US public health hospital for narcotics addiction. She began serving her time at the Federal Reformatory for Women in Alderson, West Virginia, on January 11, 1949. She was just 20 years old. As a first-time offender, and for a nonviolent crime, she was eligible for parole on July 4, 1949.[18]

Her admission file contains valuable details about Patty. She was five feet ("60 inches") tall and weighed 108½ pounds. She had "hazel" eyes with a scar over one eye that happened when someone cut her with a knife. She had hypodermic scars on her arms from shooting up. Despite this, the prison doctor considered her to be in "fairly good health." They also measured her IQ at 109, meaning she had average intelligence.[19]

Prison administrators interviewed her at least three times, building a big file on her. She seemed to fascinate them as much as she did the other men in her life. They wrote down everything she told them, though they discounted much of it as outright fabrications. She claimed to have been born in Long Beach, California, and attended Polytechnic High School there. She told another interviewer her daughter was dead, claimed that her mother had died giving birth to her, then changed her story to say her mother had remarried and her stepfather was Bunny Berigan. She also said she was a professional singer. Officials confronted her over some of her more blatant lies and finally recommended a complete psychological evaluation. Having nothing to lose, she agreed.[20]

She was examined by Dr. Vincent J. Daly, a psychologist at West Virginia's Huntington State Hospital, formerly West Virginia Asylum. If anything, being off drugs and confined made her even more erratic. She assumed a Gaelic accent and claimed to be of Irish heritage in their interviews. She also admitted using heroin and morphine and "other drugs." She frankly described how she acquired the drugs, including trading sex for drugs with anyone who could supply her. Dr. Daly administered a Rorschach test, which revealed "a pattern of constitutional psychopathy, poor basic personality, marked depression, and neurotic anxiety," which was psychobabble for a very messed up girl. His final medical report was indeed sad:

> We appear to be confronted by a 21-year-old white female who presents the picture of constitutional psychopathy, symptomized by pathological lying, narcotic addiction, and amoral and social misbehavior. In view of the history, past clinical findings, and the present Rorschach, we are inclined to believe that despite the comparative youth of this girl the pattern is well fixed and that prognosis for social rehabilitation is at best doubtful.
>
> It is very likely that this person will adjust to prison life and cause little disciplinary concern if she does not come in contact with more dominant personalities who would induce her to attempt rash actions. In view of the apparent deep-seated psychopathy, corrective psychotherapy does not seem feasible. The best social prognosis we can hope for is borderline social adjustment at the expiration of her sentence.[21]

The bottom line for the doctor was that Patty was a hopeless case for rehabilitation. She was a broken human being.

The rest of her time in federal prison passed uneventfully. She was not a discipline problem except in minor ways like not cleaning her room and practicing poor grooming and hygiene. She had a few medical problems, at least one of which was self-inflicted: she swallowed a safety pin. All prisoners were assigned to classes, and they put her in choir, knitting, Spanish, arithmetic, and current events. She did well in choir and knitting but struggled in academic subjects. A tendency to act out eventually got her dismissed from the choir. Her history of drug addiction may have affected her mind, because she had trouble remembering even simple things like the orders she took as a prisoner waitress. She was reassigned to dishwashing. She was just enough of a problem to be denied parole when she came before the parole board on June 29, 1949.[22]

She spent eighteen months at Huntington State Hospital, completing her sentence on July 4, 1950. She had been approved for parole on March 18. The conditions of her release required her to make plans for life after prison. She first proposed going back to California and working for the Culls again. She was supported in this by Mrs. Cull, who wrote a letter to the authorities saying Patricia could return to work and live with them, which was surprisingly generous. Prison authorities also received a letter from Pat Contreras inquiring about his "wife's" whereabouts. Officials did not answer the letter because they did not believe the couple had ever been married; it was just another one of Patty's lies. After further thought Patty decided not to go back to California but to settle in Fort Worth, where she would face fewer temptations to return to a drug-filled life. Presumably her probation officer would help her find a job and a place to live. She showed no interest in reconnecting to any of her blood relatives—not her mother, who lived in Harlingen, Texas, or her sister, who lived in Dallas. The attraction of Fort Worth was that Billy Harmon and her daughter were living there. As part of her release, she was given a train ticket and a little money for the trip. Someone, probably Billy, had to meet her at the train station, but where she lived after that is a mystery. If it was with Billy and Bunny, it was not for long, because they soon moved to Houston, leaving her on her own again.[23]

There is no record that Patty ever made any attempt to contact former foster parents or classmates. Having served her time, Patty was free to do whatever she wanted; she did not have to report to a parole officer. Unfortunately, the only jobs she could get were dead-end jobs. She was still nice looking and had a flirtatious personality but no longer "ash-blond" hair. The combination of looks and high-wattage personality got her hired as a barmaid. She was reportedly seen working in a "South Side tavern" and by another ex-classmate on a downtown street. "I hardly recognized her," the woman said. She had the "shifty eyes" of a cornered animal and the hardened face of an addict. Patty called the former classmate "several times," insisting she was "going to go straight."[24]

But she could not shake the old ways. She had run-ins with the law in Fort Worth, Dallas, and Abilene. Dallas police picked her up ten times, Fort Worth police at least once, and Abilene police once. Some of the charges were

Tarrant County Sheriff Harlan Wright (1953–1961). A botched investigation got his first term off to a rocky start. Author's collection.

for "vagrancy," which is police speak for prostitution. She was mug-shotted every time. In the fall of 1953, Fort Worth police were waging a vigorous campaign against prostitution. Patty was unlucky enough to be caught in the sweep of motels and massage parlors when she was arrested by Vice Squad Sergeant Raymond Chaffin on November 4 or 5. She was a small fish, so Chaffin didn't think much about it. She was carrying her "customer list" that he obligingly tossed because police were targeting prostitutes, not "johns." For this embarrassing oversight, Chaffin was busted back to the patrol division a week later.[25]

On Thursday, November 26, 1953 (Thanksgiving Day), a bloated, nude body was found wrapped in tire chains floating in Benbrook Lake near the dam. The person who found the body was never identified. Subsequent examination revealed that the victim was already dead when thrown into the lake, that she had been bludgeoned to death and in the water about two weeks.

Tracing Patty's criminal career through her mug shots:
Left: Long Beach, CA, Police Department, 1948. Credit: Harry Max Hill.

Center: Federal prison, 1949. Credit: Harry Max Hill.

Right: Fort Worth Police Department, 1953. Credit: Harry Max Hill.

(Later reports said the body was discovered in the Clear Fork of the Trinity.) Because the body was found in Benbrook, Sheriff Harlan Wright was called in. A pile of abandoned women's clothing was found in Boaz Park, a few miles from the lake, which was first reported in the newspapers as a promising clue before turning out to be unrelated to the crime. Sheriff Wright had been in office less than a year, and this would turn into the most sensational case of his tenure (1953–1961). Within twenty-four hours the story had been picked up by newspapers all over the state.[26]

Wright took personal charge of the investigation, assisted by Fort Worth police. The problem was, facts were few and suspects were zero, but that did not keep the newspapers from running with the story. They tracked down Patty's family and interviewed anyone who could claim to have ever known her. The first problem was identifying the body. Because of the extreme decomposition and the lack of any ID at the scene, the medical examiner had to use fingerprints to identify the body. Fortunately, "Patty Jenkins'" fingerprints were in Fort Worth police files for prostitution and narcotics possession. Ruby Jean McKinney, Patty's sister, confirmed the identification from a postmortem photograph. She was able to state absolutely that the body was that of her sister and provided the name of Patty's mother, Mrs. Eddie Jenkins of Harlingen. Police called in Mrs. Jenkins to claim the body. Meanwhile, Paschal officials viewed the same photograph but could not identify the victim as a former student, even with a name attached. That caused a rewrite in the *Star-Telegram* on Saturday because the morning edition had identified the body as that of an "Ex-Paschal Student." The evening edition headline changed that to say the victim "May Be Ex-Paschal Student." But at least the newspaper finally came up with her birth name, Alta Marie Hancock. [27]

In the days following the discovery of the body, the *Star-Telegram* did a better job covering the law enforcement side of the story. The *Fort Worth Press* did a better job running down former acquaintances of Patty, covering the human-interest angle to the story.

Ruby McKinney told authorities she thought Patty was living in Irving but had no idea who her friends were. When Olin Ray Tyler of Irving showed up at the funeral home where the body was initially taken to inquire about Patty, the authorities brought him in for questioning. Tyler was well-known to the authorities as an ex-con who had once been an "associate" of Raymond Hamilton after Hamilton left Bonnie and Clyde's gang. Now he was 44 years old, married, and living in Irving. Patty had been living with him and his wife when she disappeared. Police thought he was Patty's pimp. He told them he had last seen her on November 9 "at an E. Belknap tourist court," adding he had been trying to find her ever since.[28]

Justice of the Peace N. M. Nicholson ruled Patty's death "murder at the hands of person or persons unknown." With that verdict the investigation stumbled on, following one dead end after another. The body was turned over to the state crime lab. The needle scars on her arms showed Patty to be a heroin user, so the authorities focused on the drug connection as an explanation for her murder. Sadly, they had to admit, "her connections in the narcotics world are vague and difficult to trace." On Friday deputies found an abandoned car with blood-stained interior in the 4700 block of Dilworth, a street in Benbrook about two miles from the dam. Since this was before DNA testing, there was no way to tie the blood to Patty. They arrested a suspect, 21-year-old Elie Dale Gunter, who admitted using the car to drive someone to Oklahoma but said he didn't steal it and did not know Patty Harmon. He said the bloodstains were from his passenger's "nosebleed." He was released. A "coon hunter" was interviewed after it was reported he had seen a nude woman arguing with two men "on the lake shore" about two weeks previously, which was around the time the authorities figured she had been killed. It turned out the hunter only heard two men talking, did not see a woman nude or otherwise, and had no idea who the men were.[29]

On Sunday an anonymous tip was received about another body in Benbrook Lake. The Lake Worth Emergency Corps was called in to "drag the river above the lake," but who took the tip and who called it in remains a mystery. The police denied receiving the tip, and Sheriff Wright arrived on the scene after it was over. That left only one of the newspapers as the source of the story, and editors were not saying anything. One way or another, word got around, and spectators flocked to the scene to watch the lake being dragged— men, women, and children who treated it like a Sunday afternoon outing. The *Star-Telegram* described it as a "picnic atmosphere." Emergency personnel spent two hours dragging the river and the lake while an ambulance stood by. With darkness falling they gave up and packed it in. The disappointed crowd went home, and a chagrined Sheriff Wright told the *Star-Telegram* the next day, "It's going to be a long, hard investigation. We've got lots of people to talk to—and they aren't the kind of people who do much talking. . . . It's going to be rough case."[30]

In the meantime Patty's mother quietly made funeral arrangements. She arranged for her daughter to be buried at Mount Olivet Cemetery in a private, graveside service attended only by family members. They hoped to keep curiosity-seekers away, but the newspaper reported the time and place on the morning of the funeral. It thus became just another part of the circus atmosphere surrounding the crime: a brutal murder, a schoolgirl-turned-prostitute, a "dope ring" connection, clueless authorities! This stuff was catnip for crime reporters looking for headlines. They tracked down Patty's high-school photographs, to the chagrin of school authorities, and even found a 1944 photo of Patty as a leap-year baby.[31]

The name game for Patty continued to play out even after her death. The name on her gravestone is not Alta Marie Hancock but Patty Myree

Harmon. It seems neither her family nor the authorities were sure what to call her between her birth name, married name(s), and various aliases. It is debatable if she ever really knew who she was.

When Sheriff Wright said it was going to be "rough case," he had no idea. The murder investigation took a detour into Keystone Cops territory. A sheriff's department spokesman said they were conducting a "staircase investigation," explaining that meant "going from person to person" looking for clues. What that really meant was that they were flailing around trying to build a case. Sheriff Wright brought in the Texas Rangers because of the kidnapping and narcotics angles.[32]

A week after Patty's body was discovered, a Lake Worth woman in All Saints Hospital with minor injuries said she had been "abducted and beaten by members of a narcotics gang." Narcotics gangs were the bogeymen of the underworld at this time. In the public's mind they were, by definition, highly organized, ruthless, and well-funded, like the Mafia only without the Italian connection. The suspicion that Patty might have been murdered by drug dealers drove the investigation. When the mystery woman related her story, sheriff's deputies and Texas Rangers both were present to take it down. Harlan Wright told reporters that her story might be "pure fantasy," but they had to follow up on every lead. Another woman, a 40-year-old "Big Spring housewife" also came forward with "helpful" information. The Big Spring sheriff arranged for Wright to interview her on December 1. Taking along one of his deputies and a Texas Ranger, he chartered a plane and flew to Big Spring. It turned into a Keystone Cops affair when she misunderstood the arrangements and took the train to Fort Worth. They finally got together, and "Miss X," as Wright dubbed her, described Patty's underworld contacts in detail. Afterward Wright said he doubted the information would prove valuable. Another dead end. In the meantime, investigators cleared Elie Dale Gunter but continued to treat the Irving ex-con who may or may not have been one of Patty's johns as a person of interest. In February Texas Rangers took him to Austin for a lie detector test administered by their expert. Afterward, Wright conceded the man's story "appeared convincing."[33]

Just before Christmas Fort Worth police interviewed a blond hitchhiker who told a fantastic story about being abducted by two men on the Jacksboro highway, beaten, and dumped near Springtown. Police caught up with the victim at City-County Hospital, where she was being treated. One of her assailants, she said, threatened if she reported them, she would get "the same treatment as Patricia Ann." Vice officers recognized the victim as a prostitute and drug addict and put no credence in her story. They turned her over to Sheriff Harlan Wright, who interviewed her and told a reporter he could "make little sense out of her story."[34]

Other leads dangled before the press by Sheriff Wright included "associates" of Hollis Delois Green, a deceased Dallas crime boss; Olin Ray Tyler, now believed to be Patty's pimp; Mark Flannagan, a 28-year-old "police character" who brought along his lawyer when he was interrogated; and an unnamed 20-year-old car thief. None of them could be convincingly tied to the crime, though they remained persons of interest for lack of any real suspects. The authorities were grasping at straws.[35]

The investigation took another screwy turn when Tarrant County Auditor J. M. Williams refused to reimburse the $125 airfare it cost Sheriff Wright and pals to fly to Big Spring. An outraged Wright said he had received "verbal approval" from Williams and that the trip was necessary to check out a hot lead. The trio also spent the night in a Big Spring hotel before returning. Williams said they should have used their mileage allowance and gone by car. What the Star-Telegram called a "rhubarb" had to be resolved in commissioners court, and their decision left Harlan Wright with egg on his face.[36]

Through the winter of 1953–54 the investigation dragged on as one clue after another "fizzled." One male suspect after another was cleared, the Lake Worth woman's story was deemed unrelated to the case, and the Big Springs woman's purported friendship with Patty did not produce any leads either. Sheriff Wright was embarrassed by the lack of progress on the case.[37]

A year after her body was discovered, the authorities were no closer to solving Patty's murder. The Star-Telegram, never shy about juicing up the headlines, was now calling it a "Gang Style Slaying"—without any evidence to back up the assertion. The newspaper's entertainment editor, Elston Brooks, revisited the case, citing unnamed officials who also characterized it as a "gangland slaying." He theorized that she was murdered "because she threatened to talk about dope traffic here." Truth be told, no such evidence had been discovered. Authorities were chasing their tails. The rest of Brooks's story tugged at the heart strings telling how a "baby-faced" girl with big dreams wound up hooked on drugs floating in Benbrook Lake. He concluded that the case was ice-cold, though officers were still looking for her "slayers" (plural). Where facts were absent, speculation and creative writing took over.[38]

The case of 25-year-old Patty Harmon, a.k.a. Alta Marie Hancock, a.k.a. Patty Myree Harmon, has never been solved. The prime suspect, Olin Ray Tyler (her pimp?), turned up dead in 1956, his bullet-riddled body discovered on a lonely stretch of country road off Highway 114 in Denton County. His murder was never solved either. And so Patty's / Alta Marie's / Patty Myree's murder remains a cold case in the files of the Tarrant County Sheriff's Department and a gruesome story in the history of Benbrook Lake. The only mark she left on history was a long criminal record and a few newspaper stories. Rest in peace, Patty.[39]

Chapter 25

Bobby Day Tops
the Charts

Bobby Day is another one of those musical prodigies produced by Cowtown, more specifically by I. M. Terrell. Fort Worth's segregated high school also gave us Ornette Coleman, King Curtis, and Manet Harrison. Bobby Day was the stage name of the artist who gave us "Rockin' Robin," a number two national hit twice, in 1958 and 1972.

He began life as Robert James Byrd in Fort Worth on July 1, 1932, or maybe 1928, the records are not clear. Little is known of his early life before he attended I. M. Terrell High School. Years later he told *Star-Telegram* columnist Roger Kaye that he graduated at the age of 15, making him "one of the youngest graduates in the history of the high school," but like so many details of his story, that is impossible to verify. He eventually took a stage name but never really forgot his birth surname. Avian creatures in one form or another were part of his musical oeuvre for the rest of his life.[1]

He got a music scholarship to Prairie View A&M but attended for only a "short time" as he described it because he found the going "tough," so in 1947 he took off to California, settling in the Watts section of Los Angeles and enrolling in UCLA, where, he told interviewer Jeff Tamarkin, he got a music scholarship. Said Day proudly, "In mathematics and music, I got straight A's

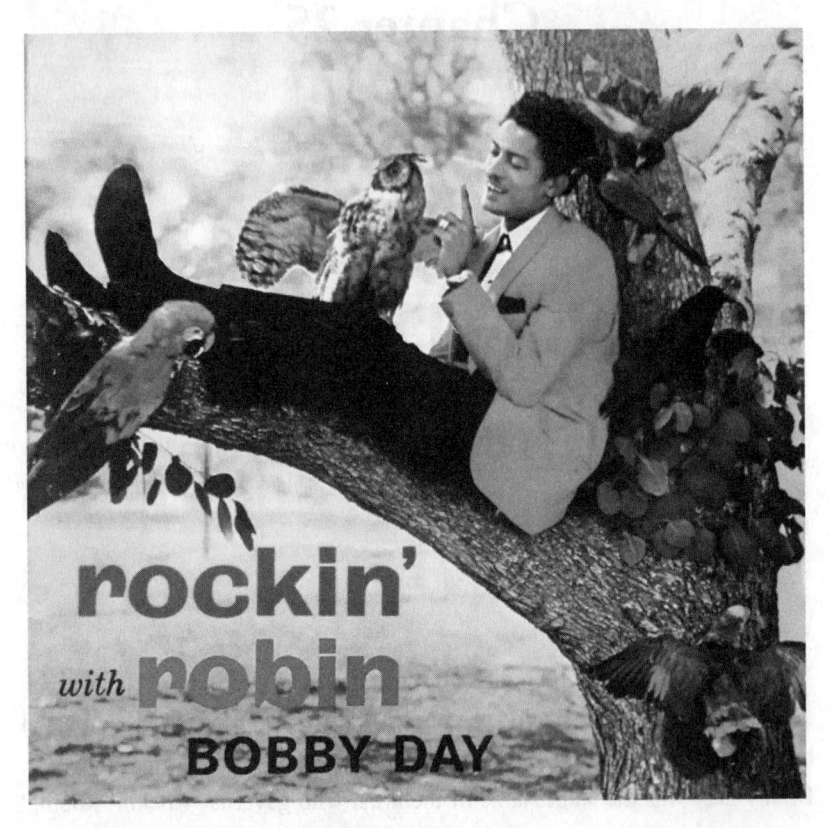

Rockin' Robin, Bobby Day's 1959 breakthrough album, its cover clearly aimed at the American Bandstand audience. Author's collection.

and one B, but I don't talk about that B." He did not graduate from college because he preferred to follow his muse. He began performing locally with another R&B singer, Earl Nelson, as The Voices. Their professional relationship would continue successively for years. R&B was the new term for what had long been known as "race music." Dubbed R&B, it was more likely to attract a white audience hungry for something new. In 1949 Byrd and Nelson hooked up with R&B pioneer Johnny Otis to form the Hollywood Flames and signed with the Selective record label. Starting in 1950 and continuing for the next seventeen years, the Hollywood Flames, under a variety of names and with an ever-changing lineup, released more than seventy-five R&B and rock and roll records on various labels.[2]

THE HOLLYWOOD FLAMES

FEATURES THEIR R&B NO. 5 AND POP NO. 11 HIT BUZZ, BUZZ, BUZZ

BUZZ, BUZZ, BUZZ

THE SINGLES COLLECTION

1950-62

78-track 3-CD set comprising most of their A & B sides from these years on the Selective, Unique, Fidelity, Specialty, Recorded in Hollywood, Spin, 7-11, Swing Time, Lucky, Aladdin, Money, Cash, Class, Ebb, Chess, Goldie and Coronet labels

Includes recordings as The Hollywood Flames, The Flames, Hollywood's Four Flames, The Four Flames, The Jets, The Question Marks, The Turks, The Ebbtides, The Pelicans and The Satellites

The Hollywood Flames (1949–1980s) were the most successful of the various groups Bobby Day was associated with, going through numerous personnel changes over the years. (Day is on the bottom left.) Author's collection.

In 1955, still as Bobby Byrd, he recorded some of his own music solo, which attracted no attention in the highly competitive R&B market. The usual approach of aspiring artists like himself was to cut a few singles and take them around to radio DJs and nightclubs in person, hoping they caught the public's ear. Bobby was still the acknowledged leader of the Flames, sharing the writing and lead singing with Earl Nelson. They wrote "Young Girl" for the group, which went nowhere. Still, the Flames had a loyal following in the Watts club scene. They also got airplay on Art Laboe's nightly R&B show on KPOP radio. That exposure helped them sign with Leon René's Class Records in 1957. That July they released their biggest hit ever, "Buzz-Buzz-Buzz," cowritten by Byrd and Earl Nelson. When the single soared to number five on the R&B charts and number eleven on the pop charts, the record label convinced him to change his name to Bobby Day, and that is how he was known thereafter.[3]

The Hollywood Flames followed up "Buzz-Buzz-Buzz" with "Crazy," another number cowritten by Day. That same year they recorded a song on the Class label written by Day's wife, Jackie, recording it as Bobby Day & the Satellites, a name they took from newspaper headlines about the space race between the US and the USSR. The song was "Little Bitty Pretty One." Day's career finally took off under René's guidance, who had been in the music business since the 1930s and had an eye for talent and an ear for what would sell. "Little Bitty Pretty One" had a catchy title and the kind of doo-wop sound that was just catching on in the mid-fifties. Still, the single only reached number fifty-seven on the pop charts and did not register on the R&B charts, though that was not the worst of it. The song was covered by another minor Black artist, Thurston Harris, and released on the Aladdin label. It became a huge hit, soaring to number two on the R&B charts and number six on the pop charts. Harris's version was pushed up the charts by his TV appearance on Dick Clark's *American Bandstand*, and "Little Bitty Pretty One" went on to become a standard, covered by everyone from the Dave Clark Five to the Jackson 5 to Huey Lewis and the News in the next twenty-five years. There was nothing unethical about what Aladdin and Harris did; that was just how the music business worked. One artist's composition could become another artist's hit record.[4]

Day left the Hollywood Flames to go solo in 1958, probably at Leon René's urging. The breakup was an amicable business decision; the star had outgrown his backups. The Flames continued to perform and record with a new lineup, even appearing at New York's Apollo Theater with other popular R&B groups. They also backed Day on some of his recordings. He continued to perform with Earl Nelson, too, as Bob & Earl. Together they wrote and recorded two undistinguished singles on the Class label, "Gee Whiz" (1958) and "Chains of Love" (1959). Their biggest hit together was the original version of "Harlem Shuffle" (1963, number forty-four on the R&B charts), which was covered by countless other groups subsequently.[5]

Day signed with Chicago's Chess Records and released the single "Come Seven," which went nowhere. As a performing artist Bobby Day had a decent voice but could not sustain a recording career. It was as a songwriter with a feel for what the rock and roll teen audience wanted that proved to be his ticket. He wrote and cowrote catchy doo-wop tunes with a pounding R&B beat that appealed to whites and Blacks alike. His muse was strongest from 1958 to 1959, when he wrote and recorded three minor R&B hits and one monster, two-sided hit that made both the R&B and pop charts. The two-sided hit was "Rockin' Robin," backed with "Over and Over" on the B side, but disc jockeys did not always follow the record labels' directions on what was the A side what was the B side. The response of listeners to "Rockin' Robin" in 1958 was overwhelming. It climbed to number one on the R&B charts and number two on the pop charts. "Over and Over" only reached number forty-one on the pop charts but number one on the R&B charts. What kept "Rockin' Robin" out of the number one spot was Tommy Edwards's smooth ballad, "It's All in the Game," which appealed to both the kids and their parents. Both sides of the single proved to have "legs," as they say. "Over and Over" became an even bigger hit for the Dave Clark 5 in 1965. The Hollies, another British Invasion group, also tapped Day's catalog for hits in the seventies.[6]

The backstory to "Rockin' Robin" is interesting all by itself. Giant hits always raise curiosity about how they came to be written. It was cowritten with his mentor, Leon René, who used the alias Jimmie Thomas, perhaps to disguise his involvement for tax purposes. Day later told an interviewer that René came up with the tune while he came up with the lyrics. They were wrestling with it when they heard birds singing outside, which inspired the title. But what kind of bird? The alliterative choice that also scanned well was the robin (Imagine: "Rockin' Sparrow" or "Rockin' Bluejay"). And that's how "Rockin' Robin" came to be written. They brought in Day's old group the Hollywood Flames to sing backup. The song's immortal intro, "tweedle-lee-dee-dee-dee," was something Day came up with on the spot. Combined with the shuffle drumbeat, trilling flute, harmonizing on "tweedle-lee-dee-dee-dee / tweet tweet," Day's tongue-twisting vocal, and the syncopated handclaps, the whole thing came together almost as if by magic. It was a rock and roll masterpiece, plus as rock historian Dave Marsh opined, it contains the cleverest metaphor for male sexual prowess ever

Left: Bobby Day, studio photo. Author's collection.

Right: Frequent Day collaborator Leon Rene. They created some great rock 'n' roll together. Author's collection.

recorded—namely, "He outbopped the buzzard and the oriole." We have to remember, "Rockin' Robin" came out at a time when sexual references still had to be disguised in music.[7]

Getting their song on record also proved challenging. Because of the primitive recording equipment of the day and the cost of studio time, they had to get it right the first time. The finished song was not only an instant rock and roll classic, but it was also Leon René's biggest hit since 1931's "When It's Sleepy Time Down South," and Class Records's biggest hit ever. It paid off for Bobby Day with an invitation to appear on *American Bandstand*, every rock and roll performer's dream. He parlayed the record's success as a single into a studio album in 1959, which included both "Little Bitty Pretty One" and "Rockin' Robin."[8]

Neither Bobby Day nor Leon René ever reached that level of success again. René's success did not last much longer than the record's time on the charts. His career was derailed in 1959 by the payola scandal investigation (record companies paying radio deejays to play their records) launched by Congress. He claimed that he was targeted because he was an industry power in recording R&B artists. His was not the only big name in the recording business brought down by the payola scandal. It also took down Alan Freed, who as "Mr. Rock and Roll" had seemed untouchable.[9]

Bobby Day rode the success of "Rockin' Robin" back to the R&B charts three more times in 1959, not even reaching the Top 40, which was the measuring stick for hit records. His biggest success was the immediate follow-up where he tried to cash in on "Rockin' Robin" with the clumsily titled, "The Bluebird, the Buzzard, and the Oriole." Radio listeners were not captivated; it only reached number fifty-four. His last charting single was "Gotta New Girl," which was another very minor hit on the R&B charts due to his name being attached.[10]

After 1960 Day concentrated on his songwriting while continuing to record occasionally with his old pal Earl Nelson. Besides the "Harlem Shuffle," they also put "Don't Ever Leave Me" on the R&B charts (number eighty-five, 1962). His muse, it would seem, had deserted him. He was never able to capture that old black magic. He did take a page from the playbook of his mentor, Leon René, by forming his own record label, Birdland, which released a string of unremarkable self-penned singles under different aliases, all of which played on his surname: "Baby Face" Byrd, The Birds, The Birdies, The Daybirds. Any hope of capitalizing on his surname died in 1965 when Roger McGuinn's chart-topping folk-rock group, The Byrds, laid claim to it.[11]

After his recording career ran out of steam, he hit the oldies circuit, touring with other R&B old-timers like Johnny Otis and Marv Johnson (dropped by Motown after a couple of hits). Promoting himself as a singer and bandleader, he found appreciative audiences in Australia and the United Kingdom, but in the United States his star had clearly set. In 1983 he returned to Fort Worth to play the Ricochet Room in the Americana Hotel backed by his old group, the Hollywood Flames, with an all-new lineup.[12]

He remained a prolific songwriter almost to the end, though none of his music (see "A Little Bird") made it onto the charts. What his later songs

Publicity photo of "the other" Bobby Day, a country-western singer, 1969.
His photo was mistakenly put out by the Associated Press in June 1990.
He was still alive and kicking. Author's collection.

revealed was that he had a deep fondness for feathered creatures. Another
nonhit in that same category, "Beep-Beep-Beep," found a different kind of
commercial success in a Kia Sorento TV commercial in 2012, earning some
rare royalties for his estate.[13]

Bobby Day died of cancer at the age of 59 (or maybe 63) on July 27,
1990, in Los Angeles. He had entered the hospital twelve days earlier
with an ulcerated stomach and never left. At the time he was still doing

the oldies circuit with the likes of Tiny Tim, another early rock and roll has-been. He was largely a forgotten man except for aficionados of early R&B. His burial in LA's Holy Cross Cemetery attracted a small group of mourners. Karen Castillo, a member of his management firm, offered the best eulogy: "He wasn't one of these kids that popped up and got lucky. He was extremely talented. . . . His rhythm and blues voice was dynamic and captivating." He was also a favorite with his fellow performers because "you never saw him without a smile." His obituaries around the country got a lot wrong. The Associated Press even made an embarrassing mistake, putting out a photograph of white country-western singer Bobby Day on July 30 with the press release announcing his death. When the error was pointed out they had to issue a correction. The mistake was not a problem for the *Star-Telegram*, which did not carry his obituary even though he was a Fort Worth product.[14]

He was survived by his wife, Jackie, and four children. His catalog after his passing was controlled by Aladdin Records before it was eventually taken over by Dutch conglomerate EMI Records. It seems there is little chance of him being inducted into the Rock and Roll Hall of Fame, but he adds to the luster of Fort Worth's musical heritage.[15]

He was part of that first generation of Black R&B artists who made the jump to rock and roll, in the process winning a vast audience of white kids unexcited by their parents' music. Along with Chuck Berry, James Brown, and Little Richard, he blurred the lines between R&B and rock and roll. "Rockin' Robin" was the same kind of hard-charging novelty record that the Coasters became famous for, but the Coasters had Jerry Leiber and Mike Stoller to keep them supplied with hits. Day never achieved the same level of fame or had a long career in the spotlight. His greatest hit turned out to be what is known in the music business as a one-hit wonder. It went on to become a children's song with hand gestures and is best known in rock and roll history for Michael Jackson's version, which went to number two on the charts in 1972 and remained on the charts for eleven weeks. "Tweedle-lee-dee-dee, tweet, tweet!"

Endnotes

Notes for Chapter 1

1. John Pratt in Tenth US Census (1880), Fort Worth, Tarrant County, TX. Cf. Ninth US Census (1870), Fort Worth, Tarrant County, TX. James Wellington Pratt in US Social Security Applications and Claims Index, 1936–2007, Feb. 1937 application. For relationship to Dick King, see recollections of Howard W. Peak, *Fort Worth Star-Telegram*, October 1, 1922.

2. "Veterans of 'Lost Cause' Paid Tribute to an Ex-Slave," *Fort Worth Star-Telegram*, October 30, 1949 (Centennial Ed.). The education of the master's son is told in Julia Kathryn Garrett, *Fort Worth: A Frontier Triumph* (Fort Worth: Texas Christian University Press, 1996), 279. She only she says it was the "youngest son" and does not say it was a college education.

3. *Fort Worth Star-Telegram*, October 1, 1922.

4. Clifford R. Caldwell and Ron De Lord, *Eternity at the End of a Rope* (Santa Fe: Sunstone Press, 2015), 196. *Fort Worth Daily Gazette*, July 11, 1895.

5. James and Nellie Payne, Twelfth US Census (1900), Fort Worth, Tarrant County, TX.

6. Mehaly [*sic*] Butler in Tenth US Census (1880), Fort Worth, Tarrant County, TX. Henry H. Butler in Twelfth US Census (1900), Fort Worth, Tarrant County, TX. Mildred [sic] Butler in Thirteenth US Census (1910), Fort Worth, Tarrant County, TX. Key life dates for entries vary from one census to another. For example, Mahalia ("Makaly") might have been 14 or 15 when she married Butler, and he might have been 32 or 38. The best age to use is one connected to a specific birth date: for Mahalia January 28, 1867, and for Henry January 18, 1843. US Death Certificates, 1903–1982, "Mildred M. Butler," Bureau of Vital Statistics, TX Dept. of Health, Austin, TX, Certificate No. 4710, filed January 4, 1939. For Butler Housing Project, see *Fort Worth Star-Telegram*, July 22, 1940.

7. *Fort Worth Daily Gazette*, September 18, 1895. The 4 HBCUs in Texas at the time (with founding dates) were Paul Quinn (1872),

Wiley College (1873), Huston-Tillotson College (1875), and Prairie View A&M College (1876).

8. For singing, see *Fort Worth Telegram*, March 9, 1906. For memorial service, see *Fort Worth Daily Gazette*, March 6, 1895. *Fort Worth Record and Register*, August 7, 1901.

9. James Pratt in Twelfth US Census (1900), Fort Worth, Tarrant County, TX.

10. For singing and marriage, see *Fort Worth Telegram*, March 9, 1906.

11. Fort Worth *City Directory*, 1936–1947, Fort Worth Library History Center.

12. Betty Steward seems to be the sister of Lena Johson Pratt. At least they shared the same name, Johnson, through marriage. Betty married Tarrant County's Clifford (Clifton?) Steward in 1895. Lena Pratt signed off on her death certificate in 1946.

13. "Proud History," a brochure explaining "The Historic Wall," Fort Worth: Trinity Railway Express, the Black Historical and Genealogical Society, and Historic Fort Worth. For Castelan's mural, see *Fort Worth Star-Telegram*, February 12, 2023.

14. For a discussion of this important aspect of the Civil Rights Movement, see Dylan C. Penningroth, *Before the Movement: The Hidden History of Black Civil Rights* (New York: W. W. Norton, 2023).

Notes for Chapter 2

1. Timothy Foote, "George Washington Slept Here," *Smithsonian Magazine*, December 1999, at smithsonianmag.com/history/George-Washington-slept-here. Bill Markley, "Billy & Jesse," *Wild West Magazine*, December 2021, 42–43. For Fort Worth's "Billy," see Tarrant County Historic Ledgers, Tarrant County Convict Records, vol. 1, 1887–1890, Case No. 6621, July 8, 1890; and Richard Selcer, *Hell's Half-Acre* (Fort Worth: TCU Press, 1991), p. 216.

2. For background on the little-known Frank James, see Mark Lee Gardner, "The Other James Brother," *Wild West Magazine*, August 2013, 30–37.

3. W. C. Jameson, *Rocky Mountain Train Robberies: True Stories of Notorious Bandits and Infamous Escapades* (Helena, MT: TwoDot, 2019).

4. *Fort Worth Daily Gazette*, August 31 and September 2, 1883.

5. *Kansas City* (KS) *Times*, May 30, 1882. There is some question about exactly when they were married, 1874 or '75. Cf. *Press of Atlantic City* (NJ), April 16, 1939.

6. Quoted in *Galveston Daily News*, November 26, 1893.
7. James's gambling habits are not detailed, but it is doubtful he ever ran with the high rollers. *Fort Worth Daily Gazette*, July 21, 1893. For dime novel, see "Roundup" column, *Wild West Magazine*, October 2013, 7.
8. *Dallas Morning News*, July 14, 1915.
9. *Fort Worth Daily Gazette*, July 20, 1886.
10. *Fort Worth Daily Gazette*, July 20, 1886. For Courtright, see Richard Selcer, "Legendary Marshal Timothy Isaiah Courtright," in *Fort Worth Characters* (Denton: University of North Texas Press, 2009), 42–47.
11. *Dallas Morning News*, June 30, 1886. *Fort Worth Daily Gazette*, June 30 and July 20, 1886.
12. *Dallas Morning News*, June 30, 1886. *Fort Worth Daily Gazette*, July 20, 1886.
13. *Fort Worth Record*, February 10, 1921. For two-year stay, see *Fort Worth Daily Gazette*, March 31 and October 12, 1887.
14. *Austin American-Statesman*, March 4, 1887. *Fort Worth Record Telegram*, May 9, 1914. *Fort Worth Star-Telegram*, May 11, 1914.
15. *Fort Worth Daily Gazette*, October 12 and 13 (2 reports), 1887.
16. *Fort Worth Gazette*, September 11, 1891.
17. *Austin Weekly Statesman*, March 10, 1892. Ford himself was gunned down in a Creede saloon three months later.
18. *Galveston Daily News*, November 26, 1893. For Sanger Brothers connection, see *Austin American-Statesman*, January 2, 1895. For popularity with the women, see Stephen Harrigan, "Metamorphosis of a Killer," *American History Magazine*, June 2012, 59.
19. Theodore Dreiser, *A Book about Myself* (New York: Boni and Liveright, 1922), chap. 19. See also Dennis Bertram, "Letters to the Editor," *Wild West Magazine*, June 2022, 8. Dreiser's autobiography is a lesser work, known today only to scholars and his most devoted fans.
20. *Fort Worth Daily Gazette*, November 17, 1888. Bunch was never apprehended. He died in Mississippi in 1893. For Bunch, see *New Orleans Daily Picayune*, January 4, 1889; and *Fort Worth Morning Register*, March 3, 1897. For Masterson and Garrett, see Gardner, "Other James Brother," 37.
21. *Austin American-Statesman*, January 2, 1895.
22. *Fort Worth Record and Register*, September 10, 1899.
23. *Fort Worth Daily Gazette*, April 23, 1893. For Wild West show, see Craig Berry, *The Hidden History of Western Kentucky* (Charleston, SC: History Press, 2011).

24. Description of appearance is a composite from several sources: *Galveston Daily News*, November 26, 1893. *Fort Worth Daily Gazette*, July 21 and October 13, 1893. *Fort Worth Record and Register*, September 10, 1899. Harrigan, "Metamorphosis of a Killer," 56.

25. *Fort Worth Star-Telegram*, March 12, 1911.

26. *Fort Worth Record and Register*, November 14, 1901.

27. *Fort Worth Record and Register*, February 12, 1902. *El Paso Times*, November 26, 1901.

28. *Fort Worth Telegram*, August 17 and October 10, 1902; and October 11, 1903. For price of Buffalo Bill's tickets, see *Houston Post*, October 5, 1902. For Wild West Show, see Gardner, "Other James Brother," 37.

29. *Fort Worth Record and Register*, February 13, 1902.

30. Quoted in *Fort Worth Record and Register*, February 12, 1902.

31. *Fort Worth Record and Register*, February 17, 1902.

32. *Fort Worth Record and Register*, November 10, 1906. *Fort Worth Telegram*, March 12, 1911.

33. Interview with C. J. E. Keller, June 7, 1938, "Federal Writers' Project, Research Data: Fort Worth and Tarrant County," vol. 2, 494–95 (microfilm), Fort Worth Library History Center, 1941.

34. For price of admission, cf. *Fort Worth Record and Register*, July 20, 1913, which says twenty-five cents. For Mary James, see *Fort Worth Record and Register*, November 21, 1900. Another source says James charged fifty cents a person. Harrigan, "Metamorphosis of a Killer," 57.

35. *Fort Worth Star-Telegram*, May 11, 1914.

36. *Fort Worth Star-Telegram*, November 22, 1914; February 19, 1915. *Fort Worth Record-Telegram*, February 20, 1915. *McKinney* (TX) *Courier-Gazette*, March 12, 1915. For church membership, see Harrigan, "Metamorphosis of a Killer," 59.

37. *Fort Worth Record and Register*, September 6, 1908. For "Outlaw State," see editor's column, *Wild West Magazine*, December 2021, 4.

Notes for Chapter 3

1. "The *Nugget*'s Story," *Wild West Magazine*, October 2001, 42–43. Neil B. Carmony, "Hello Ike! Any New War?" *Quarterly of the National Association for Outlaw and Lawman History* 26, no. 1 (January–March 2002): 31. Will McLaury's letters are in the collections of the New York Historical Society. For who was armed and who wasn't, see Paula Mitchell Marks, *And Die in the West* (New York: William Morrow, 1989), 215–16, 221. For the full story of the McLaury

brothers "told from the viewpoint of Frank and Tom," see Paul Lee Johnson, *The McLaurys in Tombstone, Arizona: An O.K. Corral Obituary* (Denton: University of North Texas Press, 2012).

2. *Arizona Weekly Citizen* (Tuscon), November 6, 1881. For headline, see Joseph Patrick, "Home at the Corral," *Historic Traveler*, Autumn 1994, 36.

3. Gregory Michno, "Worse Than the Hostile Comanches," *Wild West Magazine*, October 2021, 60.

4. *Wild West Magazine*, October 1995 (p. 52) and October 2001 (p. 43). William M. Breckenridge, *Helldorado: Bringing the Law to the Mesquite* (New York: Houghton Mifflin, 1928).

5. Frank Waters, *The Earp Brothers of Tombstone: The Story of Mrs. Virgil Earp* (New York: Bramhall House, 1960).

6. Jeff Guinn, *The Last Gunfight* (New York: Simon & Schuster, 2011), 232. Bob Stinson, "Where Legends Rest in the West," *Wild West Magazine*, October 2012, 54.

7. *Fort Worth Daily Standard*, May 28, 1877. For Greene, see *Fort Worth Telegram*, June 30, 1904 (obituary).

8. Frank and Tom's Fort Worth connection to Fort Worth comes from UNT Press author Paul Lee Johnson in email dated June 15 and July 12, 2024.

9. *Dallas Daily Herald*, July 29, 1880. Paul Lee Johnson, "The Will of McLaury," *Wild West Magazine*, October 2013, 26–33. Interview with Paul Lee Johnson(author of *The McLaurys in Tombstone, Arizona* [Denton: University of North Texas Press, 2013]), by Johnny D. Boggs, *Wild West Magazine*, October 2013, 12–13.

10. Guinn, *Last Gunfight*, 244–51. Wyatt Earp and friends set out on their "vendetta ride" in 1882 to avenge the shooting of his brothers, Virgil and Morgan. Allen Barra, *Inventing Wyatt Earp: His Life and Many Legends* (New York: Caroll & Graf, 1998), 12, 233.

11. Karen Holliday Tanner, *Doc Holliday: A Family Portrait* (Norman: University of Oklahoma Press, 1998), 171. Guinn, *Last Gunfight*, 251.

12. Matthew Bernstein, *George Hearst: Silver King of the Golden Age* (Norman: University of Oklahoma Press, 2021). The Tombstone connection is summarized in Matthew Bernstein, "The Buffalo-Bone Cane Mystery," *Wild West Magazine*, Winter 2023, 66–71.

13. *Arizona Republic* (Phoenix), March 18, 1996. Guinn, *Last Gunfight*, 264–66.

14. *Fort Worth Daily Gazette*, September 12, 1884; April 5, 1885.

15. Johnson, "Will of McLaury," 33. *Fort Worth Daily Gazette*, September 2, 1891. *New Orleans Times-Picayune*, November 118, 1893.

16. *Fort Worth Daily Gazette*, April 16, 1894. *Fort Worth Record and Register*, July 8 and 15, 1900.

17. Dan Pritchett (brother-in-law) and L. A. Trimble (son-in-law). *Fort Worth Star-Telegram*, February 17, 1913; November 11, 1931.

Notes for Chapter 4

1. Celestina Blok, *Lost Restaurants of Fort Worth* (Charleston, SC: History Press, 2017), 17–25.

2. *Dallas Daily Herald*, February 6, 1873. *Fort Worth Daily Gazette*, January 10, 1883; and August 28, 1894.

3. *Fort Worth Star-Telegram*, July 27, 1919.

4. For local cost of a smoke, see *Fort Worth Daily Gazette*, July 27, 1883.

5. *Dallas Morning News*, January 16 and 17, 1889. For legal cost on the open market, see *Fort Worth Record and Register*, July 23, 1890.

6. *Fort Worth Daily Gazette*, July 27, 1883. *Fort Worth Telegram*, August 14, 1904.

7. *Fort Worth Daily Gazette*, February 5, 1888.

8. *Fort Worth Star-Telegram*, April 26, 1931.

9. *Fort Worth Star-Telegram*, July 27, 1919; April 26, 1931.

10. *Fort Worth Star-Telegram*, April 26, 1931.

11. Lady George Munchus-Forde, "History of the Negro in Fort Worth; Syllabus for a High School Course," (master's thesis, Fisk University, 1941), 33. (The author compares the Black community in these years with other minority communities in Fort Worth.)

12. *Fort Worth Record and Register*, August 15, 1906.

13. *Fort Worth Record and Register*, August 15, 1906. *Fort Worth Star-Telegram*, July 27, 1919.

14. *Fort Worth Star-Telegram*, January 26. 1909.

15. Jacob W. Olmstead, *The Frontier Centennial: Fort Worth and the New West* (Lubbock: Texas Tech University Press, 2021), 94.

Notes for Chapter 5

1. Charlsie Poe, *Booger Red: World Champion Cowboy* (Winters, TX: privately printed, 1991), 1–2, 105–6. Even his biographer is unclear when he was born, citing different dates at different points in her story! For his business name, see *Fort Worth Telegram*, March 6, 1904.

2. Poe, *Booger Red*, 78.
3. Poe, *Booger Red*, 13.
4. *Seguin Gazette-Enterprise*, October 30, 1991.
5. Charlise Poe, who says he was born in 1858, also says he was 31 when they married in 1895. Poe, *Booger Red*, 1 and 17. If, as some accounts say, he was born in 1864, then he was just 31 years old, still a May-December romance by any standard.
6. Poe, *Booger Red*, 15.
7. Poe, *Booger Red*, 32, 38, 113.
8. Or Booger Red's Wild West & Vaudeville Show, according to Poe, *Booger Red*, 106.
9. Poe, *Booger Red*, 33, 37.
10. *Fort Worth Telegram*, March 6, 1904.
11. For a general history of these women, see Chris Enss, *Along Came a Cowgirl: Daring and Iconic Women of the Rodeo & Wild West Shows* (Helena, MT: Farcountry Press, 2022). See also "Double Billing" in *Wild West Magazine*, December 2021, 18.
12. Frederick Melton "Foghorn" Clancy, *My Fifty Years in Rodeo: Living with Cowboys, Horses, and Danger* (San Antonio: Naylor, 1952), 5–6.
13. Poe, *Booger Red*, 24. Pickett was rodeo's first celebrity black performer, known as "the Bull Dog N——" to white Southern audiences. *Fort Worth Telegram*, March 6, 1904.
14. For the world's fair, see Cindy Jones, "Privett, Samuel Thomas, Jr. [Booger Red]," *Handbook of Texas Online*, February 9, 2009, https://www.tshaonline.org/handbook/entries/privett-samuel-thomas-jr-booger-red. For the exposition, see Poe, *Booger Red*, 30, 80–81.
15. *Fort Worth Star-Telegram*, March 19, 1916.
16. Olmstead, *Frontier Centennial*, 18.
17. Poe, *Booger Red*, 31.
18. Poe, *Booger Red*, 2.
19. Poe, *Booger Red*, 37.
20. *Fort Worth Star-Telegram*, February 25, 1917; March 10, 1919.
21. *Fort Worth Star-Telegram*, March 11, 1924. Poe, *Booger Red*, ii, 1.
22. Poe, *Booger Red*, 77, 105–6, 111.
23. *Fort Worth Star-Telegram*, June 7 and July 7, 1946; January 29, 1956. Tom Mulvaney, "Booger Red's Last Ride," *Southwestern Review*, Autumn 1944; repr. in *Reader's Digest*, Vol. 8, No. 290 (June 1946).
24. Poe, *Booger Red*, 103. *Fort Worth Star-Telegram*, July 12, 2024.

Notes for Chapter 6

1. Penal Code of the State of Texas, Chapter VII, "Of Abortion," Articles 531–536, adopted by the Sixth Legislature, 1857. Cf. Under current Texas law (2023) abortion's legality is sidestepped by allowing private citizens to bring a civil lawsuit against anyone who "aids or abets" the procedure. In this way the state is not involved in deciding the constitutionality of abortion; it is a civil matter. The private citizen can sue for up to ten thousand dollars. *Fort Worth Star-Telegram*, October 31, 2021.
2. *Dallas Daily Times-Herald*, April 20 and 21, 1894.
3. *Dallas Morning News*, September 13, 1894.
4. *Dallas Morning News*, June 16; July 4, 11, and 12, 1912. *Fort Worth Star-Telegram*, June 16, 1912. *Houston Post*, July 9 and 11, 1912. *Fort Worth Record and Register*, July 12 and 14, 1912. *San Angelo* (TX) *Evening Standard*, July 14, 1912.
5. *Fort Worth Star-Telegram*, November 20, 1928 (obit). *Nashville Tennessean*, October 14, 1876 (marriage announcement). Tenth US Census, 1880, Dallas, Dallas County. Twelfth US Census, 1900, Fort Worth, Tarrant County. Thirteenth US Census, 1910, Fort Worth, Tarrant County. Fourteenth US Census, 1920, Fort Worth, Tarrant County. TX.
6. *Fort Worth Star-Telegram*, December 12, 1909. For animal trap, see William A. Link, "Animal Trap," January 14, 1913, Texas Patents, Govt. Docs. Dept, UNT Libraries, Portal to Texas History, https://texashistory.unt.edu/ark:/67531/metapth508343.
7. *Fort Worth Star-Telegram*, January 10, 1912.
8. *Fort Worth Star-Telegram*, February 6, 1911; and February 18, 1913.
9. *Fort Worth Star-Telegram*, June 27, 1913.
10. *Fort Worth Star-Telegram*, June 19, 1913.
11. *Fort Worth Star-Telegram*, June 26, 1913.
12. *Fort Worth Star-Telegram*, June 29, 1913.
13. *Fort Worth Star-Telegram*, June 26 and 29, 1913.
14. *Fort Worth Star-Telegram*, June 26 and 27, 1913.
15. *Fort Worth Star-Telegram*, July 9, 1913. *Fort Worth Record*, June 28, 1914.
16. *Fort Worth Star-Telegram*, June 29; July 1 and 5, 1913.
17. *Fort Worth Star-Telegram*, February 18, March 11, 19, and 20, 1914. For revocation of medical license, see *Fort Worth Star-Telegram*, May 1, 1916.

18. *Fort Worth Star-Telegram*, December 27, 1914; October 10, 1928.

19. *Fort Worth Record-Telegram*, October 10, 1928; and January 9, 1929. *Fort Worth Star-Telegram*, November 20, 1928.

20. *Fort Worth Star-Telegram*, November 15 and 16, 1977 (obit). Marriage Licenses, E. B. Youngblood to Miss Daisy Moore, Park City, Utah, *Fort Worth Star-Telegram*, March 12, 1918. Mary Daisy Moore Youngblood, Buried, Mount Olivet Cemetery, *Find a Grave*, accessed November 15, 2024, https://www.findagrave.com/memorial/152594395/mary-daisy-youngblood.

21. *Fort Worth Star-Telegram*, April 16, 1921.

Notes for Chapter 7

1. Sells does not have a published biography. Much of the information on him comes from his obituaries printed in several newspapers around the country. Unfortunately, some of the details in those obituaries are incorrect. The Fort Worth Library has Cato Sells Papers, 1920–1929, (Accession No. 0000.138), Fort Worth Library History Center.

2. Ely Parker was a member of the Seneca tribe. He served as aide and secretary to Ulysses Grant during the Civil War, rising to the rank of brigadier general. After being elected president, Grant appointed him to head the Bureau of Indian Affairs. After losing everything in the stock market crash, Parker lived out his last years in poverty. See Dee Brown, *Bury My Heart at Wounded Knee* (New York: Barrie & Jenkins, 1973), chap. 8. For "Godfather," see *Fort Worth Star-Telegram*. December 31, 1948 (obit.). For "Father," see *Daily Ardmore* (OK) *Ardmoreite*, January 4, 1920.

3. *Fort Worth Star-Telegram*, June 21, 1941. "Cato Hedden Sells," *Find a Grave*, accessed November 16, 2024, https://www.findagrave.com/memorial/104667038/cato-hedden-sells. For origins of name, see *Davenport* (IA) *Quad-City Times*, July 18, 1899.

4. *Fort Worth Star-Telegram*, December 31, 1948 (obit).

5. *Davenport Quad-City Times*, July 18, 1899. *Marshalltown* (IA) *Evening Times-Republican*, August 16, 1899.

6. *Fort Worth Star-Telegram*, September 26, 1920. For causes, see *Waco* (TX) *Times-Herald*, April 25, 1924; and *Fort Worth Star-Telegram*, June 21, 1941. *Fort Worth Star-Telegram*, December 31, 1948 (obit).

7. *Dallas Morning News*, February 19, 1907. *Fort Worth Star-Telegram*, December 31, 1948 (obit). *Corpus Christi Caller-Times*, December 31,

1948 (obit). For "reputation," see *Fort Worth Star-Telegram*, November 27, 1907.

8. *Fort Worth Record and Register*, October 15, 1908. *Dallas Morning News*, June 19, 1912. For spelling bee, see *Cleburne* (TX) *Morning Review*, March 21, 1909.

9. *Dallas Morning News*, July 19 and December 13, 1912. *Fort Worth Star-Telegram*, June 21, 1941. For "Immortal 40," see *Fort Worth Star-Telegram*, December 31, 1948 (obit).

10. *Dallas Morning News*, March 9, 1913. *Fort Worth Star-Telegram*, May 24, 1913. For joke, see *Wilkes-Barre* (PA) *Times-Leader*, September 15, 1913. *Fort Worth Star-Telegram*. December 31, 1948 (obit.).

11. *Lexington Herald*, December 18, 1914. *Davenport Quad-City Times*, October 19, 1915. *Fort Worth Star-Telegram*, October 22, 1915. For "busiest man," see *Los Angeles Evening Express*, August 20, 1915. For "myself" quote, see *Daily Ardmore Ardmoreite*, January 4, 1920. Thirteenth United States Census (1910) and Fourteenth United States Census (1920).

12. *Miami Herald*, March 26, 1914. *Lexington Herald*, December 18, 1914. *Fort Worth Star-Telegram*, December 31, 1948 (obit). His stand against polygamy would have put him at odds with Quanah Parker, who had eight wives, but Quanah died in 1911.

13. "Cato Heddon Sells," *Find a Grave*.

14. *Fort Worth Telegram*, November 12, 1907. *Fort Worth Star-Telegram*, July 9 and October 12, 1917; March 7, 1918. *Dallas Morning News*, March 8, 1918.

15. *Waterloo* (IA) *Courier*, April 6, 1910. *Dallas Morning News*, July 4, 1915. *Grand Forks* (ND) *Daily Herald*, March 26, 1916. *Dallas Morning News*, April 15, 1916. *Fort Worth Star-Telegram*, May 28, 1916.

16. *Dallas Morning News*, February 27, 1915; and November 22, 1918. *Fort Worth Star-Telegram*, July 9, 1917; and June 1, 1919. *Fort Worth Telegram*, April 1, 1908. For copies of Sells's speeches, see Cato Sells Papers, 1920–1929, Box 1, Fort Worth Library History Center.

17. *Fort Worth Star-Telegram*, September 19, 1916.

18. *Dallas Morning News*, February 7, 1915. Ralph A. Wooster, *Texas and Texans in the Great War* (Kerrville, TX: State House Press, 2010).

19. *Fort Worth Star-Telegram*, March 17 and April 14, 1918.

20. *Macon* (GA) *Telegraph*, November 16, 1918. *Fort Worth Star-Telegram*, November 15, 1978. *Dallas Morning News*, November 22, 1918.

21. *White Earth* (MN) *Tomahawk*, June 17, 1920. *New York Times*, December 28, 1914. *Fort Worth Star-Telegram*, December 31, 1948 (Obit). Cato Sells Papers, 1920–1929, Fort Worth Library.

22. *Wyoming State Tribune*, August 18, 1920. *Fort Worth Star-Telegram*, November 11, 1948.

23. *Fort Worth Star-Telegram*, April 24, 1921.

24. *Fort Worth Star-Telegram*, September 26, 1920; April 10 and 17, 1921. *Dallas Morning News*, September 27, 1920. For residences, see *Fort Worth Star-Telegram*, June 21, 1941; and March 8, 1948.

25. *Fort Worth Star-Telegram*, December 31, 1948 (obit). For "Special," see Cato Sells Papers, 1920–1929, Box 1, Fort Worth Library History Center.

26. Cato Sells Papers, 1920–1929, Box 1, Fort Worth Library History Center.

27. Brian A. Cervantez, *Amon Carter: A Lone Star Life* (Norman: University of Oklahoma Press, 2019), 66.

28. *Fort Worth Star-Telegram*, June 21, 1941.

29. *Fort Worth Star-Telegram*, December 31, 1948 (obit). *Corpus Christi Caller-Times*, December 31, 1948 (obit). *Wichita Falls* (TX) *Times*, December 31, 1948 (obit). "Cato Heddon Sells," *Find a Grave*.

30. *Galveston Daily News*, April 10, 1921.

31. *Fort Worth Star-Telegram*, November 6, 1927.

32. *Marshall* (TX) *News Messenger*, January 5, 1924.

33. *Fort Worth Record-Telegram*, November 20, 1922.

34. *Fort Worth Star-Telegram*, November 11, 1948. Julien Hyer, *The Land of Beginning Again* (Atlanta: Foote & Davis, 1952), 355–56.

Notes for Chapter 8

1. As a professional she never used the name "Minnia." After relocating to New York, she tried to spell it "Manette," but apparently found it easier to go with the simplified spelling, "Manet," which is how she was known for most of her adult life. See "Fowler, Manette" in Fourteenth Census of the US, 1920, Tarrant County, Fort Worth, TX, Sheet No. 14B; and "Manet H. Fowler," in Fifteenth Census of the US, 1930, Tarrant County, Fort Worth, TX, Sheet No. 15A.

2. For "Minnie," see *Fort Worth Star-Telegram*, November 18, 1915. For "Banet," see *Chicago Defender*, May 13, 1939. The first appearance of her chosen name, "Manette," appears in 1917. *Fort Worth*

Star-Telegram, May 1, 1917. After her marriage in 1915, newspapers found it easier to refer to her as "Mrs. S. H. Fowler." See *Dallas Express*, March 5, 1921. Local lore says here parents worked for B. B. Paddock, legendary editor, mayor, and civic leader of Fort Worth. The Thirteenth and Fourteenth US Census reports (1900 and 1910) say he was a "day laborer" before going to work for the US Post Office.

3. On November 17, 1915, Manet was part of a "memorial service" in Fort Worth for Booker T. Washington, who had died just two days earlier. She spoke as his "former pupil," sharing her memories of the great man. *Fort Worth Star-Telegram*, November 18, 1915. Years later Manet was considered one of Carver's most distinguished students. *New York New Age*, January 16, 1954. For "high/highest honors," see *Chicago Defender*, May 13, 1939; and Laurie E. Jasinski, "Fowler, Manet Harrison," *Handbook of Texas Online*, May 29, 2013, https://www.tshaonline.org/handbook/entries/fowler-manet-harrison. Stephen's biographical details are typically combined with Manet's. See "Manet Harrison Fowler," *Wikipedia*, accessed November 18, 2024, https://en.wikipedia.org/wiki/Manet_Harrison_Fowler; and Jasinski, "Fowler, Manet Harrison."

4. For overview of her life and education by one who knew her well, see E. Clyde Whitlock in *Fort Worth Star-Telegram*, June 10, 1962. For schools, see Richard Selcer, *A History of Fort Worth in Black & White* (Denton: University of North Texas Press, 2015), 151 and 153.

5. For children, see *Fort Worth Star-Telegram*, June 10, 1962,

6. For "director of music," see *Fort Worth Star-Telegram*, May 1, 1917. For "General Secretary" and "cooperation," see *Fort Worth Star-Telegram*, September 12 and October 7, 1919. The "Negro YMCA" was also known as the "Colored branch of the [Fort Worth] YMCA."

7. For Manet, see *Dallas Express*, March 5, 1921; and *Fort Worth Record and Register*, June 15, 1928. For Stephen, see *Fort Worth Star-Telegram*, April 2, 1921; and Fort *Worth Record*, September 28, 1922. For Pageants, see *Fort Worth Star-Telegram*, November 22 and 23, 1921; and April 30, 1930; and *Pittsburgh Courier*, August 16, 1930. For "The Voice," see the *Chicago Defender*, August 9, 1930.

8. The NANM was organized in 1919. The Texas branch was an early affiliate. *Fort Worth Star-Telegram*, June 5, 1926; and April 30, 1930. For school's mission, see also *Chicago Defender*, May 13, 1939.

9. *Fort Worth Record and Register*, June 15 and 18, 1928.

10. *Fort Worth Star-Telegram*, August 15, 1929; and November 9, 1930; and February 3, 1934. Later accounts say that first "Master School" was six weeks long (*Chicago Defender*, May 13, 1939). For Whitlock, see *Pittsburgh Courier*, February 3, 1934; and *Fort Worth Star-Telegram*, November 9, 1930; May 8, 1932; October 16, 1933; March 18, 1934; May 12 and 17, 1935; May 28, 1939; and June 10, 1962.

11. For "church music," see *Fort Worth Star-Telegram*, August 15, 1929. For TANM convention, see *Fort Worth Star-Telegram*, June 17, 1928. It was in hope of attracting more events like the 1929 NANM convention to Fort Worth that "Gooseneck Bill" McDonald opened the "Hotel Jim" in 1930. For critical praise and "dramatic soprano," see the *Chicago Defender*, August 9, 1930; and *Fort Worth Star-Telegram*, April 30, 1930; and March 1, 1932.

12. *Fort Worth Star-Telegram*, April 30, 1930; and May 17, 1935. For program, see *Fort Worth Star-Telegram*, November 9, 1930; and May 8, 1932. For "national figure," see *Pittsburgh Courier*, August 16, 1930.

13. *Fort Worth Star-Telegram*, November 9, 1930; and May 8, 1932; May 12 and 17, 1935.

14. Alternately, the word was said to mean "self-betterment." Use of the Swahili must have been because Swahili is a phonetic language (the words sound exactly as they look) whereas Yoruba is a tonal language where the same word can have as many as twenty different meanings according to how it is pronounced. The school's first location was in the Bronx. *New York New Age*, January 8, 1932; April 8, 1933; and June 25, 1938. *New York Daily News*, May 7, 1935. For "civilization," etc., see *Chicago Defender*, May 13, 1939. Harold Rich, *Fort Worth between the World Wars* (College Station: Texas A&M University Press, 2020), 209.

15. The Mwalimu Creed was published in *The Negro Musician*, official publication of the NANM, in January 1929. Emile Coué, the French psychologist and pharmacist (1857–1926), formulated the mantra, "Every day in every way I'm getting better and better," subsequently known as Couéism.

16. For origins of Mwalimu School, see *Fort Worth Star-Telegram*, March 1 and May 8, 1932; and February 3 and March 18, 1934; *Pittsburgh Courier*, February 3, 1934; and *Chicago Defender*, May 13, 1939. For curriculum, see *New York Daily News*, May 7, 1935.

17. For choral performances, see *Fort Worth Star-Telegram*, March 18, 1934; and *New York New Age*, March 24, 1934; May 2, 1936; and April 1, 1939. For oratorios, see *New York Age*, December 21, 1935. For "jungle rhythms," see *Pittsburgh Courier*, February 3, 1934.

18. *New York New Age*, June 25, 1938. For "home base," see *Fort Worth Star-Telegram*, June 10, 1962. For "African village," see *Chicago Defender*, May 13, 1939.

19. "Stephen Hamilton Fowler," *Find a Grave*, accessed November 18, 2024, https://www.findagrave.com/memorial/123097911/stephen-hamilton-fowler.

20. For Negro teachers, see *Fort Worth Star-Telegram*, November 27, 1932. For Negro YMCA, see *Fort Worth Star-Telegram*, October 16, 1933; and October 3, 1935. For resignation, see *Fort Worth Star-Telegram*, May 22, 1941. *New York New Age*, June 25, 1938.

21. For booking agency, see *Fort Worth Star-Telegram*, October 6, 1957. For reopening school, see *Fort Worth Star-Telegram*, June 10, 1962. The record also shows that Manet graduated from Tuskegee in 1913, which does not jibe with a high school graduation in 1912. She was probably just an honored guest, being a famous contemporary of the reunion class.

22. *Fort Worth Star-Telegram*, November 6, 1932; January 30, 1953; and June 10, 1962. For Manet Helen, see Rich, *Fort Worth between the World Wars*, 209.

23. *Post-Standard* (Syracuse, NY), October 26, 1965. *Poughkeepsie* (NY) *Journal*, October 27, 1965. *Chicago Defender*, November 2, 1965. For school naming, see *Fort Worth Star-Telegram*, January 26, 1989.

24. Clyde Whitlock in *Fort Worth Star-Telegram*, May 8, 1932.

25. "NANM Honors Duke Ellington and Margaret Harris [*sic*] at Confab in '72," *Chicago Daily Defender*, July 22, 1972. Cary D. Wintz and Paul Finkelman, eds., *Encyclopedia of the Harlem Renaissance*, 2 vols. (New York: Taylor and Francis, 2004), 1:523.

26. For first concert, see the *Chicago Defender*, May 13, 1939. For *Newsweek*, see *Chicago Defender*, May 28, 1939, although without a comprehensive index, it is impossible to tell which issue.

27. For pageants, see *Chicago Defender*, August 9, 1930. For radio, see *Fort Worth Star-Telegram*, December 21, 1930. For "symphonic poem," see Jasinski, "Fowler, Manet Harrison." For NANM award, see *Chicago Defender*, July 22, 1972.

Notes for Chapter 9

1. The earliest biography of Carroll was Jefferson Davis Ray, *B. H. Carroll* (Nashville, TN: Sunday School Board of the Southern Baptist Convention, 1927). The modern biography is Alan J. Lefever, *Fighting the Good Fight: The Life and Work of Benajah Harvey Carroll* (Austin: Eakin Press, 1994). For church background, see John M. Carroll, *History of Texas Baptists* (privately printed, 1923; repr., New South Wales, Australia: Generic Publications, 2020).

2. *Fort Worth Star-Telegram*, November 11, 1914 (obit). For an overview of Carroll's life, see Lefever, *Fighting the Good Fight*; and "Carroll, B. H." in Norman Wade Cox, ed., *Encyclopedia of Southern Baptists* (Nashville: Broadman, 1958), vol. 1.

3. *Dallas Morning News*, November 11, 1914.

4. Benajah Harvey/B. H. Carroll in https://www.ancestry.com. See in particular Fold3 Confederates section (https://www.fold3.com) for military service, and "Benajah Harvey Carroll Sr.," *Find a Grave*, accessed November 18, 2024, https://www.findagrave.com/memorial/8468114/benajah-harvey-carroll, for biographical details. *Dallas Morning News*, May 30, 1898. *Fort Worth Star-Telegram*, November 11, 1914 (obit). For blue and gray veterans, see *Dallas Morning News*, May 30, 1898.

5. *Fort Worth Star-Telegram*, November 11, 1914 (obit). *Houston Post*, November 15, 1914 (obit).

6. *Marshall* (TX) *Evening Messenger*, November 7, 1897 (obit); and February 10, 1899. *St. Louis Globe-Democrat*, November 6, 1897 (obit). *Fort Worth Star-Telegram*, July 18, 1938 (obit). "Benajah Harvey Carroll Sr.," *Find a Grave*. *Fort Worth Star-Telegram*, November 11, 1914 (obit). *Houston Post*, November 15, 1914 (obit).

7. *Houston Post*, November 15, 1914 (obit). *Marshall Evening Messenger*, February 10, 1899.

8. *Fort Worth Record and Register*, September 9, 1909. *Houston Post*, November 15, 1914 (obit).

9. *Fort Worth Star-Telegram*, November 11 and 12, 1914 (obits); January 28, 1921. *Dallas Morning News*, November 11 (obit) and December 28, 1914. *Tulsa Evening Sun*, November 11, 1914 (obit).

10. *Fort Worth Star-Telegram*, November 14 and 15, 1914; and July 18, 1938 (obit).

11. *Fort Worth Star-Telegram*, December 13, 1914; January 28, 1921.

12. *Fort Worth Star-Telegram*, April 1, 1922 (obit). For the school, see *Fort Worth Star-Telegram*, June 16 and October 31, 1922; and September 30 and October 3, 1941. For closing and reopening plans, see *Fort Worth Star-Telegram*, April 1, 1983, and November 12, 1984.

13. *Fort Worth Star-Telegram*, July 26, 1918; April 11 and 12, 1938 (obits).

14. *Fort Worth Star-Telegram*, September 22, 1956; and February 27, 1965.

15. For knowledge of scripture and "higher calling, " see *Houston Post*, November 15, 1914 (obit). *Fort Worth Star-Telegram*, August 27, 1945; and January 26, 1958. For critical view, see Joseph Early Jr., "B. H. Carroll," address delivered at the East Texas Historical Association–West Texas Historical Association's annual convention, Fort Worth, TX, February 26, 2010. For his "infidel" period, see B. H. Carroll, "My Infidelity and What Became of It," Biblical Addresses, and Educational and Religious Addresses Collection, ed. J. H. Crowder, Roberts Library, Southwestern Baptist Theological Seminary, Fort Worth.

16. *Fort Worth Star-Telegram*, August 27, 1945.

Notes for Chapter 10

1. *Fort Worth Star-Telegram*, June 18, 1939. The Juneteenth holiday act was signed into law by President Joe Biden on June 17, 2021 with Opal Lee was in attendance. For a history of the date, see *Fort Worth Star-Telegram*, June 19, 2022.

2. *Whitewright* (TX) *Sun*, November 24, 1916.

3. *Whitewright Sun*, November 24, 1916. *Fort Worth Star-Telegram*, October 5, 1923 (obit).

4. *Fort Worth Star-Telegram*, October 22, 1954 (obit).

5. *Fort Worth Star-Telegram*, September 4, 1943. *Fort Worth Star-Telegram*, October 5, 1923 (obit).

6. *Fort Worth Star-Telegram*, July 1, 1920; November 22, 1925; August 19, 1926; and September 4, 1943.

7. *Fort Worth Star-Telegram*, October 22, 1954 (obit). *Fort Worth Telegram*, October 17, 1904.

8. Roger N. Conger, "William Cowper Brann," in *The New Handbook of Texas*, ed. Ron Tyler, 6 vols. (Austin: Texas State Historical Association, 1996), 1:704. *Fort Worth Star-Telegram*, October 22, 1954 (obit). *Fort Worth Record*, December 25, 1918.

9. *Fort Worth Star-Telegram*, October 22, 1954 (obit).

10. *Fort Worth Star-Telegram*, March 17, 1916.

11. *Fort Worth Star-Telegram*, December 26, 1918 (with photo); January 21, 1919; August 12 and 19, 1920. *Fort Worth Record-Telegram*, September 19, 1920. *Fort Worth Record*, September 19, 1920.

12. *Fort Worth Star-Telegram*, September 16, 1934.

13. *Fort Worth Star-Telegram*, January 16, 1916; January 21 and February 2, 1919; September 1, 1937. Thirteenth US Census, 1910, for Mabel C. Curtis, Fort Worth, Tarrant County, TX. Fourteenth US Census, 1920, for Charles Lucius Stowe, Fort Worth, Tarrant County, TX. Fifteenth US Census, 1930, for Charles L. Stowe, Fort Worth, Tarrant County, TX.

14. *Fort Worth Star-Telegram*, December 26, 1918; January 21 and 25 and March 9, 1919. *Fort Worth Record-Telegram*, December 27, 1918.

15. *Wichita County Times*, reprinted in *Fort Worth Star-Telegram*, March 9, 1919. For "retired," see *Fort Worth Star-Telegram*, October 22, 1954 (obit).

16. *Fort Worth Star-Telegram*, February 15 and 28; April 7, 1933; October 22, 1954 (obit).

17. *Fort Worth Star-Telegram*, October 2, 1954 (obit).

18. *Fort Worth Star-Telegram*, July 17, 1936; September 12, 1948; and April 10, 1946.

19. *Fort Worth Star-Telegram*, May 14, 1939.

20. *Fort Worth Star-Telegram*, May 13, 14, and 16, 1939.

21. *Fort Worth Star-Telegram*, June 18, 19, 20, and 21, 1939. Later accusations of arson come from *Star-Telegram* columnist Bud Kennedy and Opal Lee herself. The woman's memory may have been shaped by popular perception dating to the civil rights era. See *Fort Worth Star-Telegram*, January 15, 2017; and June 14, 2020.

22. *Austin American-Statesman*, June 20, 1939.

23. *Fort Worth Star-Telegram*, May 13 and 14, 1939.

24. *Fort Worth Star-Telegram*, September 4, 1943.

25. *Fort Worth Star-Telegram*, July 18, 1926; September 16, 1934; October 22, 1954 (obit).

26. *Fort Worth Star-Telegram*, February 12 and 13, 1951; October 22, 1954 (obit). For Elmwood, a.k.a. the "County Home," see *Fort Worth Star-Telegram*, December 13, 1954. For Rubye Stowe, see *Fort Worth Star-Telegram*, November 10, 1914.

27. *Fort Worth Record*, December 25, 1918. For "Place 10" and "hellraiser," see *Fort Worth Star-Telegram*, October 22, 1954 (obit).

Notes for Chapter 11

1. *Fort Worth Star-Telegram*, June 1, 1936; November 1, 1936. Mike Nichols, "Cowtown Sallys Forth: The Frontier Centennial," *Hometown by Handlebar*, blog, July 18, 2022, https://hometownbyhandlebar. com/?p=10644.
2. Twelfth US Census (1900) for William Wesley Copenhaver, Chickasaw Nation, OK; Thirteenth US Census (1910) for Leonard B. Osborne, South Cement, Caddo County, OK; Fourteenth US Census (1920) for Guy A. Cotton, Rush Springs, Grady County, OK; Fifteenth US Census (1930) for E. T. Brown, Borger, Hutchinson County, TX; Sixteenth US Census (1940) for Everett Benjamin King, Amarillo, Potter County, TX. *Fresno* (CA) *Bee*, November 28, 1992 (obit).
3. Olmstead, *Frontier Centennial*, 136–37.
4. *Fort Worth Daily Gazette*, September 20, 1892.
5. *Fort Worth Star-Telegram*, March 18, and August 12, 1936.
6. *Fort Worth Star-Telegram*, June 1, 1936. Olmstead (*Frontier Centennial*, 137) says there were eighty-two contestants; the *Star-Telegram* says there were seventy-five.
7. *Fort Worth Star-Telegram*, July 18, 1936.
8. For "most beautiful," see *Fort Worth Star-Telegram*, July 10, 1949. For "one of the most beautiful," see *Fort Worth Star-Telegram*, May 31, and June 1, 1936; and *San Angelo* (TX) *Standard-Times*, May 31, 1936. For favorite activities, see Debbie M. Liles, *Will Rogers Coliseum*, Images of America Series (Charleston, SC: Arcadia, 2012), 25.
9. *Fort Worth Press*, June 4 and 8, 1936. *Fort Worth Star-Telegram*, July 29, and August 12, 1936.
10. *Fort Worth Star-Telegram*, April 2, 1937.
11. *Fort Worth Star-Telegram*, July 15, 1936. For size of stage, see *Fort Worth Star-Telegram*, July 14, 1946.
12. *Fort Worth Star-Telegram*, July 17, 18, and 19; August 3, 1936. The time was corrected after being reported incorrectly the day before. For "attendants," see *Fort Worth Star-Telegram*, July 19, 1936.
13. *San Angelo Standard-Times*, May 31, 1936. *Fort Worth Star-Telegram*, July 8, and 28, 1936. For weight of gown, see *Fort Worth Star-Telegram*, July 8, 1936; and July 14, 1946.
14. *Fort Worth Star-Telegram*, July 4, 20, and 30, 1936. *Waterloo Daily Courier*, July 23, 1936.

15. *Fort Worth Star-Telegram*, July 17 and 29, 1936.

16. *Fort Worth Star-Telegram*, September 20, 1936. For jewels, see *Fort Worth Star-Telegram*, September 23, 1936; *Corsicana* (TX) *Daily Sun*, October 3, 1936; *Chillicothe* (MO) *Constitution-Tribune*, October 5, 1936. For paper-doll designs, see *Fort Worth Star-Telegram*, October 29, November 1, and November 8, 1936.

17. *Fort Worth Star-Telegram*, June 1, 1936. Olmstead, *Frontier Centennial*, 123.

18. *Fort Worth Star-Telegram*, August 11, and November 2, 1936. President Franklin D. Roosevelt and Vice President John Nance Garner were running for reelection in 1936. One of the souvenir coins is in the collections of the Dolph Briscoe History Center for American History, University of Texas, Austin, TX.

19. *Fort Worth Star-Telegram*, August 12, 1936.

20. *Fort Worth Star-Telegram*, July 20 and 30, August 11 and 12, October 22, 1936.

21. *Fort Worth Star-Telegram*, November 6, 8, and 17, 1936.

22. *Fort Worth Star-Telegram*, November 17, 1936.

23. *Fort Worth Star-Telegram*, January 25 and February 16, 1937.

24. *Fort Worth Star-Telegram*, March 12 and 21; April 18, 1937.

25. *Fort Worth Star-Telegram*, June 8, 1937; July 4, 1939.

26. *Fort Worth Star-Telegram*, March 14, 1937. The *Star-Telegram* used both terms to describe the event. For "Fiesta," see July 5, 10, 24, 27, and 29, 1937. For "Festival," see July 7, 8, and 11, 1937.

27. *Fort Worth Star-Telegram*, March 29, and April 2, 1937; and *Fort Worth Star-Telegram*, "Time Frames," June 5, 2017.

28. *Fort Worth Star-Telegram*, April 3, 1937; and *Fort Worth Star-Telegram*, "Time Frames," June 5, 2017.

29. *Fort Worth Star-Telegram*, April 3, June 6, 11, and 28; July 1, 1937.

30. *Fort Worth Star-Telegram*, June 11 and August 7, 1937; April 30, 1941.

31. *Fort Worth Star-Telegram*, April 30, 1941.

32. *Fort Worth Star-Telegram*, July 24, 1939.

33. *Bryan* (TX) *Eagle*, February 10, 1941.

34. *Fort Worth Star-Telegram*, January 15, 1946. Their son was William Greg Shelton, born October 11, 1946.

35. *Fort Worth Star-Telegram*, July 14, 1946,

36. *Fort Worth Star-Telegram*, July 16, 1976; July 10, 1949.

37. For Elston Brooks, see *Fort Worth Star-Telegram*, July 16, 1976. For Ed Brice, see *Fort Worth Star-Telegram*, September 18, 1985.

38. *Fresno Bee*, November 28, 1992.
39. *Wichita Falls* (TX) *Times Record*, March 8, 1937.
40. Liles, *Will Rogers Coliseum*, 25.
41. Frank Jackson, "When Tinseltown Came to Cowtown," *Legacies: A History Journal for Dallas and North Central Texas* 34, no. 2 (Fall 2022): 25. Olmstead, *Frontier Centennial*, 139–40.

Notes for Chapter 12

1. Mary's story is also told by Bill Fairley in "Tarrant Chronicles," *Fort Worth Star-Telegram*, November 4, 1998, a regular column, each one on a different subject.
2. Arthur Edwin Dowell in https://ancestors.FamilySearch.org. *Fort Worth Star-Telegram*, June 8, 1921 (obit).
3. Arthur Edwin Dowell in https://ancestors.FamilySearch.org. *Fort Worth Star-Telegram*, November 3, 1921; and April 11, 1963 (obit). *Fort Worth Record-Telegram*, September 5, 1930. For Cadillac, see *Fort Worth Press*, December 2, 1925.
4. *Fort Worth Star-Telegram*, June 8, 1942 (obit in 2 stories).
5. *Fort Worth Record-Telegram*, February 25, 1923. *Fort Worth Star-Telegram*, June 1, 1923; July 8, 1924. *Fort Worth Press*, March 7, 1927.
6. *Fort Worth Star-Telegram*, January 27, 1927.
7. *Fort Worth Star-Telegram*, April 10, 1937.
8. *Fort Worth Star-Telegram*, October 13, 1938 (2 stories). *Dallas Morning News*, October 13, 1938.
9. *Fort Worth Star-Telegram*, June 8 (2 stories) and 9, 1942 (obits).
10. *Fort Worth Star-Telegram*, April 10 and 11, 1963 (obits). Bill Fairley column "Tarrant Chronicles," *Fort Worth Star-Telegram*, November 4, 1998. For "statuesque," see *Fort Worth Star-Telegram*, April 4, 1944. For "Junoesque," see *Dallas Morning News*, May 19, 1938. (Juno was the Roman goddess of marriage and fertility, always depicted as a full-figured woman.) Lisa Wilder, "The Story of Mary Dowell, Famous Stuttering Showgirl," *Canadian Stuttering Association*, September 2, 2020, https://stutter.ca/articles/2020/09/story-mary-dowell-famous-stuttering-showgirl.
11. *Fort Worth Star-Telegram*, April 11, 1963 (obit).
12. Jerry Flemmons, *Amon: The Texan Who Played Cowboy for America* (Lubbock: Texas Tech University Press, 1998), 184. Fairley, *Fort Worth Star-Telegram*, November 4, 1998.

13. Jan Jones, *Billy Rose Presents Casa Manana* (Fort Worth: TCU Press, 1999), 120–21 and 134–35. *Fort Worth Star-Telegram*, June 24, 1936; May 31 and June 11, 1937.

14. *Fort Worth Star-Telegram*, September 25, 1936.

15. *Fort Worth Star-Telegram*, October 11, 1936.

16. *Fort Worth Star-Telegram*, April 14, 1937.

17. Jan L. Jones, *Renegades, Showmen & Angels* (Fort Worth: TCU Press, 2006), 123.

18. *Fort Worth Star-Telegram*, May 31, July 26, August 10, and August 29, 1937.

19. *Fort Worth Star-Telegram*, August 10, and September 21, 1937.

20. *Fort Worth Star-Telegram*, August 29, 1937.

21. See two years of *Fort Worth Star-Telegram* articles starting March 22, 1938 (evening ed.) through August 28, 1939. Jack Gordon followed her in the *Fort Worth Press* from November 24, 1936, to April 3, 1944. See also *Dallas Morning News*, August 7, 1937.

22. Another tall actress (5'9") with a speech impediment, Kay Francis, managed to overcome her liabilities to become a star of both stage and screen from the 1920s through the 1940s. Lynn Kear and John Rossman, *Kay Francis* (Jefferson, NC: McFarland, 2006), 29–30.

23. *Fort Worth Star-Telegram* series, March 22, 1938–August 28, 1939. *Fort Worth Press*, November 24, 1936–April 3, 1944 (Jack Gordon). For Ginger Rogers, see *Fort Worth Star-Telegram*, November 22, 1939.

24. *Fort Worth Star-Telegram*, April 6, 1938; and April 1, 1944. For Garbo, see Wilder, "Story of Mary Dowell."

25. *New York Daily News*, February 15 and 18; July 26; and August 11, 1940. *Fort Worth Press*, August 9, 1941. *Fort Worth Star-Telegram*, August 3, 1940.

26. *Billboard*, June 10, 1940. Jan Jones Papers, "Stuttering Sam" files, nos. 27–29, AR 764, Box 3, UTA Special Collections, University of Texas at Arlington. *New York Daily News*, September 16, 1940.

27. The story is related by Jack Gordon in the *Fort Worth Press*, May 13, 1938, without any sense of outrage. Sam does not name the senator, but it had to be either Homer Bone (D) or Lewis B. Schwellenbach (D).

28. *Dallas Morning News*, May 20, 1938; February 19 and 24, 1940. For Carter quote, see *Fort Worth Star-Telegram*, December 12, 1938. For "propositions," see *Time Magazine* obituary, April 9, 1963.

29. *Fort Worth Star-Telegram*, May 13, 1943; February 24, 1944.

30. *New York Times*, May 9, 1943. *Dallas Morning News*, May 7, 1943. Dan Parker, "Stutterin' Sam," *Collier's Magazine*, July 10, 1943, 19*ff*. *Fort Worth Press*, July 20, 1938.

31. *Fort Worth Star-Telegram*, April 1 and 2, 1944. For Hawks, see Wilder, "Story of Mary Dowell."

32. *Fort Worth Star-Telegram*, February 24 (pm edition), and April 1, 1944. For "cattle rancher," see *Seattle Star*, April 4, 1944.

33. *Fresno Bee*, February 24, 1944. *Los Angeles Evening Citizen-News*, March 14, 1944. *Fort Worth Star-Telegram*, February 24, 1944.

34. *Fort Worth Star-Telegram*, April 2 and 12, 1944. *Seattle Star*, April 4, 1944. *Miami News*, April 9, 1944. *Los Angeles Evening Citizen-News*, April 3, 1944. *Pittsburgh Press*, April 2, 1944.

35. *Fort Worth Star-Telegram*, September 10, 1954; April 10 and 11, 1963.

36. *Time Magazine*, April 9, 1963. *Fort Worth Star-Telegram*, June 9, 1942 (obit); April 10 and 11, 1963 (obits). For "college," see *Dallas Morning News*, February 24, 1940. For "toy business executive," see *Dallas Morning News*, September 10, 1954; and April 11, 1963.

37. Flemmons, *Amon*, 184–85. Fairley, *Fort Worth Star-Telegram*, November 4, 1998.

38. For Billy Rose recollections, see *Fort Worth Star-Telegram*, January 22, 1960. For Sobol, see Fairley, *Fort Worth Star-Telegram*, November 4, 1998.

Notes for Chapter 13

1. *Fort Worth Star-Telegram*, August 5, 1953; and November 15, 1955. Gary Hartman, *The History of Texas Music* (College Station: Texas A&M University Press, 2008), 204–5. Laurie E. Jasinski and Casey Monahan, *The Handbook of Texas Music*, 2nd ed. (Austin: Texas State Historical Association, 2012).

2. *Fort Worth Star-Telegram*, August 5, 1953.

3. *Fort Worth Star-Telegram*, August 5, 1953. *Panama City* (FL) *News Herald*, April 4, 1998.

4. *Fort Worth Star-Telegram*, August 5, 1953; and September 10, 1983. *Time Magazine*, September 5, 1949.

5. Anthony J. Gribin and Matthew M. Schiff, *The Complete Book of Doo Wop* (Narberth, PA: Collectables Record, 2009), 180.

6. *Fort Worth Star-Telegram*, May 23, 1955; and September 10, 1983.

7. *Fort Worth Star-Telegram*, September 30, 1976; and September 10, 1983.

8. *Fort Worth Star-Telegram*, July 27, 1994 (obit.)

Notes for Chapter 14

1. Martin Donnell Kohout, "Smith, Major Bill," in Jasinski and Monahan, *Handbook of Texas Music*, 561–62. *Fort Worth Star-Telegram*, July 17, 1990.

2. *Fort Worth Star-Telegram*, September 1, 1948; February 14, 1949 (want ads for sound engineers); September 13, 1983; March 19, 1991 (Herring obit).

3. *Fort Worth Star-Telegram*, October 16, 1959; December 28, 1999 (Bud Kennedy column). Kohout, "Smith, Major Bill," 561.

4. Diana Finlay Hendricks, *Delbert McClinton: One of the Fortunate Few* (College Station: Texas A&M University Press, 2017), 72.

5. Sharpe was really discovered by Lester Sill and Lee Hazlewood in Las Vegas. Norm N. Lite, *Rock On: The Illustrated Encyclopedia of Rock N Roll* (New York: Thomas Y. Crowell, 1974), 357. Hendricks, *Delbert McClinton*, 78.

6. Hendricks, *Delbert McClinton*, 78. *Fort Worth Star-Telegram*, December 28, 1999.

7. *Fort Worth Star-Telegram*, July 17, 1990; December 28, 1999.

8. *Fort Worth Star-Telegram*, May 11, 1986; and December 28, 1999.

9. *Fort Worth Star-Telegram*, December 28, 1999. Joel Whitburn, *The Billboard Book of Top 40 Hits: 1955 to the Present* (New York: Billboard Publications, 1983), p. 57.

10. *Fort Worth Star-Telegram*, February 9, 1987. *Longview* (TX) *News-Journal*, October 10, 1967. The exact sales numbers of "Hey Paula" are hard to verify. Smith would later say sales "approached the five million mark" and "the biggest American record ever in Italy." Liner notes of LP record *Texas Gold as Mined by Major Bill Smith*, Le Cam Records, Inc., Fort Worth.

11. *Fort Worth Star-Telegram*, February 9, 1987. Whitburn, *Billboard Book of Top 40 Hits*. For "sugar pop," see Dave Hawkins, "The Man Who'll Listen to Your Song," *Dallas Morning News*, October 18, 1973, quoting Marvin "Smokey" Montgomery, coauthor of "Hey, Baby."

12. Whitburn, *Billboard Book of Top 40 Hits*, 295. Wayne Jancik, *The Billboard Book of One-Hit Wonders* (New York: Watson-Guptill, 1990),

161–62. Patrick Beach, "One More 'Last Kiss'—Long before Pearl Jam's Hit. . . . ," *Austin-American Statesman*, June 7, 1999. Kohout, "Smith, Major Bill," 561.

13. Smith released at least eighteen Rondels singles between 1963 and 1970, sometimes recording different versions of the same song, anything to get another hit. Hendricks, *Delbert McClinton*, 70 and 79.

14. *Fort Worth Star-Telegram*, August 5, 1979.

15. For Elvis and Bobby Vinton, see Whitburn, *Billboard Book of Top 40 Hits*. *Fort Worth Star-Telegram*, February 6, 1963.

16. Kohout, "Smith, Major Bill," 561.

17. *Fort Worth Star-Telegram*, November 7, 15, and 16, 1963.

18. "Elvis Booster Bill Smith Dies," obituary, *Dallas Morning News*, September 14, 1994. Congressional tribute reported in *Fort Worth Star-Telegram*, September 13, 1983.

19. "Elvis Booster Bill Smith Dies," *Dallas Morning News*, September 14, 1994. *Fort Worth Star-Telegram*, January 11, 1981; July 17, 1990. Kohout, "Smith, Major Bill," 561. For lawsuit, see *Dallas Morning News*, March 19, 1994. It was settled out of court shortly before Smith's death. Chapman quote from the sleeve notes for the LP record *Texas Gold as Mined by Major Bill Smith*, Le Cam Records, Inc., Fort Worth.

20. *Dallas Morning News* obituary, September 14, 1994.

21. *Fort Worth Star-Telegram*, September 13, 1983.

22. For Phil Record, see *Fort Worth Star-Telegram*, September 13, 1994 (obituary).

23. *Fort Worth Star-Telegram*, September 13, 1994 (obit). Quote is from sleeve notes for the LP record *Texas Gold as Mined by Major Bill Smith*, Le Cam Records, Inc., Fort Worth.

Notes for Chapter 15

1. Jacquelyn Masur McElhaney, *Pauline Periwinkle and Progressive Reform in Dallas* (College Station: Texas A&M University Press, 1998). Samantha Dodd, "Legendary Lady of the Law: Louise Ballerstedt Raggio and the Reform of Texas Marital Property Law," *Legacies: A History Journal for Dallas and North Central Texas* 35, no. 1 (Spring 2023): 38–50. For "girl reporter," see *Fort Worth Star-Telegram*, October 20. 1963. For anyone wondering, Amon Carter did not take control of the *Star-Telegram* until 1923.

2. *Brownsville* (TX) *Herald*, August 18, 1908.

3. *Brownsville* (TX) *Daily Herald*, January 13 and 15, 1909. *Fort Worth Star-Telegram*, November 9 and December 12, 1930; January 25, 1931; August 31, 1932.

4. Katie Sherrod, "High-Heeled Times in the Newsroom," in *Grace & Gumption: Stories of Fort Worth Women*, ed. Katie Sherrod (Fort Worth: TCU Press, 2007), 262. *Austin American-Statesman*, September 20, and December 19, 1909. *Houston Post*, May 14, 1911. The North Texas Female College and Conservatory of Music was founded in 1877. Its distinguished president for many years was Lucy Kidd-Key. In 1919, after her death, the school was renamed Kidd-Key College. It closed in 1935. Larry Wolz, "Kidd-Key College," in Jasinski and Monahan, *Handbook of Texas Music*, 345–46. *Fort Worth Record and Register*, August 11, 1907. *Fort Worth Record-Telegram*, August 29, 1915. *Whitewright Sun*, July 11, 1919. *Austin Daily Texan*, May 14 and 18, 1910. For alumnus activism, see *Fort Worth Star-Telegram*, June 22, 1915.

5. *San Antonio Daily Express*, January 15, 1911.

6. *San Antonio Daily Express*, January 15 and March 5, 1911. *Austin American-Statesman*, March 12, 1911.

7. *Fort Worth Star-Telegram*, February 3 and 4, 1912. For "Beeswax," see *Fort Worth Star-Telegram*, April 27, 1913; March 7, 1915; and *Waco* (TX) *News-Tribune*, May 17, 1920.

8. *Fort Worth Star-Telegram*, February 3 and 6, 1912.

9. *Fort Worth Star-Telegram*, November 12, 1912.

10. *Fort Worth Star-Telegram*, February 4, 1912.

11. *Fort Worth Star-Telegram*, July 21, 1912; July 10, 24, 26, and 28; November 9, 1913. For Record's involvement, see *Fort Worth Star-Telegram*, October 20, 1963.

12. *Fort Worth Star-Telegram*, January 28, 1913; April 20, 1913.

13. *Fort Worth Star-Telegram*, April 14 and 16, 1913.

14. *Galveston Daily News*, July 16, 1911. *San Antonio Light*, September 24, 1912. *Fort Worth Star-Telegram*, September 29 and October 27, 1912; February 25, 1913. *McKinney Courier-Gazette*, October 26, 1912. *Glens Falls* (NY) *Post-Star*, October 22, 1912.

15. *Fort Worth Star-Telegram*, February 25, 1913.

16. *Fort Worth Record*, October 16, 1920. *Fort Worth Star-Telegram*; May 19, 2024 (Richard Gonzales column).

17. *Fort Worth Star-Telegram*, November 1, 1913; and August 3, 1970 (obit). *Fort Worth Record-Telegram*, November 2, 1913. *Austin American-Statesman*, November 3, 1913.

18. Sherrod, "High-Heeled Times in the Newsroom," 262–63. *Fort Worth Star-Telegram*, December 12 and 16, 1915.

19. Sherrod, "High-Heeled Times in the Newsroom," 262–63. *Frederick (OK) Leader*, July 31, 1921. For "Midwest," see *Fort Worth Star-Telegram*, July 11, 1921. For new publication, see *Fort Worth Star-Telegram*, February 6, 1919.

20. *Fort Worth Star-Telegram*, June 28, 29, 30; July 2, 4, 9, 11, 12, 16, 31; August 15, 22, 26; and September 4, 1921. This is not a comprehensive listing of all the columns, only a representative selection. Joan Givner, *Katherine Anne Porter: A Life* (Athens: University of Georgia Press, 1982).

21. *Fort Worth Star-Telegram*, July 9 and August 15, 1921.

22. *Fort Worth Star-Telegram*, June 29, 1921.

23. *Fort Worth Star-Telegram*, July 2, 1921. For "lost years," see *Fort Worth Star-Telegram*, July 16, 1921.

24. *Fort Worth Star-Telegram*, June 28; July 2, 12, and 31, 1921.

25. *Fort Worth Star-Telegram*, July 2, 4, and 31, 1921. *Frederick Leader*, July 31, 1921.

26. *Fort Worth Star-Telegram*, September 4, 1921; and November 3, 1923; May 1, 1927; November 9, 1930; February 25, 1940; and August 27, 1982 (obit). Howard W. Peak, *A Ranger of Commerce, Or 52 Years on the Road* (San Antonio: Naylor Printing, 1929).

27. *Fort Worth Star-Telegram*, September 21, 1921; February 25, 1940; and August 27, 1982 (obit).

28. *Fort Worth Star-Telegram*, April 26, 1937. *Corsicana Daily Sun*, June 23, 1937. *Arlington (TX) Citizen-Journal*, August 6, 1970.

29. *Fort Worth Star-Telegram*, October 20, 1963; and August 3, 1970, morning ed. (obit). *Arlington Citizen-Journal*, August 6, 1970.

30. *Fort Worth Star-Telegram*, August 27, 1982 (obits on 2 pages).

Notes for Chapter 16

1. *Bryan Eagle*, December 22, 1921; January 9, 1946; June 2, 1938. *Fort Worth Star-Telegram*, January 7, 1938. William Brogdon's obituary in the *Bryant Eagle* says he settled in Brazos County in 1876. *Bryant Weekly Eagle*, December 22, 1921.

2. *Beaumont (TX) Enterprise*, February 18, 1903; and October 3, 1908. *Beaumont City Directory*, 1909. *Chicago Inter-Ocean*, April 15, 1910. *Bryan Eagle*, May 2, 1960 (obit). *Fort Worth Star-Telegram*, January 7, 1938.

3. *Houston Post*, December 3, 1910. *Waco Times-Herald*, December 6, 1910. *Bryan Eagle*, November 20, 1911.

4. US postmasters, state of Texas, 1912. Beaumont *City Directory*, 1914. World War I draft registration, Stansell Tenyson [*sic*] Brogdon, Muskogee, OK, September 12, 1918.

5. *Fort Worth Star-Telegram*, August 3 and November 5, 1920; and June 18, 1922. *Waco Times-Herald*, July 15, 1922.

6. *Fort Worth Star-Telegram*, November 5, 1920; May 16, 1929; February 9, 1930.

7. *Fort Worth Star-Telegram*, June 18; December 18 and 19, 1922.

8. *Fort Worth Star-Telegram*, September 3, 1922.

9. *Fort Worth Star-Telegram*, July 14, 1922. *Waco Times-Herald*, July 15, 1922.

10. *Fort Worth Star-Telegram*, July 14, 1922.

11. *Fort Worth Star-Telegram*, July 14 and 18, 1922. *Morning Tulsa* (OK) *Daily News*, July 23, 1922.

12. *Fort Worth Star-Telegram*, May 20, 1926; and January 7, 1938. *Lubbock* (TX) *Morning Avalanche*, March 24, 1938.

13. *Fort Worth Star-Telegram*, July 17 and August 9, 1927. *Marshall News Messenger*, July 8, 1927. *Waco News-Tribune*, August 9,1927.

14. *Waco Times-Herald*, June 12 and October 2, 1927. *Dallas Morning News*, January 7, 1931. *Fort Worth Star-Telegram*, March 27 and July 13, 1930.

15. *Dallas Morning News*, January 7, 1931. *Fort Worth Star-Telegram*, February 25, 1931; March 6 and May 15, 1932.

16. *Fort Worth Star-Telegram*, March 7, 1930; May 16 and 26, 1929; and June 29, 1933.

17. *Fort Worth Star-Telegram*, October 9, 1933.

18. *El Paso Times*, January 8, 1938. *Austin American-Statesman*, March 7, 1938. *Fort Worth Star-Telegram*, March 7, 1938. For "music composer," see *Bryan Eagle*, May 2, 1960 (obit).

19. *Kerrville* (TX) *Mountain Sun*, May 19, 1938. *Waxahachie* (TX) *Daily Light*, April 23, 1938. *Fort Worth Star-Telegram*, January 7, March 6 and 7, 1938.

20. *Bryan Eagle*, June 2, 1938. *Austin American-Statesman*, July 3, 1938. *El Paso Times*, January 8, 1938. *Austin American-Statesman*, January 8, March 7, and July 17, 1938. *Fort Worth Star-Telegram*, March 7, June 20, and July 1, 1938. For old-age pension and Confederate home, see *Fort Worth Star-Telegram*, July 1, 1938.

21. *Fort Worth Star-Telegram*, June 20 and 30; and July 1 and 17, 1938. *Brownsville Herald*, July 20, 1938.

22. *Harlingen Valley* (TX) *Morning Star*, July 21, 1938. *Brownsville Herald*, July 20, 1938.

23. *Fort Worth Star-Telegram*, August 7, 1938.

24. *Houston Chronicle*, May 21 and June 16, 1946. *Waco* (TX) *Tribune-Herald*, November 29, 1959. *Hearne* (TX) *Democrat*, June 2, 1961. *Bryan Eagle*, November 26, 1961. For annexation proposals, see *Austin American*, July 3, 1938; and *Houston Chronicle*, May 21, 1946.

25. US Death Certificates, 1903–1982, TX Dept. of Health, Bureau of Vital Statistics, "Stansell L. (*sic*) Brogdon," May 3, 1961, Travis County, TX. *Bryan Eagle*, May 2 and 3, 1960.

26. *Hearne Democrat*, June 2, 1961. *Bryan Eagle*, November 26, 1961.

Notes for Chapter 17

1. *Fort Worth Star-Telegram*, May 28 and November 14, 1916.

2. *Fort Worth Star-Telegram*, October 3, 1912; November 12, 1913; November 11, 1915; November 14, 1916. J'Nell Pate, *North of the River: A Brief History of North Fort Worth* (Fort Worth: TCU Press, 1994), 133–34, 179n21.

3. *Fort Worth Star-Telegram*, November 14, 1916. For Myers and Littick, see *Danville* (KY) *Advocate*, January 8, and August 25, 1917; *Danville* (KY) *Advocate-Messenger*, March 30, and September 11, 1917; and *Lexington Herald-Leader*, September 16, 1917.

4. *Fort Worth Star-Telegram*, December 26, 1920; and December 21, 2003. *Madison* (WI) *Capital Times*, December 2, 1924. For Moran's A&M days, see *Fort Worth Star-Telegram*, November 28, 1965. Some sources say Moran helped develop the great Jim Thorpe while coaching at Carlisle. This is not true, as Thorpe graduated before Moran arrived. Cf. *Fort Worth Star-Telegram*, June 15, 1949 (obit).

5. *Fort Worth Star-Telegram*, November 14, 1916.

6. *Danville Advocate*, November 5, 1917.

7. *Fort Worth Star-Telegram*, January 23, 1916; June 15, 1949; November 28, 1985. *Long Beach* (CA) *Press-Telegram*, December 21, 1922.

8. *Danville Advocate*, February 18, 1918.

9. *Fort Worth Star-Telegram*, October 31, 1943. *Louisville Courier-Journal*, November 1, 1919.

10. *Danville Advocate-Messenger*, December 5, 1919.
11. *Fort Worth Star-Telegram*, October 31, 1943; and April 1, 1952 (obit). *Danville Advocate*, November 16, 1917. *Danville Advocate-Messenger*, February 14, 1923.
12. *Minneapolis Star*, November 23, 1920. *Austin Austin-American*, December 22, 1920. *Fort Worth Star-Telegram*, October 31, 1943.
13. Bill Fairley, "When Bo McMillin Slew Goliath," *Fort Worth Star-Telegram*, April 4, 2007.
14. *Fort Worth Star-Telegram*, October 31, 1943; January 8, 1967. *New Britain* (CT) *Herald*, October 21, 1922.
15. For size of teams, see *Minneapolis Star*, December 22, 1920; and *Philadelphia Inquirer*, October 26, 1923. For Texas football players, see *Tulsa World*, November 26, 1922.
16. *Fort Worth Star-Telegram*, April 1, 1952 (obit).
17. *Fort Worth Star-Telegram*, October 3, 1912; December 10, 1935; and December 21, 2003. For Greines boys in particular, see Hollace Weiner column, *Fort Worth Star-Telegram*, March 3, 2024.
18. *Fort Worth Star-Telegram*, June 15, 1949 (obit).
19. *Fort Worth Star-Telegram*, March 18, 1915; October 22, 1920. *Louisville Courier-Journal*, November 1, 1919.
20. Michael K. Bohn, *Heroes & Ballyhoo: How the Golden Age of the 1920s Transformed American Sports* (Lincoln: University of Nebraska Press, 2009), 6–7.
21. *Fort Worth Star-Telegram*, November 27 and 29, 1946.

Notes for Chapter 18

1. The current bronze bust was put in place during a WPA-funded restoration in 1934.
2. *Dallas Morning News*, May 31, 1890. Cf. reminiscences of Fort Worth resident Howard Peak, *Fort Worth Star-Telegram*, August 13, 1922, which differs in significant details.
3. B. B. Paddock created the myth that Hayne leaped from a second-story window, breaking both his ankles. B. B. Paddock, *History of Texas: Fort Worth and the Texas Northwest Edition* (Chicago: Lewis Publishing, 1922), perpetrated by Amos Melton in "Fire Hero Is Without Statue," *Fort Worth Star-Telegram*, March 30, 1930. For short biography of Hayne, see Selcer, *Fort Worth Characters*, 88–106 (chap. 5).

4. "Williams, J.," Tenth US Census, 1880, Fort Worth, Tarrant County, TX, Enumerator District 89, sheet 6B, line 22. For "Black Exodus," see Alferdteen Harris, ed., *Black Exodus: The Great Migration from the American South* (Oxford: University Press of Mississippi, 1992).

5. *Fort Worth Daily Gazette*, June 4, 1890.

6. *Fort Worth Daily Gazette*, June 5, 1890. The Dallas newspapers did not mention Jesse.

7. *Dallas Morning News*, May 31, 1890. *Fort Worth Daily Gazette*, June 4, 1890. For other (white) heroes of the fire, see *Dallas Weekly Times-Herald*, May 31, 1890.

8. The *Gazette* mentions "different theories" without blaming anyone in particular. *Fort Worth Daily Gazette*, June 4 and 5, 1890. Cf. the recollections of Clay Sandidge, a volunteer fireman interviewed by reporter Mack Williams for the *Fort Worth Press* many years later, and an account of the fire by *Star-Telegram* columnist Amos Melton also many years later. *Fort Worth Star-Telegram*, March 30, 1930. *Fort Worth Press*, May 27, 1957.

9. *Fort Worth Gazette*, June 3, 4, 5, and 6 1890. Selcer, *History of Fort Worth in Black & White*, 128n59.

10. *Fort Worth Telegram*, April 8, 1905. *Fort Worth Star-Telegram*, June 4, 1950 (morning ed.); March 30, 1930. *Fort Worth Press*, May 27, 1957.

Notes for Chapter 19

1. *Fort Worth Star-Telegram*, March 5, 1939; February 24, 1940. Edward H. Miller, *A Conspiratorial Life: Robert Welch, the John Birch Society, and the Revolution of American Conservatism* (Chicago: University of Chicago Press, 2021), 153.

2. Miller, *Conspiratorial Life*, 153.

3. *Time* Magazine, April 14, 1961, "Nation" section. Miller, *Conspiratorial Life*, 154. *Macon Telegraph*, September 14, 1945 (obituary).

4. Miller, *Conspiratorial Life*, 155.

5. *Fort Worth Star-Telegram*, April 2, 1961.

6. Miller, *Conspiratorial Life*, 6.

7. *Fort Worth Star-Telegram*, April 2, 1961.

8. *Fort Worth Star-Telegram*, January 1, 1967.

9. For Schlafly, see Andrew Jackson Grant, *1973: Rock at the Crossroads* (New York: Thomas Dunne Books, 2019), 303. *Time* Magazine, April 14, 1961, "Nation" section.

Notes for Chapter 20

1. *Galveston Daily News*, July 12, 1890. Hubert H. Bancroft, *History of the Northern Mexican States and Texas*, vol. 2 (1889; repr., Forgotten Books, 2018), 578. *Fort Worth Star-Telegram*, January 20, 1913 (obit); and November 13, 1931 (obit). *Dallas Morning News*, August 19, 1892. *Lampasas (TX) Daily Leader*, January 20, 1913 (obit). Octavia Pendleton became the third wife of Van Zandt on October 8, 1885. *Fort Worth Daily Gazette*, October 10, 1885. Patricia P. Kinkade, "Khleber Miller Van Zandt," in Tyler, *New Handbook of Texas*, 6:707.

2. *Fort Worth Daily Democrat*, July 26, 1876. For law practice, see *Fort Worth Daily Standard*, September 21 and November 9, 1876; May 8 and July 20, 1877; *Fort Worth Daily Gazette*, March 17, 1884; January 1 and March 8, 1886; March 1 and 11, 1890. *Fort Worth City Directory*, 1883–84, Fort Worth Library History Center. For Powell, see *Fort Worth Star-Telegram*, March 8, 1938 (obit). For Chapman, see *Fort Worth Daily Gazette*, February 24, 1886. For Courtright, see Robert K. De Arment, *Jim Courtright of Fort Worth* (Fort Worth: TCU Press, 2004), 90 and 146.

3. *Fort Worth Daily Standard*, November 9, 1876. *Fort Worth City Directory*, 1883–84, Fort Worth Library History Center. For business ventures, see *Fort Worth Daily Gazette*, October 7, 1885; May 24, June 25, and September 8, 1887; January 29, April 20, and June 17, 1888; February 24 and July 31, 1889. For New Mexico venture, see *Santa Fe Daily New Mexican*, March 22, 1889. For inventions, see *Fort Worth Gazette*, October 9, 1890.

4. For Goethe quote, see *Dallas Morning News*, July 15, 1890. For residences, see *Fort Worth Daily Gazette*, June 5, 1884; and October 16, 1887, which give E. Weatherford as the address. Cf. *Fort Worth Daily Gazette*, March 30, 1890; and *Fort Worth Star-Telegram*, "Home Section," October 30, 1949 that place the residence on W. Seventh.

5. For legislature, see *Fort Worth Daily Gazette*, January 10 and February 16, 1885. *Dallas Morning News*, August 1, 1887.

6. *Fort Worth Daily Democrat-Advance*, March 7, 1882. *Houston Daily Post*, September 29, 1883. *Galveston Daily News*, December 8, 1886. For finances, see *Dallas Morning News*, July 14, 1890.

7. Tenth US Census, 1880, for "W. S. Pendleton," Fort Worth, Tarrant County, TX. *Fort Worth Daily Gazette*, March 3, 1883. *Galveston Daily News*, July 12, 1890. For Pendleton's physical description, see

Memphis Daily Commercial, July 19, 1890. *Fort Worth Star-Telegram*, August 16, 1911 (Lizzie Pendleton's obit).

8. For social life, see *Galveston Daily News*, April 20, 1885; *Fort Worth Daily Gazette*, February 25 and August 7, 1887. For Anna Shelton, see Ruth Karbach, "The Modern Woman," in Sherrod, *Grace & Gumption*, 70–71.

9. For George Pendleton, see *Fort Worth Daily Gazette*, April 22, 1890. For oratory, see *Fort Worth Daily Gazette*, July 6, 1886. For Bailey, see *Fort Worth Daily Gazette*, February 3, 1889; April 22, 1890; and *Dallas Morning News*, February 12, 1896. For son's death, see *Fort Worth Daily Gazette*, March 26, 28, and 30, 1890. For Pendleton's victory, see *Fort Worth Daily Gazette*, April 2 and 9, 1890; *Dallas Morning News*, March 31 and April 2, 1890; *Fort Worth Star-Telegram*, September 13, 1936; and October 14, 1949.

10. *New York Sun*, December 22, 1890. Ninth and Tenth US Census reports, 1870 and 1880, for "John Cullen," Adams County, MS. Tenth US Census, 1880, for "Anna Cullen," Fort Worth, Tarrant County, TX. Fort Worth *City Directory*, 1888–89, Fort Worth Library History Center. Her four sisters were Mary, Annie, Katie, and Stella. For Fanning, see *Fort Worth Daily Gazette*, April 26, 1885. For family members, see also *Dallas Morning News*, July 15, 1890.

11. *Dallas Weekly Times-Herald*, July 26, 1890. *Galveston Daily News*, July 12, 1890. *Sacramento Bee*, July 12, 1890. *Dallas Morning News*, July 15, 1890. For unhappy marriage, see *Galveston Daily News*, July 12, 1890; *Memphis Daily Commercial*, July 19, 1890; and *Indianapolis Journal*, July 19, 1890. Their fifth child would only live twenty-two months.

12. *Galveston Daily News*, July 12, 1890. *Sacramento Bee*, July 12, 1890. *Memphis Daily Commercial*, July 19, 1890. For George Maurice, see *Fort Worth Daily Gazette*, March 28 and 30, 1890. For Father Guyot, see *Dallas Morning News*, July 12, 1890. For bogus divorce, see *Jackson* (MS) *Clarion-Ledger*, December 25, 1890.

13. *Galveston Daily News*, July 12, 1890. *Dallas Morning News*, July 13 and 15, 1890. *Dallas Weekly Times-Herald*, July 26, 1890. Different newspapers report her going to Kentucky or Tennessee. Since she had relatives in Kentucky, that was more likely her original destination. For Kentucky see *Dallas Weekly Times-Herald*, July 19, 1890. For Tennessee see *Dallas Morning News*, July 16, 1890. For gifts see

Dallas Weekly Times-Herald, July 26, 1890; and *Chicago Inter-Ocean*, October 23, 1890.

14. For Lizzie finding out, see *Dallas Morning News*, July 13, 1890. *Chattanooga* (TN) *Daily Times*, July 20, 1890.

15. For national news, see *New York Sun*, December 22, 1890; and *Sacramento Bee*, July 12, 1890. *Galveston Daily News*, July 12, 1890. *Dallas Morning News*, July 12 and 13, 1890. *Indianapolis Journal* (from New Orleans), July 19, 1890. For "fatal infatuation," see *Dallas Morning News*, July 13, 1890.

16. *Dallas Morning News*, July 12, 1890. *Galveston Daily News*, July 12, 1890. *Austin American-Statesman*, July 13, 1890. *Jackson Clarion-Ledger*, July 15, 1890. For losing his mind, see *Austin American-Statesman*, July 13, 1890; *St. Louis Globe-Democrat*, July 18, 1890; *Laredo* (TX) *Times*, July 15, 1890; *Abilene* (TX) *Reporter*, July 18, 1890. For obstacles and sympathy, see *Dallas Morning News*, July 12 and 13, 1890. For unfamiliarity with defeat, see *Dallas Morning News*, July 13, 1890.

17. *Galveston Daily News*, July 12, 1890. *Austin American-Statesman*, July 13, 1890.

18. *Dallas Morning News*, July 13, 14, and 18, 1890. *Austin American-Statesman*, July 13 and 17, 1890. *Laredo Times*, July 15, 1890. *Dallas Weekly Times-Herald*, July 19, 1890.

19. *Dallas Morning News*, July 18, 1890. *Memphis Daily Commercial*, July 19, 1890. *Chicago Tribune*, July 20, 1890. *Dallas Weekly Times-Herald*, August 9, 1890. *Chicago Inter-Ocean*, October 23, 1890.

20. *Memphis Daily Commercial*, July 19, 1890.

21. *Dallas Morning News*, July 15, 1890. *Memphis Daily Commercial*, July 19, 1890. It makes the mistake of thinking her trip was originally to Tennessee.

22. *St. Louis Globe-Democrat*, July 18, 1890. *Chattanooga Daily Times*, July 20, 1890. *Chicago Tribune*, July 20, 1890. *Dallas Weekly Times-Herald*, July 26, 1890. *Dallas Daily Times-Herald*, October 6, 1890. *Dallas Morning News*, October 7, 1890. For removal from office, see *Dallas Weekly Times-Herald*, July 26, 1890. For divorce mills, see *New York Sun*, December 22, 1890.

23. *Fort Worth Daily Gazette*, August 5, 1890.

24. *Dallas Morning News*, October 6, 1890.

25. *Dallas Morning News*, October 7, 1890.

26. *Laredo Times*, July 15, 1890.

27. *Chicago Inter-Ocean*, October 23, 1890.

28. *Jackson Clarion-Ledger*, December 25, 1890.

29. *Shawnee* (OK) *News*, June 25. 1906. *Shawnee Herald*, June 26, 1906.

30. *Shawnee News-Herald*, October 22, 1907. *Shawnee Herald*, October 24, 1907.

31. *Oklahoma City Daily Oklahoman*, March 23, 1933 (obit). For other obits, see *Shawnee County Democrat*, March 23, 1933; *Okmulgee* (OK) *Daily Times*, March 23, 1933; *Shawnee Times-Record*, March 24, 1933; *Shawnee Evening Star*, April 13, 1933; *Muskogee* (OK) *Daily Phoenix and Times-Democrat*, March 23, 1933; *Fort Worth Star-Telegram*, March 21, 1933; and *Dallas Morning News*, March 22, 1933.

32. Fort Worth *City Directory*, 1890–1899, Fort Worth Library History Center. Thirteenth US Census, 1910, for "Belle Pendleton," Fort Worth, Tarrant County, TX. For reminiscences of Belle Pendleton, see Henry Hunter McLean, *From Ayr to Thurber: Three Hunter Brothers and the Winning of the West* (Fort Worth: Fort Worth Genealogical Society, 1978), 52–54.

33. *Fort Worth Star-Telegram*, August 16, 1911. *Fort Worth Record and Register*, August 16 and 17, 1911.

Notes for Chapter 21

1. Twelfth US Census, 1900, for "Robert H. Howard," Scurry County, TX. Thirteenth US Census, 1910, for "Robert H. Howard," Erath County, TX. For Robert Howard, see C. R. Nichol, *Gospel Preachers Who Blazed the Trail* (1899; repr., Houston: Firm Foundation, 1966), 89; and *Holdenville* (OK) *Daily News*, November 27, 1931 (obit).

2. *Fort Worth Star-Telegram*, October 10 and 22, 1914. She would later claim that she worked as a "detective" in several cities before coming to Fort Worth, but there is no evidence to support this. For Nellie Bly, see Matthew Goodman, *Eighty Days: Nellie Bly's and Elizabeth Bisland's History-Making Race around the World* (New York: Ballantine Books, 2013).

3. *Fort Worth Star-Telegram*, October 10, 1914. For Mays & Mays, see *Fort Worth Star-Telegram*, October 22, 1916; and November 2, 1959 (obit). For Ollie Hargrave, see *Fort Worth Telegram*, May 31, 1907.

4. *Fort Worth Star-Telegram*, October 10, 1914.

5. *Fort Worth Star-Telegram*, October 10, 1914. For Van Buren sisters, see "Months Past" section, *History Today*, September 2019, 26.

6. *Fort Worth Star-Telegram*, October 22, 1914.

7. *Fort Worth Star-Telegram*, October 22, 1914.

8. *Fort Worth Star-Telegram*, October 22, 1914.

9. *Fort Worth Star-Telegram*, November 4 and 10, December 1, 1914.

10. *Fort Worth Star-Telegram*, November 20, 1914.

11. *Fort Worth Star-Telegram*, January 17, 1915.

12. Fourteenth US Census, 1920, for "Dudley M. Culley," El Paso County, TX. El Paso *City Directory*, 1925 (Dudley M. and Sammy [*sic*] E. Culley). US passport application for Mrs. Sammie Ezell Culley, El Paso, TX, November 15, 1920. *Salem* (OR) *Capital Journal*, April 23, 1937 (marriage announcement). Marriage license, Clark County, WA, April 24, 1937. Sixteenth US Census, 1940, for "Claude T. Springs," Stockton, San Joaquin County, CA. Stockton *City Directory*, 1940 (Claude T. and Sammie Springs). *Holdenville Daily News*, November 27, 1931. *Salem Capital Journal*, April 23, 1937. *Modesto* (CA) *Bee*, January 26, 1971 (obit).

13. *Fort Worth Star-Telegram*, October 10, 1914.

14. *Fort Worth Star-Telegram*, April 18, 1915; and April 12, 1918. *Fort Worth Record-Telegram*, April 16, 1915. For women volunteers, see *Fort Worth Star-Telegram*, December 14, 1910.

Notes for Chapter 22

1. *Harlingen Valley Morning Star*, July 13, 1958 (obit for Virginia Wheat). For Cleburne, see *Fort Worth Telegram*, November 20, 1906.

2. *Fort Worth Daily Gazette*, December 15, 1885. *Dallas Morning News*, November 22, 1906 (obit). For church affiliation, see *Harlingen Valley Morning Star*, July 13, 1958 (obit). Fort Worth *City Directory*, 1888, 1892, Fort Worth Library History Center. For church membership, see *Fort Worth Daily Gazette*, May 9, 1891. For Scheuber, see *Fort Worth Daily Gazette*, December 5, 1885.

3. *El Paso Herald*, May 26, 1900. For full story of Frank Fossett, see Richard Selcer, "Murder at the Palais Royal," *Wild West Magazine*, June 2011, 54–61. For birthday party, see *Fort Worth Daily Gazette*, March 20, 1892.

4. *Fort Worth Record and Register*, December 1, 1901. *Fort Worth Star-Telegram*, July 13, 1958 (Virginia Wheat's obit).

5. *Fort Worth Star-Telegram*, May 6, 1939; October 30, 1949; and May 7, 1965. For "elegance," see *Fort Worth Daily Gazette*, May 2, 1890. For James, see *Fort Worth Daily Gazette*, November 4, 1935 (obit). For poker game, see *Fort Worth Star-Telegram*, April 23, 1972. For Martin-Brown advertising, see *Fort Worth Daily Gazette*, February 18, 1884; and August 29, 1885. For Fort Worth Loan & Construction's problems, see *Fort Worth Daily Gazette*, October 10, 1890; and April 11, 1891. Martin-Brown's former home at Seventh and Main was turned into a men's clothing store and "elegant hotel," *Fort Worth Gazette*, June 12, 1890. For construction cost, see *Dallas Morning News*, March 12, 1901.

6. *Dallas Morning News*, March 12, 1901. *Fort Worth Telegram*, November 6, 1902. For poker game legend, see *Fort Worth Star-Telegram*, May 28, 1940. For real estate transfer, see *Dallas Morning News*, March 20, 1901. For remodeling work, see *Fort Worth Record and Register*, June 7, 1901; and April 10, 1902; and *Fort Worth Morning Register*, May 30, 1901; and *Austin American-Statesman*, October 16, 1903.

7. For NY Life, see *Fort Worth Morning Register*, March 7, 1902. For Frisco, see *Fort Worth Record and Register*, July 9, 1901.

8. *Fort Worth Telegram*, November 20, 1906 (obit). *Fort Worth Star-Telegram*, April 23, 1972.

9. *Fort Worth Telegram*, January 1, 1905; August 19, 1906. For Stag Saloon, see Fort Worth *City Directory*, 1899, Fort Worth Library History Center. Wheat was co-owner with Courtney Kenney, Lemuel Day, and Peter Currie.

10. *Fort Worth Telegram*, November 6, 1902.

11. *Fort Worth Telegram*, July 30, 1904.

12. *Fort Worth Record and Register*, April 10, 1902. *Fort Worth Telegram*, October 27, 1903. *Fort Worth Star-Telegram*, April 23, 1972.

13. *Fort Worth Telegram*, December 30, 1902; and February 24, 1903. *Fort Worth Star-Telegram*, May 7, 1965.

14. *Fort Worth Telegram*, May 1 and October 27, 1903.

15. *Fort Worth Telegram*, October 27, 1903; February 24, 1903. *Fort Worth Star-Telegram*, April 23, 1972.

16. *Fort Worth Record and Register*, October 28, 1899. *Fort Worth Telegram*, July 24, 1902; June 4, 1904; and March 27, 1906.

17. *Fort Worth Telegram*, November 20, 1906. For property holdings, see *Dallas Morning News*, November 21, 1906. *Fort Worth Record and Register*, November 22, 1906 (obit). *Dallas Morning News*,

November 22, 1906 (obit). For cause, see death certificate of Joseph G. [*sic*] Wheat, Bexar County, Texas, US Death Certificates, 1903–1982, #5166.
18. *Fort Worth Telegram*, September 5, 1908.
19. *Dallas Morning News*, November 21, 1906. For will, see *Dallas Morning News*, December 1, 1906.
20. *Fort Worth Star-Telegram*, March 23, 1935.
21. *Fort Worth Star-Telegram*, May 6, 1939; May 14 and 29, 1940; April 23, 1972.
22. *McAllen* (TX) *Monitor*, July 13, 1958 (obit). *Fort Worth Star-Telegram*, July 13, 1958 (obit).
23. *Fort Worth Telegram*, November 21, 1904; and December 21, 1908. *Fort Worth Star-Telegram*, April 23, 1972.

Notes for Chapter 23

1. Kinkade, "Khleber Miller Van Zandt," in Tyler, *New Handbook of Texas*, 6:707. John McVey and Laurie E. Jasinski, "Van Zandt, Townes," in Jasinski and Monahan, *Handbook of Texas Music*, 646–47.
2. Bud Kennedy, "Celebrate 80 Years of Country Music Great Van Zandt," *Fort Worth Star-Telegram*, March 3, 2024.
3. McVey and Jasinski, "Van Zandt, Townes," 646.
4. McVey and Jasinski, "Van Zandt, Townes," 646. *Fort Worth Star-Telegram*, June 29, 1999.
5. "Townes Van Zandt," AllMusic.com, accessed November 21, 2024, https://www.allmusic.com/artist/townes-van-zandt-mn0000744796. *Fort Worth Star-Telegram*, June 29, 1999.
6. Information on his marriages has been gathered from various sources, collected on "Townes Van Zandt—Frequently Asked Questions," pnwpest.org, accessed November 21, 2024, http://pnwpest.org/coopl/tvzfaq.html.
7. John Nova Lomax, "The Way of the Gun—Living up to His Famous Father is a Tall Order for J. T. Van Zandt," *Dallas Observer*, October 24, 2002, http://wwwdallasobserver.com/2002-10-24/music. For "hobo saint," see Bruce Pollock, *By the Time We Got to Woodstock* (New York: Backbeat Books, 2009), 242.
8. McVey and Jasinski, "Van Zandt, Townes," 646–45.
9. *Daily Telegraph* (London), January 4, 1997. *Fort Worth Star-Telegram*, June 29, 1999.

10. *Daily Telegraph*, January 4, 1997. *Murfreesboro* (TN) *Daily News-Journal*, January 8, 1997. *Fort Worth Star-Telegram*, June 29, 1999.
11. Kennedy, "Celebrate 80 Years of Country Music Great Van Zandt."
12. Kennedy, "Celebrate 80 Years of Country Music Great Van Zandt."
13. John Kruth, *To Live's to Fly: The Ballad of the Late, Great Townes Van Zandt* (New York: Da Capo, 2008); Robert Earl Hardy, *A Deeper Blue: The Life and Music of Townes Van Zandt* (Denton: UNT Press, 2008); Brian T. Atkinson, *I'll Be Here in the Morning: The Songwriting Legacy of Townes Van Zandt* (College Station: Texas A&M University Press 2012).

Notes for Chapter 24

1. Most of the heavy research on this one was done by retired Fort Worth librarian Harry Max Hill.
2. Birth certificate for Estalene Hancock, Texas Board of Health, Bureau of Vital Statistics, Dublin, Erath County, TX, file #15099.
3. *Edna Hancock vs. Lawrence Hancock*, divorce suit, Forty-Eighth District Court, Tarrant County. *Comanche* (TX) *Chief*, March 6, 1942 (obit). Death certificate for Ruby Jean McKinney, US Death Certificates, 1903–1982, State of Texas, Bureau of Vital Statistics, Tarrant County, February 18, 1983, Certificate #09182.
4. Thomas Monroe Gatlin, Fifteenth US Census (1930), Comanche County, TX.
5. *Fort Worth Press*, November 28, 1953. *Fort Worth Star-Telegram*, February 24, 1944; November 28, 1953 (evening edition). Death certificate for "Alta Myree Harmon," Tarrant County, State of Texas, Bureau of Vital Statistics, file #58604.
6. Letter between George Grammer and Harry Max Hill, October 20, 2011.
7. *Fort Worth Press*, November 28, 1953.
8. *Fort Worth Press*, November 28, 1953.
9. Paschal High School *Pantherette*, March 14, April 25, May 2, and May 23, 1944. Billy W. Sills Center for Archives, Fort Worth Independent School District, Fort Worth, TX. DeMolay was a branch of the Masonic Order for teenagers.
10. George Grammer to Harry Max Hill, October 20, 2011.

11. Fifteenth US Census, 1930, for Thomas Gatlin, Comanche County, TX. *Fort Worth Star-Telegram*, February 24, 1944 (evening edition).

12. *Fort Worth Star-Telegram*, November 28, 1953 (morning edition). Billy J. Harmon's military record, National Archives and Record Administration, Washington, DC. For Patty in graduation robe, see *Fort Worth Star-Telegram*, February 24, 1944.

13. Patricia Ann Contreras's prison record, Federal Bureau of Prisons, US Department of Justice, Washington, DC. Consists of 109 pages on her background and time behind bars, including medical records. Obtained in 2007 by Harry Max Hill through a Freedom of Information Act request (hereafter cited as Contreras prison file).

14. Contreras prison file.

15. Contreras prison file.

16. Contreras prison file.

17. US Customs report, January 13, 1949, in Contreras prison file.

18. Contreras prison file. (The US Public Health Hospital for men was and still is in Fort Worth, TX.)

19. Admission summary, March 17, 1949, Contreras prison file.

20. Contreras prison file.

21. Report of Psychological Examinations of Patricia Contreras, March 29, 1949, Contreras prison file.

22. Contreras prison file.

23. Correspondence between A. J. Contreras and Huntington prison, April 8 and 19, 1950, Contreras prison file.

24. *Fort Worth Press*, November 28, 1953.

25. *Fort Worth Star-Telegram*, October 30, 1953; November 28, 1953 (morning edition). *Fort Worth Press*, December 4, 1953.

26. *Kilgore* (TX) *News Herald*, November 27, 1953. *San Angelo Evening Standard*, November 27, 1953. *Waco Times-Herald*, November 27, 1953. *Paris* (TX) *News*, November 27, 1953. *Abilene* (TX) *Reporter-News*, November 27, 1953. *Wichita Falls Times*, November 27, 1953. *Corsicana Daily Sun*, November 27, 1953. *Vernon* (TX) *Daily Record*, November 27, 1953.

27. *Fort Worth Press*, November 28, 1953. *Fort Worth Star-Telegram*, November 28, 1953 (morning and evening editions). Cf. *Fort Worth Star-Telegram*, December 3, 1953

28. *Fort Worth Star-Telegram*, November 28, 1953 (morning and evening editions). *Fort Worth Press*, December 1, 1953.

29. *Fort Worth Star-Telegram*, November 28 (morning and evening editions), November 30 (morning edition), and December 3, 1953. For narcotics connection, see *Fort Worth Star-Telegram*, November 30, 1953.

30. *Fort Worth Star-Telegram*, November 30, 1953 (morning edition).

31. *Fort Worth Star-Telegram*, February 24, 1944 (evening edition); November 29 and November 30 (morning edition), 1930.

32. *Fort Worth Star-Telegram*, November 29, and December 3, 1953.

33. *Fort Worth Press*, December 2, 1953. *Fort Worth Star-Telegram*, December 3, 1953; February 25, 1954.

34. *Fort Worth Star-Telegram*, December 24, 1953.

35. *Fort Worth Press*, December 2 and 4, 1953.

36. *Fort Worth Star-Telegram*, February 17, 1954.

37. *Fort Worth Star-Telegram*, December 3, 1953.

38. *Fort Worth Star-Telegram*, November 25, 1954.

39. *Fort Worth Star-Telegram*, August 9, 1956. *Fort Worth Press*, August 6, 1956.

Notes for Chapter 25

1. The sources disagree on the year of his birth. For 1928, see Nick Talevski, *Rock Obituaries: Knocking on Heaven's Door* (London: Omnibus Press, 2006), 123. For 1932 see Jancik, *Billboard Book of One-Hit Wonders*, 54. *Fort Worth Star-Telegram*, May 19, 1983.

2. The Hollywood Flames' recordings have been collected on a compact disc released by the label Acrobat.

3. Jancik, *Billboard Book of One-Hit Wonders*, 55. *Fort Worth Star-Telegram*, May 25, 1984. According to rock lore, Laboe coined the phrase "oldies but goodies."

4. Hugh Gregory, *Soul Music A–Z* (London: Blandford Books, 1991), 59. Charlie Gillett, *The Sound of the City: The Rise of Rock and Roll*, 3rd ed. (New York: Souvenir Press, 2011), 105. Jancik, *Billboard Book of One-Hit Wonders*, 55. *Fort Worth Star-Telegram*, May 25, 1984. Dave Marsh, *The Heart of Rock & Soul: The 1001 Greatest Singles Ever Made* (New York: New American Library, 1989), 429.

5. *Fort Worth Star-Telegram*, May 25, 1984. Gillett, *Sound of the City*, 105. *San Bernadino County* (CA) *Sun*, July 16, 1959. *Baltimore Evening Sun*, July 30, 1990 (obit).

6. Colin Larkin, ed., *The Guinness Encyclopedia of Popular Music* (London: Guinness Publishing, 1992), 648–49. Marsh, *Heart of Rock & Soul*, 429. Gillett, *Sound of the City*, 74. *Fort Worth Star-Telegram*, May 25, 1984. For origins of song's name, see *Tacoma News Tribune*, July 30, 1990 (obit).

7. Marsh, *Heart of Rock & Soul*, 429.

8. Jancik, *Billboard Book of One-Hit Wonders*, 55. *Fort Worth Star-Telegram*, May 19, 1983. Marsh, *Heart of Rock & Soul*, 429.

9. *Los Angeles Eagle*, January 7, 1960.

10. *Fort Worth Star-Telegram*, May 19, 1983; May 25, 1984.

11. Jancik, *Billboard Book of One-Hit Wonders*, 55. *San Bernadino County Sun*, July 16, 1959. *Baltimore Evening Sun*, July 30, 1990.

12. *Alexandria* (LA) *Town Talk*, July 30, 1990.

13. *Fort Worth Star-Telegram*, May 25, 1984. *Tacoma News Tribune*, July 30, 1990.

14. *Tacoma News Tribune*, July 30, 1990. Cf. *Los Angeles Times*, August 1, 1990. For eulogy, see *Abilene Reporter-News*, July 30, 1990.

15. "The Great Doo-Wop Vocal Groups," https://www.pinterest.com/.

Bibliography

Archives and Collections

Austin History Center, Austin Public Library, Austin, TX.

Beaumont Main Library, Beaumont, TX.

Biblical Addresses, and Educational and Religious Addresses Collection. Roberts Library, Southwestern Baptist Theological Seminary, Fort Worth, TX

Billy W. Sills Center for Archives. Fort Worth Independent School District, Fort Worth, TX.

Bureau of Vital Statistics. Texas Board of Health, Austin, TX.

Dolph Briscoe History Center for American History. University of Texas, Austin, TX.

El Paso Public Library Main Branch, El Paso, TX.

Fort Worth Public Library History Center, Fort Worth, TX.
   Cato Sells Papers, 1920–1929

Gregory Dow Collection, Fort Worth, TX.

National Archives and Record Administration, Washington, DC.
   Records of the Selective Service System, 1917–1939
   US Military Service Records

New York Historical Society, New York, NY.

Prison records. Federal Bureau of Prisons. US Department of Justice, Washington, DC.

Southwestern Baptist Theological Seminary, Fort Worth, TX.
   B. H. Carroll Presidential Papers
   Roberts Library

Special Collections. University of Texas at Arlington, Arlington, TX.
   Byron C. Utecht Papers
   Fort Worth Star-Telegram Collection
   Jan L. Jones Papers

Tarrant County Historic Ledgers. Tarrant County, TX.

Newspapers

Abilene (TX) *Daily Reporter*

Abilene (TX) *Reporter*

Abilene (TX) *Reporter-News*

Alexandria (LA) *Town Talk*

Arizona Republic (Phoenix)
Arizona Weekly Citizen (Tucson)
Arlington (TX) *Citizen-Journal*
Austin American-Statesman
Austin Daily Texan
Austin Weekly Statesman
Baltimore Evening Sun
Beaumont (TX) *Enterprise*
Billboard
Brownsville (TX) *Daily Herald*
Brownsville (TX) *Herald*
Bryan (TX) *Eagle*
Chattanooga (TN) *Times*
Chicago Defender
Chicago Inter-Ocean
Chicago Tribune
Chillicothe (MO) *Constitution-Tribune*
Cleburne (TX) *Morning Review*
Comanche (TX) *Chief*
Corpus Christi Caller-Times
Corsicana (TX) *Daily Sun*
Corsicana (TX) *Semi-Weekly Light*
Daily Ardmore (OK) *Ardmoreite*
Daily Telegraph (London)
Dallas Daily Herald
Dallas Daily Times-Herald
Dallas Express
Dallas Morning News
Dallas Times-Herald
Dallas Weekly Times-Herald
Danville (KY) *Advocate*
Danville (KY) *Advocate-Messenger*
Davenport (IA) *Quad-City Times*
El Centro (CA) *Imperial Valley Press*
El Paso (TX) *Herald*
El Paso (TX) *Times*
Fort Worth Democrat-Advance
Fort Worth Daily Democrat-Advance
Fort Worth Daily Gazette

Fort Worth Daily Standard
Fort Worth Gazette
Fort Worth Morning Register
Fort Worth Press
Fort Worth Record
Fort Worth Record and Register
Fort Worth Record-Telegram
Fort Worth Star
Fort Worth Star-Telegram
Fort Worth Telegram
Frederick (OK) *Leader*
Fresno (CA) *Bee*
Galveston Daily News
Glens Falls (NY) *Post-Star*
Grand Forks (ND) *Herald*
Harlingen Valley (TX) *Morning Star*
Hearne (TX) *Democrat*
Hobart (OK) *Democrat-Chief*
Holdenville (OK) *Daily News*
Houston Chronicle
Houston Daily Post
Houston Post
Indianapolis Journal
Jackson (MS) *Clarion-Ledger*
Kansas City (KS) *Times*
Kerrville (TX) *Mountain Sun*
Kilgore (TX) *News Herald*
Lampasas (TX) *Leader*
Laredo (TX) *Times*
Lexington Herald
Lexington Herald-Leader
Long Beach (CA) *Press-Telegram*
Longview (TX) *News-Journal*
Los Angeles Eagle
Los Angeles Evening Citizen-News
Los Angeles Evening Express
Louisville Courier-Journal
Lubbock (TX) *Morning Avalanche*
Macon (GA) *Telegraph*

Madison (WI) *Capital Times*
Marshall (TX) *News*
Marshall (TX) *Evening Messenger*
Marshall (TX) *News-Messenger*
Marshalltown (IA) *Evening Times-Republican*
McAllen (TX) *Monitor*
McKinney (TX) *Courier-Gazette*
Memphis Daily Commercial
Miami Herald
Miami News
Minneapolis Star
Modesto (CA) *Bee*
Morning Tulsa (OK) *News*
Murfreesboro (TN) *Daily News-Journal*
Muskogee (OK) *Daily Phoenix and Times Democrat*
Nashville Tennessean
New Britain (CT) *Herald*
New Orleans Daily Picayune
New York Daily News
New York New Age
New York Sun
Odessa (TX) *American*
Oklahoma City Daily Oklahoman
Okmulgee (OK) *Times*
Pampa (TX) *Daily News*
Panama City (FL) *News*
Panama City (FL) *News Herald*
Paris (TX) *News*
Philadelphia Inquirer
Phoenix Republican
Pittsburgh Courier
Pittsburgh Press
Post-Standard (Syracuse, NY)
Poughkeepsie (NY) *Journal*
Press of Atlantic City (NJ)
Sacramento Bee
Salem (OR) *Capital Journal*
San Angelo (TX) *Evening Standard*
San Angelo (TX) *Standard-Times*

San Antonio Daily Express
San Antonio Light
San Bernadino County (CA) *Sun*
Santa Fe Daily New Mexican
Seattle Star
Seguin (TX) *Gazette-Enterprise*
Shawnee (OK) *County Democrat*
Shawnee (OK) *Evening Star*
Shawnee (OK) *Times-Record*
Shawnee (OK) *Herald*
Shawnee (OK) *News*
Shawnee (OK) *News-Herald*
St. Louis Globe-Democrat
Syracuse (NY) *Post Standard*
Tacoma News Tribune
Tulsa Evening Sun
Tulsa World
Tyler (TX) *Morning Telegraph*
Vernon (TX) *Daily Record*
Victoria (TX) *Advocate*
Waco (TX) *News-Tribune*
Waco (TX) *Times-Herald*
Waco (TX) *Tribune-Herald*
Waterloo (IA) *Courier*
Waxahachie (TX) *Light*
White Earth (MN) *Tomahawk*
Whitewright (TX) *Sun*
Wichita County (TX) *Times*
Wichita Falls (TX) *Times*
Wichita Falls (TX) *Times Record*
Wilkes-Barre (PA) *Times-Leader*
Wyoming State Tribune

Books

Atkinson, Brian T. *I'll Be Here in the Morning: The Songwriting Legacy of Townes Van Zandt*. College Station: Texas A&M University Press, 2012.

Bancroft, Hubert H. *History of the Northern Mexican States and Texas*. Vol. 2. 1889. Reprint, Forgotten Books, 2018.

Barra, Allen. *Inventing Wyatt Earp: His Life and Many Legends*. New York: Carroll & Graf, 1998.

Barrow, Blanche Caldwell, and John Neal Phillips. *My Life with Bonnie and Clyde*. New York: Simon & Schuster, 2009.

Berry, Craig. *The Hidden History of Western Kentucky*. Charleston, SC: History Press, 2011.

Bernstein, Matthew. *George Hearst: Silver King of the Gilded Age*. Norman: University of Oklahoma Press, 2021.

Blok, Celestina. *Lost Restaurants of Fort Worth*. Charleston, SC: History Press, 2017.

Bohn, Michael K. *Heroes & Ballyhoo: How the Golden Age of the 1920s Transformed American Sports*. Lincoln: University of Nebraska Press, 2009.

Breakenridge, William M. *Helldorado: Bringing the Law to the Mesquite*. New York: Houghton Mifflin, 1928.

Brown, Dee. *Bury My Heart at Wounded Knee*. New York: Barrie & Jenkins, 1973.

Caldwell, Clifford R., and Ron DeLord. *Eternity at the End of a Rope*. Santa Fe: Sunstone Press, 2015.

Carroll, John M. *History of Texas Baptists*. Privately printed, 1923. Reprint, New South Wales, Australia: Generic Publications, 2020.

Cervantez, Brian. *Amon Carter: A Lone Star Life*. Norman: University of Oklahoma Press, 2019.

Clancy, Frederick Melton "Foghorn." *My Fifty Years in Rodeo: Living with Cowboys, Horses, and Danger*. San Antonio: Naylor, 1952.

Cox, Norman Wade, ed. *Encyclopedia of Southern Baptists*. 2 vols. Nashville: Broadman, 1958.

De Arment, Robert K. *Jim Courtright of Fort Worth*. Fort Worth: TCU Press, 2004.

Dreiser, Theodore. *A Book about Myself*. New York: Boni and Liveright, 1922. Reprinted as *Newspaper Days*. NY: Horace Liveright, 1931.

Enss, Chris. *Along Came a Cowgirl: Daring and Iconic Women of the Rodeo & Wild West Shows*. Helena, MT: Farcountry Press. 2022.

Flemmons, Jerry. *Amon: The Texan Who Played Cowboy for America*. Lubbock: Texas Tech University Press, 1998.

Garrett, Julia Kathryn. *Fort Worth: A Frontier Triumph*. Fort Worth: Texas Christian University Press, 1996.

Gatewood, Jim. *J. Frank Norris, Top o' Hill Casino, Lew Jenkins, and the Texas Oil Rich*. Garland, TX: Mullaney, 2006.

Gillett, Charlie. *The Sound of the City: The Rise of Rock and Roll*. 3rd ed. New York: Souvenir Press, 2011.

Givner, Joan. *Katherine Anne Porter: A Life*. Athens: University of Georgia Press, 1982.

Goodman, Matthew. *Eighty Days: Nellie Bly's and Elizabeth Bisland's History-Making Race around the World*. New York: Ballantine Books, 2013.

Grant, Jackson. *1973: Rock at the Crossroads*. New York: Thomas Dunne Books, 2019.

Gregory, Hugh. *Soul Music A–Z*. London: Blandford Books, 1991.

Gribin, Anthony J., and Matthew M. Schiff. *The Complete Book of Doo Wop* (Narberth, PA: Collectables Record, 2009.

Guinn, Jeff. *Go Down Together: The True Story of Bonnie and Clyde*. New York: Simon & Schuster, 2009.

Guinn, Jeff. *The Last Gunfight*. New York: Simon & Schuster, 2011.

Hardy, Robert Earl. *A Deeper Blue: The Life and Music of Townes Van Zandt*. Denton: University of North Texas Press, 2008.

Harris, Alferdteen, ed. *Black Exodus: The Great Migration from the American South*. Oxford: University Press of Mississippi, 1992.

Hartman, Gary. *The History of Texas Music*. College Station: Texas A&M University Press, 2008.

Hendricks, Diana Finlay. *Delbert McClinton: One of the Fortunate Few*. College Station: Texas A&M University Press, 2017.

Hyer, Julien. *The Land of Beginning Again*. Atlanta: Foote & Davis, 1952.

Jameson, W. C. *Rocky Mountain Train Robberies: True Stories of Notorious Bandits and Infamous Escapades*. Helena, MT: TwoDot, 2019.

Jancik, Wayne. *The Billboard Book of One-Hit Wonders*. New York: Watson-Guptill, 1990.

Jasinski, Laurie E., and Casey Monahan. *The Handbook of Texas Music*. 2nd ed. Austin: Texas State Historical Association, 2012.

Johnson, Paul Lee. *The McLaurys in Tombstone, Arizona: An O.K. Corral Obituary*. Denton: University of North Texas Press, 2012.

Jones, Jan L. *Billy Rose Presents Casa Mañana*. Fort Worth: TCU Press, 1999.

Jones, Jan L. *Renegades, Showmen & Angels*. Fort Worth: TCU Press, 2005.

Kear, Lynn, and John Rossman. *Kay Francis*. Jefferson, NC: McFarland, 2006.

Kruth, John. *To Live's to Fly: The Ballad of the Late, Great Townes Van Zandt*. New York: DaCapo Press, 2008.

Larkin, Colin, ed. *The Guinness Encyclopedia of Popular Music*. London: Guinness Publishing, 1992.

Lefever, Alan J. *Fighting the Good Fight: The Life and Work of Benajah Harvey Carroll*. Austin: Eakin Press, 1994.

Liles, Debbie M. *Will Rogers Coliseum*. Images of America Series. Charleston, SC: Arcadia, 2012.

Lite, Norm N. *Rock On: The Illustrated Encyclopedia of Rock N Roll*. New York: Thomas Y. Crowell, 1974.

Marks, Paula Mitchell. *And Die in the West*. New York: William Morrow, 1989.

Marsh, Dave. *The Heart of Rock & Soul: The 1001 Greatest Singles Ever Made*. New York: New American Library, 1989.

McElhaney, Jacquelyn Masur. *Pauline Periwinkle and Progressive Reform in Dallas*. College Station: Texas A&M University Press, 1998.

McLean, Henry Hunter. *From Ayr to Thurber: Three Hunter Brothers and the Winning of the West*. Fort Worth: Fort Worth Genealogical Society, 1978.

Miller, Edward H. *A Conspiratorial Life: Robert Welch, the John Birch Society, and the Revolution of American Conservatism*. Chicago: University of Chicago Press, 2021.

Nichol, C. R. *Gospel Preachers Who Blazed the Trail*. 1899. Reprint, Houston: Firm Foundation, 1966.

Olmstead, Jacob W. *The Frontier Centennial: Fort Worth and the New West*. Lubbock: Texas Tech University Press, 2021.

Paddock, B. B. *History of Texas: Fort Worth and the Texas Northwest Edition*. Chicago: Lewis Publishing, 1922.

Pate, J'Nell. *North of the River: A Brief History of North Fort Worth*. Fort Worth: TCU Press, 1994.

Peak, Howard W. *A Ranger of Commerce, Or 52 Years on the Road*. San Antonio: Naylor Printing, 1929.

Penningroth, Dylan C. *Before the Movement: The Hidden History of Black Civil Rights*. New York: W. W. Norton, 2023.

Poe, Charlsie. *Booger Red: World Champion Cowboy*. Winters, TX: privately printed, 1991.

Pollock, Bruce. *By the Time We Got to Woodstock*. New York: Backbeat Books, 2009.

Ray, Jefferson Davis. *B. H. Carroll*. Nashville, TN: Sunday School Board of the Southern Baptist Convention, 1927.

Rich, Harold. *Fort Worth between the World Wars*. College Station: Texas A&M University Press, 2020.

Selcer, Richard. *Fort Worth Characters*. Denton: University of North Texas Press, 2009.

Selcer, Richard. *Hell's Half-Acre*. Fort Worth: Texas Christian University Press, 1991.

Selcer, Richard. *A History of Fort Worth in Black & White*. Denton: University of North Texas Press, 2015.

Sherrod, Katie, ed. *Grace & Gumption: Stories of Fort Worth Women*. Fort Worth: TCU Press, 2007.

Talevski, Nick. *Rock Obituaries: Knocking on Heaven's Door*. London: Omnibus Press, 2006.

Tanner, Karen Holliday. *Doc Holliday: A Family Portrait*. Norman: University of Oklahoma Press, 1998.

Tyler, Ron, ed. *The New Handbook of Texas*. 6 vols. Austin: Texas State Historical Association, 1996.

Waters, Frank. *The Earp Brothers of Tombstone: The Story of Mrs. Virgil Earp*. New York: Bramhall House, 1960.

Whitburn, Joel. *The Billboard Book of Top 40 Hits: 1955 to the Present*. New York: Billboard Publications, 1983.

Wintz, Cary D., and Paul Finkelman, eds. *Encyclopedia of the Harlem Renaissance*. 2 vols. New York: Taylor and Francis, 2004.

Wooster, Ralph A. *Texas and Texans in the Great War*. Kerrville, TX: State House Press, 2010.

Articles, Chapters, and Theses

Bernstein, Matthew. "The Buffalo-Bone Cane Mystery." *Wild West Magazine*, Winter 2023.

Bertram, Dennis. "Letters to the Editor." *Wild West Magazine*, June 2022.

Boggs, Johnny D. Interview with Paul Lee Johnson. *Wild West Magazine*, October 2013

Carmony, Neil B. "Hello, Ike! Any New War?" *Quarterly of the National Association for Outlaw and Lawman History* 26, no. 1 (January–March 2002): 31.

Conger, Roger N. "William Cowper Brann." In Tyler, *New Handbook of Texas*, 6:704.

Dodd, Samantha. "Legendary Lady of the Law: Louise Ballerstedt Raggio and the Reform of Texas Marital Property Law." *Legacies: A History*

Journal for Dallas and North Central Texas 35, no. 1 (Spring 2023): 38–50.

"Double Billing." *Wild West Magazine*, December 2021.

Early, Joseph, Jr. "B. H. Carroll." Address presented at the annual state convention of the East Texas–West Texas Historical Association, 2010.

Foote, Timothy. "George Washington Slept Here." *Smithsonian Magazine*, December 1999. https://smithsonianmagazine.com/history/george-washington-slept-here.

Gardner, Mark Lee. "The Other James Brother." *Wild West Magazine*, August 2013.

Harrigan, Stephen. "Metamorphosis of a Killer." *American History Magazine*, June 2012.

Jackson, Frank. "When Tinseltown Came to Cowtown." *Legacies: A History Journal for Dallas & North Central Texas* 34, no. 2 (Fall 2022): 18–27.

Jasinski, Laurie E. "Fowler, Manet Harrison." *Handbook of Texas Online*, May 29, 2013. https://www.tshaonline.org/handbook/entries/fowler-manet-harrison.

Johnson, Paul Lee. "The Will of McLaury." *Wild West Magazine*, October 2013.

Karbach, Ruth. "The Modern Woman." In Sherrod, *Grace & Gumption*, 63–85.

Kinkade, Patricia A. "Van Zandt, Khleber Miller." In Tyler, *New Handbook of Texas*, 6:707.

Kohout, Martin Donnell. "Smith, Major Bill." In Jasinski and Monahan, *Handbook of Texas Music*, 561–62.

Markley, Bill. "Billy & Jesse." *Wild West Magazine*, December 2021.

McVey, John, and Laurie Jasinski. "Van Zandt, Townes." In Jasinski and Monahan, *Handbook of Texas Music*, 646–47.

Michno, Gregory. "Worse Than the Hostile Comanches." *Wild West Magazine*, October 2021.

"Months Past." *History Today*, September 2019.

Mulvaney, Tom. "Booger Red's Last Ride." *Southwestern Review*, Autumn 1944. Reprinted in *Reader's Digest* 8, no. 290 (June 1946).

Munchus-Forde, Lady George. "History of the Negro in Fort Worth, A Syllabus for a High School Course." Master's thesis, Fisk University, 1941.

"Mwalimu Creed." *Negro Musician*, January 1929.

"The *Nugget*'s Story." Wild West Magazine, October 2001.

Parker, Dan. "Stutterin' Sam." *Collier's Magazine*, July 1943.

Patrick, Joseph S. "Home at the Corral." *Historic Traveler*, Autumn 1994.

"Roundup." *Wild West Magazine*, October 2013.

Selcer, Richard. "Murder at the Palais Royal." *Wild West Magazine*, June 2011.

Stinson, Bob. "Where Legends Rest in the West." *Wild West Magazine*, October 2012.

Wolz, Larry. "Kidd-Key College." In Jasinski and Monahan, *Handbook of Texas Music*, 345–47.

Index